Best regards,

Jim Wetzel

In this study James Wetzel details the emergence of Augustine's concept of will out of his reflections on virtue, grace, and the good life. Other studies have acknowledged Augustine's role in the creation and transmission of an essentially new concept of will, foreign to classical philosophy, but they have tended to apply to his work an anachronistic distinction between theology and philosophy. Wetzel argues for continuity between Augustine's initial philosophical interests in human freedom and virtue and his subsequent focus on the nature and necessity of grace. By setting Augustine's doctrine of grace in the context of his Platonism, Wetzel is able to provide a philosophical assessment of his concept of will as it takes shape first in response to pagan philosophy and second in reaction to Pelagian theology.

AUGUSTINE AND THE
LIMITS OF VIRTUE

AUGUSTINE AND THE LIMITS OF VIRTUE

JAMES WETZEL

Assistant Professor of Philosophy and Religion,
Colgate University, Hamilton, New York

CAMBRIDGE
UNIVERSITY PRESS

Published by the Press Syndicate of the University of Cambridge
The Pitt Building, Trumpington Street, Cambridge CB2 1RP
40 West 20th Street, New York, NY 10011-4211, USA
10 Stamford Road, Oakleigh, Melbourne 3166, Australia

First published 1992

Printed in Great Britain at the University Press, Cambridge

*A cataloguing in publication record for this book is available from the British
Library*

Library of Congress cataloguing in publication data
Wetzel, James.
Augustine and the limits of virtue/James Wetzel.
p.   cm.
Revision of the author's thesis (Ph.D.) – Columbia University.
Includes bibliographical references and index.
ISBN 0 521 40541 6
1. Augustine, Saint, Bishop of Hippo.   2. Virtue – History.
3. Grace (Theology) – History of doctrines – Early church, ca.
30–600.   4. Free will and determinism – History.   I. Title.
B655.Z7W47 1992
170–dc20   91–32635   CIP

ISBN 0 521 40541 6 hardback

To my students

Tu autem bonum nullo indigens bono semper
quietus es, quoniam tua quies tu ipse es. Et hoc
intellegere quis hominum dabit homini?

Conf. XIII

Death is not an event in life: we do not live to experience death.

If we take eternity to mean not infinite temporal duration but timelessness, then eternal life belongs to those who live in the present.

Our life has no end in just the way in which our visual field has no limits.

Wittgenstein, Tractatus 6.4311

Contents

Preface

I tend to approach philosophy theologically, and so it is not surprising that I am drawn to Augustine. His was the greatest attempt in late antiquity and perhaps of any time thereafter to find in the greatest philosopher of antiquity, Plato, a theologian *manqué*. But I was not able to appreciate the ingenuity and profundity of Augustine's Platonism until I was able to appreciate Platonism. For that I have to thank Iris Murdoch and Martha Nussbaum, whose portraits of Plato in *The Sovereignty of Good* and *The Fragility of Goodness* respectively converted me to Platonic philosophy. Murdoch is a fellow Platonist but not a fellow theist; Nussbaum is neither Platonist nor theist. I doubt whether either philosopher would find the Platonism I ascribe to Augustine very congenial. Anyone familiar with their works will nevertheless recognize their pervasive influence on what I have written.

Augustine's Platonism led me to consider in particular his conception of will. The theme of willing and limits to willing runs throughout his writings, not as a constant fixed by a set of definitions, but as an increasingly intricate web of connections between knowledge, virtue, grace, and the philosophical quest for happiness. In my attempt to reconstruct this web and display its marvelous coherence, I found it impossible to maintain a sharp distinction between interpretation and reconstruction. This is likely to bother only those who see philosophy and the history of philosophy as two entirely different preoccupations. My excuse for mixing them here is that I could not make sense of what Augustine said without sometimes having to consider what he was trying to say, what he might have said, or even on occasion what he ought to have said. I have no general theory to offer of the role of philosophy in history or vice versa, and therefore my style of analysis must stand or fall on its particular ability to illuminate Augustine's thought.

This book began as a dissertation, and I would like to acknowledge the readers on my examination committee. Richard Norris, Charles Larmore, Robert Somerville, Herbert Deane, and Wayne Proudfoot read my work carefully and critically, pointing out places of infelicitous expression, obscure argumentation, and dubious translation. I have benefited from their encouragement and from the seriousness with which they took their task. Wayne Proudfoot, my principal adviser, has been a good friend and mentor, and over the course of my graduate career at Columbia University, he helped me to hone my skills as a philosopher of religion. And were it not for my compatriots David Wisdo, Eric Brandt, and Ava Chamberlain on the one hand and for the Charlotte Newcombe Fellowship Foundation on the other, my graduate career would have seemed and been longer than it was. My compatriots filled my time at Columbia with fellowship and conversation, and Charlotte Newcombe funded a year of writing.

In the trek from dissertation to book, I happily incurred further debts. I have learned a great deal about Augustine from J. Patout Burns and William Babcock, with whom I have corresponded since 1987, when we met at a conference at Trinity College, University of Toronto. My understanding of Augustine's theology of grace would have been much impoverished without Burns, and I have come to approach Augustine's early work largely through Babcock's questions. Jerry Balmuth, my colleague in Philosophy and Religion at Colgate University, displayed an unsettling ability to see what I was saying before I had even thought of saying it, and I am in his debt for some of the connective tissue in my argument. Maude Clark, also a colleague, kept me honest with her Nietzschean skepticism of Augustine. Many of my revisions of Augustine were first tested on my students in Medieval Philosophy, much to their bemusement, I fear, but I thank them none the less.

My editor at Cambridge, Alex Wright, who heard me promise to meet one deadline after another, and my wife, Pamela Biel, who read my typescript and disentangled my prose when she could, impressed me greatly with the virtue of patience. Pauline Marsh, my congenial copy-editor, impressed me with her prudence.

Academic etiquette has long recognized a form of Augustinian wisdom. We claim our vices as our own and share the credit of our virtues with others. I have come to understand and value this wisdom over the course of having written this book.

Abbreviations

De spir. et litt.	*De spiritu et littera* (*The Spirit and the Letter*)
De Trin.	*De Trinitate* (*The Trinity*)
De ver. rel.	*De vera religione* (*On True Religion*)
Propp.	*Expositio quarundam propositionum ex epistula ad Romanos* (*Exposition of Selected Propositions from Letter to the Romans*)
Retrac.	*Retractationes* (*Reconsiderations*)
Sol.	*Soliloquia* (*The Soliloquies*)

EDITIONS

CCSL	Corpus Christianorum Series Latina
CSEL	Corpus Scriptorum Ecclesiasticorum Latinorum
OSA	Œuvres de Saint Augustin

Introduction: Augustine and philosophy

> If Plato has said that the sage is the one who imitates,
> knows, loves God, participation in whom brings happiness,
> what need is there to examine other philosophers? None
> have come closer to us than the Platonists.[1]

Hannah Arendt once remarked of Augustine that he turned to
religion out of philosophical perplexity.[2] Augustine's account in
the *Confessiones* of his discovery of philosophy lends support to
her judgment. In book III he recalls his reaction at age nineteen
to Cicero's *Hortensius*, an exhortation to philosophy. "Truly
that book," he reports, "changed my disposition."[3] Judging
from the earlier sections of the *Confessiones*, Augustine's former
disposition had inclined him towards experimenting with sin, a
disposition so puzzling in its motivations that he can hardly
recollect it with a semblance of intelligibility. When Cicero
converts him to philosophy, Augustine turns the mystery of his
own perversity into an object of study. Thereupon begins his
intensely personal and profoundly philosophical preoccupation
with evil. What was its nature, its origin, its end? – questions
not unrelated in his mind to God's conceivability.

For a considerable stretch of the narrative in the *Confessiones*,
Augustine describes himself as having been bound in imagination to a material God, and, by consequence, to evil as the
material antithesis of God's substance. This Manichaean
outlook on good and evil as eternally opposed natures seemed to

---

[1] *De civ. Dei* 8.5 (CCSL 47, 221, 1–7): "Si ergo Plato Dei huius imitatorem cognitorem
amatorem dixit esse sapientem, cuius participatione sit beatus, quid opus est excutere
ceteros? Nulli nobis quam isti propius acesserunt."
[2] *The Life of the Mind*, vol. II (New York: Harcourt, Brace, Jovanovich, 1978), 84.
[3] *Conf.* 3.4.7. (CCSL 27, 30, 6–7): "Ille uero liber mutauit affectum meum."

Augustine, for a long while, to make sense of his own struggle against apparently intractable vice. Ultimately he would find the dualistic view of good and evil obfuscating, its power to explain illusory. He speaks of his perceptual breakthrough in book VII, after he has read the books of the Platonists (*libri Platonicorum*). Their words direct his attention inwards, and with his mind's eye he catches sight of God's immaterial light. No longer bound to a material imagination, Augustine removes good and evil from external space and places them in his newly discovered interior space, the realm of his will.

Most philosophers who have taken an interest in Augustine, Arendt not least among them, have looked to his creation of our modern concept of will out of the Latin *voluntas*. His conceptual innovation seems to have coincided with his departure from a crude Platonism, which would have confused knowing with willing. Augustine understood all too well from his own case that knowledge of the good did not necessarily result in the appropriate transformation of motivation. Virtue could in discomforting ways lag behind vision. The dénouement of his remarkable vision in book VII, for instance, was not conversion but the intransigence of habit: "I did not stand fast to enjoy my God; I was but carried off to you by your beauty, and soon I was torn from you by my own weight... this weight, the habit of my flesh."[4]

If we take Augustine's reason to have been the conduit of his desire for God, and his habits to have been the product of his untutored appetites (i.e., those desires of his formed independently of his knowledge of God), then his predicament in book VII cannot usefully be described as a conflict between reason and appetite. For Augustine's conflict, according to his account of his own conversion in book VIII, is resolvable in reason's favor, and were the conflict in book VII merely one of reason with appetite, the resolution never would have come. His problem in book VII, it seems, is not that he needs more or better knowledge of God, but that he lacks the ability to modify his habitual appetites to fit his new knowledge. His new knowledge,

---

[4] *Conf.* 7.17.23 (CCSL 27, 107, 2–4): "et non stabam frui deo meo, sed rapiebar ad te decore tuo moxque diripiebar abs te pondere meo...; et pondus hoc consuetudo carnalis."

in so far as it is knowledge of the good, has motivational content. But if that content fails either to integrate or to eliminate his habitual desires, Augustine will find himself caught between two contrary and irreconcilable sources of motivation. Doubtless in such a conflict he would want to identify himself with his rational desires, and yet his reason's sole means of control over irrational appetite – the motivating power of knowledge – will have run up against an absolute limit.

A less-than-absolute limit suggests the presence of a mediating faculty, the will, which could determine itself in accord with either rational or irrational desires while retaining its independence from both. One way Augustine might be supposed to have opened up separate conceptual space for the will, separate from space held by knowledge and desire, is to have given choice a measure of independence from desire. Let our desires of themselves determine our disposition and activity, and what we will have is habitual action. Moreover there is no guarantee, as Augustine illustrates in his own case in book VII, that those habits will defer to rational judgment or superior knowledge. The power of knowledge to motivate is not enough to determine action. We must *choose* to be motivated by rational rather than habitual desires, and if our choice fails to carry into action, we have not the triumph of appetite over reason, but a failure of will. Augustine's commentators are fond of describing his Platonic vision of God in book VII as the conversion of his intellect, and his commitment to the Christian life in book VIII as the conversion of his will. The two conversions mark Augustine's debt to and departure from Platonism.

Much of what I discuss in this book can be described as my attempt to recollect Augustine the philosopher, to locate the knot of his philosophical perplexity and then follow his efforts at disentanglement. In large part this will be a story about Augustine's "discovery" of the will, for I firmly believe, as many have before me, that his reflections on willing brought about a revolution in philosophy. After Augustine, Plato's legacy never could be quite the same. I assess the nature of his debt to and departure from Platonism differently than most, however. The conventional wisdom, which I have suggested in brief above, credits Platonism with having introduced Augustine to his inner depths, the reality once hidden by the sensual imagery of his imagination. Having turned within, Augustine enters the labyrinth of his will, where he encounters himself torn between sin and grace, longing for reunion with God but still caught in habitual diversions. His way out is not through knowledge but through love – God's responsive love for Augustine – and there marks Augustine's departure from Platonism. He responds in will to God's willing of his redemption. If Augustine were strictly a Platonist, he should have had need for only one conversion, that of his intellect.

Augustine's debt to Platonism certainly had to do in part with its revelation to him of reality beyond the sensible. He says as much in the *Confessiones*, and there is no reason not to take him at his word. Yet Augustine owes an even profounder debt to Platonism which is easy to overlook. Plato and his interpreters introduce him to the seductive power of the good. It enters his awareness in the form of God's power to transform the being of God's beholder. When he recounts his vision of God in book VII, however, he gives no indication of having been able to retain his own power to respond or to incorporate God's agency into his own. He communicates instead the frightening experience of being transformed despite himself and therefore of feeling alienated from the person transformed: "And when I recognized you for the first time, you raised me up so that I might see the reality of what I could see, and not yet was I the person who could see."[5] In describing the dawning of his vision, Augustine uses surprisingly violent language: "You beat back the infirmity of my power of seeing, radiating your light forcibly upon me, and I shook with love and with horror."[6] The momentary vision, for all its immediate seductiveness and power, fails to take hold. Augustine, in transport, snatched up and carried off by God's beauty, finds himself not with God but in a place far removed, a *regio dissimilitudinis*, not only from God but also from himself. This time of exile cannot last. God's voice calls Augustine from on high and invites him to become like God, but

[5] *Conf.* 7.10.16 (CCSL 27, 103, 13–15): "Et cum te primum cognoui, tu assumpsisti me, ut uiderem esse, quod uiderem, et nondum me esse, qui uiderem."
[6] *Conf.* 7.10.16 (CCSL 27, 103, 15–17): "Et reuerberasti infirmitatem aspectus mei radians in me uehementer, et contremui amore et horrore."

Augustine's habits, which express the self he has known, soon bring him back to earth. It is his memory of God, and not his vision, which must now do the work of transformation.

I do not say that Augustine's profounder debt to Platonism is easily overlooked because the sheer seductiveness of the good is easily overlooked in Augustine's experience of God. Quite the contrary: seductiveness is so overwhelmingly present in his description of God's incorporeal light that we tend to be blinded to anything else. We cannot see, in particular, the manner in which Augustine is supposed to take shape in God's light. But if as readers we are left with no knowledge of Augustine's transformation in his transport to God, it is neither because Augustine has chosen to omit the relevant details from his narration nor because his self-knowledge in transport simply cannot be communicated across the experiential gulf between first and third person. His readers admittedly might lack the benefit of incorporeal light in reading of his experience, but Augustine never leads us to believe that had we such il-lumination, we would know something about him which we could not otherwise learn from reading the *Confessiones*. In fact, we seem to be no more significantly alienated from Augustine's experience of God than he himself was at the time of his experience. In retrospect he tells us how little he felt a part of what he saw. It was as if he was not yet the person who had experienced the rapture of transcendent vision. As narrator of his own life, Augustine needs some intelligible way of describing this odd doubling of himself, which allowed him to be paradoxically both present and absent in the same experience. To resolve the paradox without ignoring the phenomenon on which it is based, he will need to move beyond the conceptual resources of his Platonic inheritance.

Plato, to Augustine's mind, had unified philosophy's two greatest ambitions – to know the world and its causes and to live the good life – when he discovered the world's foundation in the good, which Augustine was only too happy to redescribe as God.[7] But neither Plato nor his followers ever solved the problem of mediation. The problem emerged from the disparity

[7] See especially *De civ. Dei* 8.4.

between the sublime perfection of the good and the human mind's powers of representation. Supposing that we were to have the representation of the good as sublimely perfect, still we could do nothing with the representation until we managed to connect it with our habitual pursuits of goods. In other words, to appropriate the good into our power of agency, we would have to be able in some way to include *ourselves* in the good's representation. The flawless Platonic God, more real to Augustine than his own fleeting existence, called back to itself the perfection in Augustine. But since Augustine's identity was as much a matter of his infirmities as his virtues, most of him was left behind. When his conversion does come, and its moment is famously described in the garden scene of book VIII, when Augustine answers to a command to "take up and read" ("tolle, lege"), we need to ask as readers why so much more of Augustine seems to be included in this turn to God rather than in the other. Why does an unmediated vision of God bring him internal division, while a mediated calling ushers in his conversion?

Augustine's extended discussion of his will's internal division in book VIII, which sets the stage for his moment of inner healing, draws our attention to the importance of his concept of will. We would not be wrong to expect to find his departure from Platonism somewhere in the elaboration of this concept. We would be wrong, however, and fundamentally wrong, were we to suppose that Augustine introduces room for the will by diminishing his Platonic confidence in the power of knowledge to motivate and thereby to conform human agency to the good. He retains this confidence undiminished not only in the *Confessiones*, but for the remainder of his career as a theologian, and it is what I have referred to as his profounder debt to Platonism. Most of Augustine's commentators, I think it fair to say, would disagree with me wholeheartedly. They tend to read him in the *Confessiones* and especially in his later polemical works against the Pelagians, his archenemies in theology, as having denied the sufficiency of knowledge for personal transformation. And so where I see a debt to Platonism, they would mark a departure.

I admit that there is an immediate appeal to the reading contrary to my own. The moral of Augustine's description of his vision of God in book VII seems to be that even the most compelling presentation of knowledge cannot determine the response of the knower to the knowledge. God's reality is the most compelling reality imaginable, and yet when this reality presents itself to Augustine's inner gaze, his vision effaces his will, and he becomes passive instead of receptive to what he is seeing. His bypassed agency, left out of the encounter, soon interrupts his vision with its customary claims on his attention. What better way for Augustine to reintroduce his human response to God than in book VIII to add choice to knowledge? He could (and should) still retain a modest confidence in the motivational contribution of his knowledge, but not so much that his knowledge alone could be supposed to unify his will. When he enters the scene of his conversion with his divided will, let God be supposed to strengthen his resolution to live up to his knowledge, but let Augustine retain the capacity to refuse the help. He will not refuse, of course, since his knowledge of the good confirms his desire to conform himself to God, but his power to refuse will allow him to be receptive to transformation. *Voluntas* enters into Augustine's conversion as his commitment to his knowledge of the good, a commitment informed but not determined by the motivational contribution of his knowledge. At this point we will have come to an understanding of the will as the power of choice – the power to choose one's own motives. In order for this sort of power to exist, willing will have to be conceptually distinct from desiring. If it were not, we would will to have some desire determine our action only to have our will determined by some prior desire.

There are at least two reasons for rejecting this account of the will. The first is that it is incoherent. The second is that it is not Augustine's. I mention both reasons because Augustine worked through the notion of will as choice before finding it unserviceable and moving on to a far more complex understanding. He never denied, of course, that we make choices and can be held responsible for what we choose. But choice did not capture for him the way in which our wills registered knowledge of the good. Whenever we act, Augustine would contend, we act under some representation of the good. If we willfully refuse to act in accordance with what we judge to be best, then we become unintelligible to ourselves, at least in so far as our refusal outruns our available motives. It adds absolutely nothing to the attribution of agency, then, to incorporate an unexpressed power of refusal into every agent's consent to whatever good has served to motivate a particular course of action. The theory of will as the power of choice, informed by but independent of desire, makes every action to some degree unintelligible, for if the theory were true, no action would ever be sufficiently explained by its motives. We would have to add the agent's free-floating choice of motives to complete the explanation.[8] Augustine condemned the Pelagians for this reification of choice, not only because it gave them rather than God the last word on their redemption, but because it amounted in essence to a denial of God's power to transform human agents. No matter what God could supply human beings with in the way of motives, they could hold back from acting on their motives, even if it meant refusing to acknowledge what they knew for themselves to be good. The Pelagian will, as I shall describe it for the time being, did not merely exacerbate the problem of mediation; it rendered it insoluble in principle. I submit that the Pelagian will is a fiction. There is no faculty of will, distinct from desire, which we use to determine our actions.

Augustine abandons this fiction when he comes to the conclusion, early in his long career as a theologian, that God can call sinners irresistibly to a new way of life.[9] The irresistibility of grace ensures that God's presentation of the good to human agents necessarily meets with the appropriate response – the conformity of living to knowing. Augustine's

---

[8] This point needs minor qualification. If the action to be explained were habitual, we could bypass choice and appeal directly to the agent's unreflective acquiescence to familiar patterns of behavior. This, however, would be to explain the habitual action *qua* habit. If we wished to explain the habitual action *qua* action, we would have to trace the habit to an original intentional action, whose motives could then be attributed to the agent. The theory of will, as I have outlined it above, purports to account for the attribution.

[9] See Augustine's second response to Simplician in *Ad Simpl.*, written circa 396. I discuss this work and its relationship to the *Confessiones*, which comes on its heels, at length in chapter 4.

interpreters, especially the philosophically minded, have as a rule tended to distance him from his theological commitment to the sufficiency of grace for moral regeneration. They reserve his intimations of God's unlimited control over human redemption for his doctrine of predestination, whose final form awaited his last years, when the old bishop, having tired of controversy, supposedly gave into an authoritarian impulse and preached the value of human slavery to God. Even Arendt, who praised Augustine for having held on to philosophy throughout this life, disavowed any interest in his doctrine of predestination, which she dismissed in passing as "the most dubious and also most terrible of his teachings."[10] Predestination, to hear Augustine tell of it, is simply grace from God's point of view.[11] As a doctrine it has little more content than the assertion that human freedom poses no limit to God's power to redeem. It cannot be dismissed altogether, however, without the dismissal of the philosophical interest of grace. Arendt and like-minded commentators do Augustine the dubious favor of saving his philosophy from his theology. They take grace's irresistibility to indicate Augustine's abdication of human freedom and sacrifice of philosophy (worldly wisdom) to God, when in fact it better expresses his attempt to salvage Platonism's naive and uninformed confidence in the power of knowledge to motivate. God is the good guaranteeing its own reception in the human will. Described from the human point of view, this reception can be called grace.

It is in his brilliant theological analyses of grace that Augustine "discovers" the will and suggests an answer to the problem of mediation. We cannot, however, hope to understand him here, unless we first reduce the antagonism between where he starts in philosophy and where he finishes in theology. Recollecting Augustine the philosopher will require bringing into continuity his two distinct personae, long familiar to scholars – that of the young devotee of philosophical knowledge and that of the elderly doctor of grace. We must, to achieve this, call to mind his unresolved philosophical perplexities before we seek to determine the direction and end of his theological

---

[10] Arendt, *The Life of the Mind*, vol. II, 105.   [11] *De praed. sanct.* 10.19.

development. Otherwise we will tend to "compensate" for the apparent extremity of his doctrine of grace and read back the Pelagian fiction into his conception of *voluntas*.

Pelagius and Augustine shared the same ambition in philosophy. Each wanted to describe the way in which human beings were capable of defining themselves in a world not of their own making. This ambition merged normative and metaphysical concerns, for it was metaphysical in its attempt to fathom the source of human autonomy and normative in its attempt to identify the good life with the autonomous life. Augustine and Pelagius were in their common ambition the heirs of Hellenistic thought, and their respective theologies took root in the soil of its philosophy, especially Stoicism, whose unbounded confidence in the autarky of reason colored the ethics of an entire era. Because Pelagius seemed in the end to deny that there were ever significant obstacles to living the good life, once reason had illuminated its nature, he stood in more obvious continuity with the philosophical tradition than Augustine, who came to disparage the worldly wisdom of pagan philosophy for its overconfidence. In book xix of *De civitate Dei* he denies that the *philosophi* will ever be able to secure human happiness in the embrace of wisdom. Cutting at the heart of philosophical ambition this way, he seems at the same time to be severing himself from philosophy. But Augustine's invective against philosophy should be set in the context of his family quarrel with past philosophers and not dramatized into his rejection of philosophy per se. The elderly doctor of grace remained a Platonist to the end, and he pursued his quest for the source of human autonomy and well-being in his own unique variant of Platonism.

When I insist on Augustine's Platonism, I allude broadly to his philosophical orientation and not narrowly to his ties to the Neoplatonism of Porphyry and Plotinus. I do not dismiss the importance of the latter by any means, but nor have I found it terribly useful for my purposes to take Augustine's measure as a Platonist against standards set by the third-century Neoplatonists. Stoic rather than Neoplatonic influence informed his early views of virtue, autonomy, and the good life, and disposed him to think Stoically about ethics throughout his career as a

philosopher and theologian. In putting Stoicism before Neoplatonism, my intention is not to contrast Stoic and Platonic
influences on Augustine but to highlight his Stoic appropriation
of Plato. The Stoics took from Plato the figure of Socrates as the
paradigmatic sage, whose wisdom made him virtuous and
whose virtue made him invulnerable to suffering. Socrates, at
least in his Stoic incarnation, knew how to live in the world so
as never to depend for happiness on commitments beyond his
control. His virtue made him invulnerable in the sense that it
expressed his reason's ability to free him from concern for
material losses. As for virtue itself, that remained an expression
of his wisdom, accessible to him at all times. Especially in his
early writings, Augustine embraced the Stoic convergence of
virtue, autonomy, and happiness in wisdom. It set for him
philosophy's ideal, and he would reckon the success of individual
philosophies against it. When he read the work of the
Neoplatonists, who freed his imagination from corporeal paradigms, he discovered the metaphysical basis of the Stoic
convergence – the transcendent good, or what he described in
the *Confessiones* as the incorporeal God. Having encountered this
God, for however fleeting a moment, Augustine gained a
philosophical insight lost on Stoics, namely, that the source of
human wisdom must transcend the world's changing material
nature. Otherwise, conforming ourselves to wisdom would be
conforming ourselves to that which changes, without having
control over the changes.

Augustine's broadly Platonic sensibilities take shape as three
philosophical presuppositions. First is his conviction that human
autonomy has its source in something of supreme value outside
of humanity. Second is his conviction that the source of supreme
value must be free of whatever limits human autonomy. Third
is his conviction that we can be made over into the image of the
good we know, and once in the image of the unlimited good, we
will cease to experience limits to our autonomy. The notion of
autonomy which enters into each of these presuppositions bears
a family resemblance to the rational self-sufficiency of the Stoic
sage. The saint, no less than the sage, would in freedom have to
be motivated by the right sort of desires, or rational desires.
Desires are rational when they are informed by wisdom, only

wisdom of a sort unimagined by Stoics, whose sense of the real remained confined to the material. The supreme good, un-known to Stoics but known to Platonists, liberates those who come to apprehend it by motivating them to live the good life, which is by nature rational. Augustine lavished a great deal of attention on the object and nature of the apprehension. His second presupposition led him to describe the object of this apprehension – the supreme good – as the ideal expression of agency. It makes sense to speak of the source of supreme value as free from limits to autonomy only if the source can be represented as having the capacity to act. God expresses the good in action, without limitation. Human beings take on the image of God when they similarly act without limits to their own autonomy. Limits to autonomy, mentioned in the second and third of Augustine's Platonic presuppositions, refer not to external impediments to action but to failures of wisdom. Not to know the good, or to refuse to acknowledge the good we know, is to compromise our autonomy by having to act, by default or by perversity, on the wrong sorts of desires. God has no such limits, being the source of wisdom. Human beings, by contrast, are capable of evil.

G. R. Evans, in her highly regarded study of Augustine's reflections on evil, brings together the diversity of his thinking under the principle that evil works on the mind to obstruct reason and obfuscate understanding.[12] Sinners do not reason well, nor do they apprehend the world aright, especially when it comes to the discernment of higher goods. Evans rightly emphasizes the cognitive deficiencies of evil agency in her interpretation of Augustine. Going wrong is never far in Augustine's mind from being wrong. Nevertheless, too thorough an assimilation of evil to error would obscure evil's character as an expression of human agency. It is too simple a picture of evil, for instance, to suppose that sinners sin because they misperceive the nature of the good and consequently choose their course of action badly. The picture distorts because it separates mis-perceiving from willing and leaves Augustine on the horns of a false dilemma. Either sinning lies in misperceiving and not

---

[12] *Augustine on Evil* (Cambridge: Cambridge University Press, 1982).

willing, in which case no one who knew the good would act against it, or sinning lies in willing and not misperceiving, in which case anyone who acted on the good would have to have chosen to be motivated by it. The first horn of the dilemma would have Augustine deny the obvious fact, illustrated amply in his own *Confessiones*, that agents do not (and perhaps cannot) always will what they know to be good. The second horn would have him embrace the Pelagian fiction of the faculty of will, distinct from reason and desire, and independent in its operation from the motivating power of the good. Augustine chose neither horn, for his own, more nuanced, understanding of willing put him in a position to recognize the falsity of the dilemma.

It is not my intention to charge Evans with simplifying or distorting Augustine. I applaud her emphasis on his "epistemology of evil," for it brings to the fore Augustine's unflagging commitment to a broadly Platonic metaphysics and theory of knowledge, which is easy to lose sight of when he starts to explore the intricacies of grace. If, however, we are to understand Augustine on willing (which was not the aim of Evans), we must try to see his reflections on grace, not as addenda to his Platonic commitments, but as substantive reformulations of them. Augustine as a Platonist preoccupied himself with the psychology of willing. That makes him a Platonist of a different type. Plato and his Neoplatonic heirs had no such preoccupation. How, then, does it originate and develop in Augustine?

As a general approach to this question, I plan to focus on the dual aspect of virtue in Augustine's thought. One aspect is cognitive. Augustine takes the Platonic trope of virtue as vision very seriously. For example, in the *Soliloquia*, an early work, he defines virtue as the "proper and perfected act of looking, or looking which leads to vision."[13] The sort of vision Augustine has in mind transforms human desires to align them with the object of vision, the good. This brings up the other aspect of virtue, its volitional aspect, or more precisely, its role in the expression of human autonomy. Agents whose desires have been conformed to their knowledge of the good are, for Augustine,

---

[13] *Sol.* 1.6.13 (CSEL 89, 21, 11–12): "aspectus rectus atque perfectus, id est, quem visio sequitur, virtus vocatur."

autonomous or free agents. It is perhaps a truism, in no need of argument, that virtue expresses appropriately coordinated powers of perception and volition. But matters become far less obvious once someone asks for an explication of "appropriately" in this context. The best available answer often takes the form of an excursus into inappropriate coordination, or failures of virtue. Part of what makes Augustine's Platonism unusual is his tendency to trace lack of virtue to human refusal to acknowledge the good rather than to the absence or unavailability of practical knowledge – to a disposition of will rather than to a cognitive deficit. The two need not be unrelated, of course, for perverse dispositions can artificially produce cognitive deficits, and cognitive deficits (for instance, ignorance of the good) can lead to perverse dispositions. My point is that Augustine tends to redescribe problems of knowledge, in particular difficulties in knowing the good, as problems of will or agency, thereby making the appropriation of knowledge and not knowledge per se his explanandum.

In chapter 1, I hope to illustrate this Augustinian turn of mind in the context of book XI of the *Confessiones*, which on a first reading seems to discuss, without much resolution, the problem of how we manage to be cognizant of time. I will argue that Augustine's main concern in this book is with self-knowledge, or his efforts as a creature in time to gain some representation of himself over time. His failure to acquire an adequate representation, which he clearly admits, must be diagnosed as a problem of will. In two respects his mode of arguing in book XI can be taken as paradigmatic of his philosophizing. First he shifts Platonic representation away from the categories of materiality and immateriality to the related but by no means identical categories of time and eternity. Second he treats the problem of representation, of having temporal realities signify eternal verities, as the problem of having to convert self-knowledge into knowledge of God.

Chapter 1 is supposed to introduce some of the important conceptual links between Augustine's interests in knowing and representing on the one hand, and willing and desiring on the other. It is stage-setting, and as such is set out *in medias res*, without much regard for changes and developments in his point of view. In subsequent chapters, I discuss the origins and development of Augustine's interest in virtue, and because of his association of virtue with autonomy, that is to attend as well to his interest in the will and its freedom. The extraordinary complexity of his views on willing makes it especially important to situate them in their developmental context. To this end, chapters 2–5 offer what amounts to a genealogy of Augustine's conception of will. In chapter 2, I am concerned in particular with his Stoic attempt to describe the convergence between virtue and happiness. The convergence is important because without it his metaphysical concerns with autonomy stand apart from his normative interests in human flourishing, and it then becomes hard to understand why he would have viewed failures of virtue as failures, rather than expressions, of autonomy. Much of my analysis of Augustine in chapters 2 and 3 details his abortive attempts to fit his Stoic conception of virtue into an adequate moral psychology. Augustine discovered that his philosophical inheritance, whether Stoic or Platonic, came up short when he turned to it to explicate the psychology of moral struggle. Pagan philosophers seemed to have little appreciation for the difficulties creatures of habit and passion would have in appropriating philosophical wisdom. Augustine made it his business to explore this uncharted terrain. By the end of chapter 3 I will have covered his initial fascination and eventual disillusionment with Stoic virtue, and more generally, with philosophical prescriptions for happiness. Along the way from fascination to disillusionment, Augustine gains an acute appreciation for human affections and their power to subvert the motivations he or anyone else receives from coming to know the good. His diagnosis of the corrupting influence of affections on virtue marks his break with pagan philosophy and begins to give content to his own conception of will and its connection to conceptions of virtue and autonomy. But it is not until Augustine rehabilitates the affections and reintegrates them into the life of virtue that we have his complete conception of will. Chapters 4 and 5, focusing on conversion and moral regeneration, follow Augustine through the labyrinth of grace and end with his reaffirmation of the transformative power of knowledge. Needless to say, his reaffirmation will have been informed by his attention to the problem of mediation, or of our having to translate eternal wisdom into time-bound willing and representing.

The phrase "the limits of virtue," which appears in the title of my book, has two intended connotations. I mean it to refer negatively to Augustine's dissatisfaction with pagan virtue and its blindness to the psychology of inner conflict, and positively to his theistic reformulation of virtue as the motivational integrity of graced willing. The connotation shifts abruptly from the former to the latter once I begin to focus on Augustine's acknowledgment of God's full control over human redemption. His notoriously thick notion of grace never compromises his interest in human autonomy; on the contrary, this particular interest necessitates his doctrine of grace. Commentators who have seen the matter otherwise too often, I think, overlook the continuity between his early philosophical preoccupation with virtue and human freedom and his later theological preoccupation with grace. The theological preoccupation is an extension of, and not a reaction against, the philosophical preoccupation, as I try to make clear in the opening section of chapter 4. True, the doctor of grace indicts the *philosophi* for their unrealistic assessment of the human condition. But he never gives up the ideal, common to much of late antique philosophy, of bringing together virtue, autonomy, and human flourishing. What changes in his philosophy is not the nature of the ideal but the manner of its appropriation.

I hope in what follows to interpret and critique Augustine as a philosopher of antiquity. This is certainly a sufficient undertaking for a single book. I am nevertheless confident that renewed attention to Augustine can be of significance to contemporary philosophical investigation of human autonomy. I am not prepared in this work to argue that point at length, but rather than leave the reader with only a vague promissory note, I will by way of conclusion attempt to situate Augustine's thinking on autonomy in the context of some current and representative work on free will.

CHAPTER I

Time-bound

The cornerstone of Augustine's natural philosophy is his distinction between sensibility and intelligence. Human beings share with other animals the ability to perceive the material world via the senses. Through the senses we take into our minds mental representations of sensibilia, or physical objects. On the basis of these representations, which either take place in the presence of their objects or are called up in memory, we can situate ourselves in time and space and become aware of our physical surroundings. But if our modes of knowing were confined solely to sensibilia, we would have very limited capacities for judgment. We could, for instance, judge whether material conditions were favorable or likely to be favorable to the satisfaction of our needs or desires, but we could not judge whether the desires we happened to have in response to some set of circumstances were appropriate or worthy of satisfaction. For evaluative judgments we need to have representations, not simply of sensibilia, but of sensibilia under some aspect of the good. Mental representations of goods, intelligibilia, inform a mode of knowing unavailable to nonrational animals. Via their intelligence, human beings can perceive the physical world in its vileness or beauty, its evil or its goodness.

Augustine credits the Platonists for having brought the intelligibilia into proper philosophical focus. Following their lead, he associates sensibilia with what we can sense by the sight and touch of a body (*uisu tactuque corporis*), intelligibilia with what we comprehend through the mind's eye (*conspectu mentis*).[1]

---

[1] *De civ. Dei* 8.6.

The contrast between two kinds of perceiving, one mental and the other physical, fails in itself to elucidate the difference in representational content between sensibilia and intelligibilia. It is not enough for Augustine to note that we perceive material forms with our physical senses and intelligible forms with our mind's eye, for no matter what the source of our representations, they register mentally. But although it would not be wrong to say that our senses can give us access to intelligibilia and our mind to sensibilia, it would be an imprecise manner of speaking. Sensible representations have their basis in our sensible encounters with the physical world, and intelligible representations have their basis in paradigmatic forms which physical particulars (sensibly perceived) more or less adequately instantiate.[2] Sensible representations can be subsumed under intelligible ones, but the reverse is impossible.

Temporal realities, subject to change, furnish the representational content of sensibilia. We sense things in time and space. It is harder to interpret what Augustine supposes the representational content of intelligibilia to be. He sometimes speaks as if there were two sorts of objects to be represented – the ones able to be perceived by the senses and the ones revealed in God, the light of the human mind (*lux mentium*).[3] I am nevertheless disinclined to read him as placing intelligibilia in an invisible world "behind" the visible, material world, as if, in a thing of beauty, beauty were a special sort of object existing apart from the thing. For the most part Augustine resists confusing a difference in representational content with a difference in worlds. We do not have as many worlds as we have modes of perception; we have but one world, whose comprehension requires different modes of perception.

To begin to see why Augustine's intelligibilia need not and should not be thought to require the duplication of the material

---

[2] In *De lib. arb.* 2.8.22, Augustine uses knowledge of numbers to illustrate the difference between the two sorts of representation. Although we can sensibly perceive the physical integrity of an object, he argues that we do not (odd as it may at first seem) similarly perceive the object's numerical unity. All corporeal objects can be partitioned in some way, while true numerical unity has no countable parts. Countability presupposes the partless unit. Numerical unity is therefore something other than physical form, and requires for its cognition intelligible representation. Augustine's argument parallels Plato's argument in book VII of the *Republic* (523b–526a).   [3] *De civ. Dei* 8.7.

world in spirit, let us look more intently at the anatomy of intelligible judgment, using as our example the intelligibility of beauty. In *De civitate Dei* he observes that "there is no physical beauty, whether still, as in a shape, or in motion, as in a tune, which is judged other than by mind."[4] Imagine a difference in judgment between a musicologist and her student on the aesthetic merit of the Adagio movement of Mozart's Piano Concerto in A Major. The teacher deems the movement beautiful, and her student deems it uninspired and plodding. Both listeners have access to the same recording, and so their sensible representations of the movement do not differ in content. It is at the level of intelligibility, in this case the intelligibility of beauty, that teacher and student part company. What in Augustine's view would account for the difference in their respective judgments, and more specifically for the possibility of one judgment being more adequate than the other?[5]

For there to be judgments about physical beauty, not simply arbitrary decisions, Augustine contends first of all that beauty in representation (*species pulchritudinis*) must transcend the spatial and temporal diversity of its physical instantiation. When student and teacher hear Mozart's Adagio, for instance, their sensible representations supply them with a temporal sequence of sounds; but before they can pass judgment on the music's beauty, they must transform their sensible impressions into a unified representation of the music in its integrity. The adequacy of their respective representations will depend in part on the adequacy of the norms they each use to represent the unity of the object of beauty, in part on their respective abilities to use those norms. Augustine's second contention about the nature and possibility of intelligible judgment invokes the need for normative standards. If representations of beauty admit of better and worse, then the "paradigmatic representation," he claims, "cannot be in the realm of things, where it would be

---

[4] *Ibid.*, 8.6 (CCSL 47, 223, 30–2): "Nulla est enim pulchritudo corporalis siue in statu corporis, sicut est figura, siue in motu, sicut est cantilena, de qua non animus iudicet."

[5] My provisional answer to this is drawn largely from *De civ. Dei* 8.6.

demonstrably subject to change."[6] God's mind, because it is not subject to change, sets the standard for all human representations of beauty. We adopt this standard in so far as we are able to see the world as God sees it, or in God's light, as it were. Were there no immutable mode of seeing the world (God's mode), there would be no principled way to relate changes in mind to improvements in judgment, no way to admit the aspiration to truth into the disagreement between the musicologist and her student.

Augustine's appeal to a divine standard for human judgment will, of course, be idle unless he can give us some reason to believe that human beings have access to God's point of view. But before we can address epistemological issues raised by his account of intelligibilia, we need further clarification on the logic of his position. When Augustine situates Platonic forms or ideas in the mind of a creator, he frees himself from the need to explicate truth as a correspondence between corporeal and incorporeal objects and suggests in its place a correspondence between divine and human judgment. I have suggested thus far that Augustine's intelligibilia are not immaterial objects, reference to which determines the truth or falsity of our evaluative judgments. In fact, the distinction between corporeal and incorporeal reality, dear to the heart of Platonists, enters into Augustine's theory of truth only tangentially. Much more important to him is the distinction between mutable and immutable reality. God cannot be material, because matter is mutable, and nothing mutable can supply standards for truth. Augustine ranks the Platonists over the Stoics and Epicureans because the latter, being materialists, are constrained to ground truth on a shifting foundation. His critique rests on his assumption that whatever is material is susceptible to change. He does not, however, assume that immateriality implies immutability. Philosophers who try to base truth on standards set by the judgments of mutable, immaterial minds, human minds, for instance, fare no better in Augustine's eyes than the Stoics and Epicureans.[7]

Platonists fare best in his eyes largely because he has been

---

[6] *De civ. Dei* 8.6 (CCSL 47, 223, 41–42): "non esse in eis rebus primam speciem, ubi mutabilis esse conuincitur."   [7] *De civ. Dei* 8.5.

disposed from the time of his youth, when he listened in Milan to the sermons of Ambrose, to adopt them as fellow theists, Plato included.[8] Plato, needless to say, would have been surprised to learn that he shared Augustine's conception of a creator God.[9] Be that as it may, Augustine labored under the assumption that Platonists all sought, as he did, an adequate conception of God, and however this assumption may have distorted his view of pagan Platonism, it profoundly influenced his appropriation of Platonic metaphysics. Above all else, the theistic context of his Platonism inclined him to associate representations of intelligibilia with exercises of practical, rather than speculative, reason. In his Platonic theism, the world is intelligible only when we represent it to ourselves as God's creative act, and we represent it to ourselves as created only when we create (act) in imitation of God. Augustine weds his theory of truth to his doctrine of creation.

The conceptual links between willing and representing in Augustine's Platonism are, to say the least, intricate. His doctrine of creation forges the strongest links, whose importance can be suggested indirectly if we remove his Platonism from its theistic context and then try to make sense of intelligible representation. The intelligibility of music's beauty, to return to our original example, would still require having some representation in our minds of the unity of the object of beauty. But what is the object of beauty? The obvious candidate is the music itself, or the temporally dispersed organization of sounds. These sounds, however, are registered in our minds sensibly, and sensations refer us to the material world. Platonism tells us that beauty does not have its referent in the material world. Its paradigmatic representation transcends spatial and temporal particulars altogether, and this paradigm sets the standard for all representations of physical beauty. At this point it seems paradoxical to speak of *physical* beauty or of goodness *in* the world, for the world is evidently left behind whenever beauty or goodness is represented. This would not be the case were there

---

[8] See *Conf.* 5.13 for Augustine's introduction to Ambrose and Peter Brown, *Augustine of Hippo: A Biography* (Berkeley: University of California Press, 1967), 79–87.

[9] Augustine himself seemed surprised. In *De civ. Dei* 8.11 he entertains (but reluctantly dismisses) the possibility that Plato may have met the prophet Jeremiah or read at least parts of the Hebrew Scriptures.

some correspondence in form between the physical world and paradigmatic forms of beauty and goodness, but it is very hard to imagine what sort of isomorphism could hold between corporeal and incorporeal forms. They "resemble" one another in none of their features. In sum, Platonism's attempt to transcend the material world, when pursued outside of theism, will tend to end (perhaps inescapably) in its rejection of the physical. Augustine's misplaced appreciation of Plato's conception of God did not, in fact, keep him from criticizing Platonists for their inability to see the body other than as an encumbrance to the mind.[10] In that regard, at least, he did respond to pagan Platonism's blindness to creation.

Now let us consider directly the importance of theism to Augustine's Platonism. "God is Truth" has, for Augustine, a very precise meaning. God imparts value and significance to the world in the act of creating it, and in our evaluative judgments we seek to discover the substance of what God has imparted. In representing value we must draw upon our own capacity for creating and imagining creation, for the world manifests God's wisdom in a manner akin to that in which artifacts manifest the wisdom of their artisans. There is no way, as the analogy between human craft and divine creation suggests, to represent wisdom apart from its material incarnations. When we do move beyond the world's materiality to arrive at some representation of its intelligibility, it is not by having to exit into a self-contained immaterial world. Instead we subsume the world we are given under the wisdom that has informed it and, like apprentice artisans, learn to discern the values of our craft in the works of the master. These values are not themselves material things, yet neither are they immaterial things. Their reality emerges out of the act of significant creation, and they serve to enliven the physical world with intelligence.

The craft analogy, for all its suggestiveness, is only an analogy, and lest it mislead, we need to bear in mind its fundamental shortcoming. Human artisans learn their trade from other artisans, and their work as artisans can be judged by standards of value they as individuals have had little if any role

---

[10] See, for example, *De civ. Dei* 12.27, 13.20, 14.3, and 14.5.

in creating. More generally, human agents, in seeking to live worthy lives, exercise their practical reason in the context of preexisting values, whose nature and appropriate expression in their lives they hope to discover. God, by contrast, never expresses values in creating, but rather in creating brings values (which we can discover) into being. In God there is simply no distinction between willing and representing the good. The good is represented by whatever God wills. Augustine explains as follows:

"God saw that it was good." – What else should be understood by these words, which are said of all things, if not the approbation of work done with the practical skill of God's wisdom? It is so far from true, however, that God learned of its goodness just when it was made, that had God not known of it, none of it would have come to be. When, therefore, God sees that it is good – the world which never would have come to be at all had God not had envisioned it before it was made – God does not learn of its goodness but causes its goodness to be known.[11]

I take Augustine to have invoked in his interpretation of creation a logical or conceptual connection between the good and God's will. The good would not be in the world unless God willed the world to be. Unlike human agents, who act in the context of an objective order of values, God acts (logically) prior to the formation of the objective order, and therefore no external standards of value can inform divine willing. Whatever falls outside of creation not only is ipso facto without value, but is ipso facto without existence.[12]

The passage I have cited above is nevertheless not without ambiguity. We might take Augustine to mean not that God wills the good into existence but that God wills into existence only that which is good. Each option allows God to remain the sovereign creator of the good, but the choice between them leaves Augustine with something like Euthyphro's dilemma. Is

---

[11] *De civ. Dei* 11.21 (CCSL 48, 339, 1–7): "Quid est enim aliud intellegendum in eo, quod per omnia dicitur: 'Vidit Deus quia bonum est,' nisi operis adprobatio secundum artem facti, quae sapientia Dei est? Deus autem usque adeo non, cum factum est, tunc didicit bonum, ut nihil eorum fieret, si ei fuisset incognitum. Dum ergo uidet quia bonum est, quod, nisi uidisset antequam fieret, non utique fieret: docet bonum esse, non discit."

[12] Hence evil cannot have positive ontological status. It can be only a negation or perversion of what is.

the good good because God wills it, or does God will the good
because it is good? Choose the first horn, and you seem to
confuse goodness with arbitrary fiat; choose the second, and
you face the daunting task of having to define the good. I have
no doubt that Augustine would have opted for the first horn.
"God must be loved," he writes, "not as this or that good, but
as the good in itself."[13] When he insists that God is Wisdom, or
Truth, or the Good, he is not merely indulging in pious
declamations. He is making a logical point about the foundations of judgment. The proposition "God is good," for instance,
does not predicate goodness to God but rather identifies God
with goodness. It would be misguided to predicate goodness to
the standard of goodness, for predications of goodness are
possible only in reference to the standard. If the standard were
allowed to serve as a subject of predication, it would cease to be
the standard for whatever predicate we applied to it. As long as
God sets the standard for wisdom and goodness, we cannot *judge*
whether God is wise or good; in reference to God we judge
whether other realities have wisdom or goodness.[14]

The first horn of Euthyphro's dilemma is uncomfortable only
for those who miss the logic of Augustine's position. Many
divine-command ethicists, for instance, have been made uncomfortable by questions like the following: "If God approves
of cruelty, would that make cruelty good?" Behind the question
stands the suggestion that goodness could have no logical
connection to what God wills if it were logically possible for God
to approve of whatever happens to offend our deepest moral
intuitions. The suggestion, however, is either innocuous or false.
It is innocuous if we are assuming that God's will changes over
time. In that case God no longer sets the standard for goodness
(standards must be fixed), and it becomes logically possible for
God to approve of acts we would deem evil in reference to some
other standard of goodness. But the logical connection between
God and the good depends on God's will serving as the *standard*
for goodness. If we take this into account, the suggestion is false.
There is nothing incoherent in the assertion that we could be

---

[13] *De Trin.* 8.3.4 (50, 272, 21–22): "Sic amandus est deus, non hoc et illud bonum, sed
ipsum bonum."
[14] Augustine argues along these lines in *De lib. arb.* 2.12.34 and *De Trin.* 8.3.4.

mistaken in any of our evaluative judgments relative to a divinely fixed standard of value, for the question of what we can know relative to an objective standard of value is not identical to the question of what makes a standard of value objective. When Augustine links God logically to the good, he answers the latter, but leaves open the answer to the former.

In the broader context of his philosophy he does not, of course, simply leave the question of knowing the good open. He is too much of a Platonist not to be consumed by it. But because he is a Platonic *theist*, the question takes the particular form of whether human beings can gain even limited access to the way God sees the world. Having attended to the logic of Augustine's theism, we know that viewing the world in God's light is not viewing the world apart from its materiality but viewing it as a unity under the aspect of eternity, *sub specie aeternitatis*. It seems incontestable that time-bound minds, such as ours, cannot unify the sum of the world's temporal and spatial diversity into a single, timeless representation. Nevertheless, we can, as far as Augustine is concerned, aspire to having images of eternity in time, and these images supply us with representations of the world's intelligibility to whatever extent they replicate the unity of God's timeless point of view. In taking this line, Augustine will face two formidable challenges. First, since it is far from obvious that temporally situated beings have any access to timeless perspectives, he will have to clarify what it would mean for us to have representations of eternity. Second, since we do not in any case have access to God's timeless perspective, he will have to account for how we know when our time-bound representations increase in intelligibility.

For the remainder of this chapter, I focus primarily on the first issue, the matter of eternity's representation in time. In *Confessiones* XI Augustine turns his attention to his apparently paradoxical ability to represent time to himself – i.e., his measuring of time. Over the course of his analysis of time's measurement, he begins to notice the necessary insinuation of eternity (timelessness) in all of his representations of realities in time, including and especially himself. He recollects or represents time as a unity whenever he comes to measure it, and similarly he recollects or represents himself as a unity whenever he comes to take the measure of himself over time. *Confessiones* XI supplies us with Augustine's paradigm for representing eternity in time, but it ends on a note of failure. The temporal insinuations of eternity fall well short of their ideal in God, and Augustine discovers much disorder and disunity in his representation of himself. Reasons for the disunity, for the inadequacy of Augustine's self-knowledge, move us into deeper waters. In this chapter I introduce but do not elaborate at length the connection Augustine draws between inadequate self-knowledge and perversity of will. In God, willing and representing the good necessarily go together; in humans the connection must be recovered.

THE ENTROPY OF PERSONAL IDENTITY

Augustine's famous investigation of time in *Confessiones* XI occupies chapters 14 through 28. These sections lend themselves as a group to independent treatment, even though at least ostensibly they form part of an extended meditation on creation (Gen. 1:1) and are framed in book XI by meditations on God's timeless eternity. The investigation of time proper raises what, by Augustine's day, have become standard skeptical doubts about time's existence. It advanced by reformulating those doubts as worries about the possibility of measuring time, and it concludes with what many have taken to be Augustine's answer to skepticism.

In his commentary on book XI, E. P. Meijering cautions us not to divorce Augustine's speculative agenda on the question of time from his existential interest in time's status as a created reality. Augustine's investigation of time has no independence, ultimately, from its theological setting.[15] While Meijering's caution is important, it is nevertheless useful to see how far a more circumscribed approach to time can be taken. It is somewhat of a mystery why Augustine would have chosen in the midst of a confession to pursue a skeptical problem having no obvious significance for human redemption. But his motives for

---

[15] E. P. Meijering, *Augustin über Schöpfung, Ewigkeit und Zeit: Das Elfte Buch der Bekenntnisse* (Leiden: E. J. Brill, 1979), 115.

digressing cannot be fathomed until we have given consideration to what he says in digressing. The separate sections on time in any case invite analysis apart from time's connection with eternity.[16] If the loss of surrounding context frustrates our ability to interpret Augustine's remarks on time, then a diagnosis of the frustration can lead us to consider why Augustine takes up the problem of time where he does.

Augustine opens the issue of time with the question, "What, then, is time?"[17] Rather than attempt any direct answer to this, he uses it as an occasion to raise puzzles about time's existence that go at least as far back as the fourth book of Aristotle's *Physics*.[18] Time seems to have no independent existence of its own. In the future it is yet to be, in the past it no longer is, and in the present it reduces to a moment having no duration. The claim about the status of the present may seem counterintuitive, but Augustine reasons that if the present had any duration, it would extend into the past or into the future, neither of which are presently in existence:

If some slice of time is understood to be incapable of division, even into the most minute portions of moments, that time alone is called "the present." That, however, is what passes from future to past so rapidly that its passing has no duration. For if there is duration, it divides up into past and future, and the present is left without length.[19]

Time passes through the point of the present either towards that which no longer exists or towards that which does not yet exist. Augustine wonders bemusedly whether time exists solely in its tendency not to exist ("tendit non esse").[20]

Time's tendency towards nonexistence does not have the air

---

[16] Paul Ricœur has explored Augustine's remarks on measuring time largely apart from their broader context in book XI. See his *Time and Narrative*, vol. I (Chicago: University of Chicago Press, 1984), 3–30, and III (Chicago: University of Chicago Press, 1988), 12–22.

[17] *Conf.* 11.14.17 (CCSL 27, 202, 38): "Quid est ergo tempus?"

[18] For a brief history of classical and late antique reflection on time's reality, see Richard Sorabji, *Time, Creation, and the Continuum: Theories in Antiquity and the Early Middle Ages* (Ithaca: Cornell University Press, 1983), 7–32.

[19] *Conf.* 11.15.20 (CCSL 27, 204, 48–53): "Si quid intellegitur temporis, quod in nullas iam uel minutissimas momentorum partes diuidi possit, id solum est, quod praesens dicatur; quod tamen ita raptim a futuro in praeteritum transuolat, ut nulla morula extendatur. Nam si extenditur, diuiditur in praeteritum et futurum: praesens autem nullum habit spatium." [20] *Conf.* 11.14.17.

of paradox until Augustine attempts to account for his ordinary
ability to measure time and meaningfully employ temporal
concepts. If we assume, as Augustine does, that our divisions of
time into long and short and our comparisons between times
have some basis in reality, then what is it that we are measuring
and comparing? Augustine points out that whatever can be
measured must also exist, and exist with definite boundaries.
Time *ex hypothesi* does not exist in the past and future and has no
boundaries in the present, since the present has no duration to
be bounded. Occasionally Augustine attempts to soften the
paradox by suggesting that time can be measured in passing,[21]
but he recognizes that nothing with a measurable duration can
be held up for measure in a durationless present. It passes into
the past, where it no longer exists.

Not long into the investigation it becomes clear that
Augustine's primary concern will be with the temporal present
– the locus of whatever control we have over time. In an
economizing move, he suggests that references to past and
future time can be redescribed as modes of reference to the
present:

Now that it is clear and evident that things exist neither in the future
nor in the past, there are not, strictly speaking, three times – past,
present, and future. Perhaps we might say, strictly speaking, that there
are three times – the present of things past, the present of things
present, and the present of things future.[22]

This would give us three kinds of "present" time, each accessed
by a discrete mental activity. Remembering operates on the
present of things past, expecting on the present of things future,
and perceiving on the present of things present. Though perhaps
bizarre-sounding (Augustine does not expect us to give up the
less cumbersome way of referring to past and future[23]), his

[21] *Ibid.*, 11.16.21, 11.26.33.
[22] *Ibid.*, 11.20.26 (CCSL 27, 206–7, 1–5): "Quod autem nunc liquet et claret, nec
futura sunt nec praeterita, nec proprie dicitur: tempora sunt tria, praeteritum,
praesens et futurum, sed fortasse proprie diceretur: tempora sunt tria, praesens de
praeteritis, praesens de praesentibus, praesens de futuris."
[23] *Conf.* 11.20.26 (CCSL 27, 207, 8–10): "Dicatur etiam: 'Tempora sunt tria,
praeteritum, praesens et futurum,' sicut abutitur consuetudo." ("Let it still be said,
'There are three times, past, present, and future,' in the manner of our customary
misusage.")

suggestion amounts to no more than the observation that our command over the past and future depends on what we control at present in the form of memory and expectation. In drawing our attention to this, Augustine indicates how the problem of the nonexistence of the past and future will be taken care of with the solution to the problem of the durationless present. The present "contains" the past and the future and lends its being to theirs.

If Augustine is to redeem time's measurement from the poverty of a durationless present, he needs to associate the temporal present with some sort of *distentio*. The basic meaning of *distentio* is that of a stretching out or an extension. It is tempting to read the *distentio* of Augustine's interest as extension in the sense of temporal duration, since the lack of such duration is apparently what makes the temporal present problematic. It turns out, however, that he seeks another sort of *distentio*, having nothing to do with duration.

The term does not actually appear in book XI until the twenty-third chapter, where Augustine begins consideration of the classical habit of associating time with the regularity of celestial motion.[24] Over the course of the argument, he dismisses the idea that time is the motion of a physical body. Movement, he reasons, occurs in time, but time does not cease when movement ceases; therefore time cannot *be* physical motion.[25] Though simple, his reasoning is telling. If Augustine's interests in *distentio* were directed towards finding an acceptable standard for temporal measurements, the association of time's *distentio* with regular physical motion, such as celestial motion, would be a logical choice. But he indicts the classical view for irrelevance, not for error. Since his own interests in the problem of time turn on how standards can be used at all, appeals to *distentio* as simple duration are idle.[26] He will need to invoke *distentio* not as time

---

[24] Noted and discussed by Ricœur, *Time and Narrative*, vol. I, 15–16. On the matter of Augustine's access to classical views connecting time and motion, see Meijering, *Augustin*, 79–88, who presents a synopsis of the scholarship.

[25] *Conf.* 11.24.31.

[26] Ricœur, *Time and Narrative*, vol. III, 13, criticizes Augustine for missing the distinction between the crude thesis that time is the movement of bodies and Aristotle's "infinitely more subtle thesis" that time, though not motion, cannot be understood

extended and fixed in reference to the regularity of motion, but as control over time, exemplified in his ability to perceive temporal order and make measurements. That sort of *distentio* can only be a *distentio animi*, his mind's encompassment of time.[27]

The problem of the durationless present, in the wake of *distentio*'s disassociation from simple duration, turns on how the human mind orders time in the temporal present. In the celebrated climax of his investigation, Augustine explicates his own mind's act of ordering past, present, and future:

> It is in you, my mind, that I measure times. Do not clamor at me, or rather, do not clamor at yourself, with the disorderly throng of your impressions. In you, I say, I measure times. What I measure in the present is the impression which things passing by make in you and leave behind after they have passed. I do not measure the things themselves whose passage occasioned the impression; it is the impression that I measure when I measure times. This therefore is either what times are, or I do not measure them.[28]

Augustine has told us earlier that past and future could be packed into the present if redescribed as modes of occurrent mental activity: namely, the activities of remembering and expecting. There was at least implicit in this redescription of past and future the suggestion that the present might afford a sufficient perspective for the mind to orient itself in time. In the passage cited above, Augustine draws out the suggestion explicitly. If he is to have awareness of time, his mind must be able to order its own mental contents, and in particular order the impressions that things deposit in its temporal present. *Distentio animi* can be his mind's encompassment of time only if it represents as well his mind's encompassment of itself.

It might reasonably be asked what his mind's self-encompassment involves. For now, I will suggest only a minimal answer to

---

apart from motion. It is fair to say that Augustine overlooks the distinction, but I fail to see how the more subtle thesis would advance his interests in time any better than the crude thesis he refutes.   [27] *Conf.* 11.26.33.

[28] *Ibid.*, 11.27.36 (CCSL 27, 213, 46–52): " In te, anime meus, tempora metior. Noli mihi obstrepere, quod est: noli tibi obstrepere turbis affectionum tuarum. In te, inquam, tempora metior. Affectionem, quam res praetereuntes in te faciunt et, cum illae praeterierint, manet, ipsam metior praesentem, non ea quae praeterierunt, ut fieret; ipsam metior, cum tempora metior. Ergo aut ipsa sunt tempora, aut non tempora metior."

this. Augustine associates his mind's control over its contents with his power of attention.[29] Ideally he should, in concentrating upon his experience of the present, be able to perceive and differentiate properly all of his impressions in their variety, including those having temporal significance. To the extent that he manages this, he approaches an encompassing perception of his mind's contents. Though minimal, this answer is sufficient to test the viability of Augustine's analysis of time's measurement. Has he in fact supplied a firm foundation for a practice shaken by skeptical doubts?

Let us take Augustine at his word and treat time's measurement as the measurement of mental impressions. When he registers lengths of time in his mind, he translates the problematic idiom of past, present, and future into the idiom of the enduring present, where impressions of the past and future can be held on to and measured. Sounds promising, but Augustine is short on details. He gives us no account of how he manages to perceive impressions as having a temporal aspect to them. How does he pick out from his mental contents a memory, percept, or anticipation, and then on the basis of his recognition "measure" the time embodied in impression? Nor does he explain how impressions get their temporal significance in the first place. It is not an explanation merely to say that the impressions are caused by the passing of time. What is it exactly that passes, if the terms of time's analysis leave us with a nonexistent past and future and a present without duration? Impressions are left as the expression of a nonexistent cause on a durationless present. It looks as if Augustine cannot connect the two idioms of temporality (one of events and one of impressions) without begging the very questions he has raised to render time's measurement paradoxical.[30]

---

[29] *Conf.* 11.28.37 (CCSL 27, 214, 8–10): "Et quis negat praesens tempus carere spatio, quia in puncto praeterit? Sed tamen perdurat attentio, per quam pergat abesse quod aderit." ("Who denies that the present lacks duration, since it goes by in an instant? But attention nevertheless endures, and through it what will be hastens on to what has been.")

[30] I am, of course, not the only one to have noticed lacunae in Augustine's analysis. See Ricœur, *Time and Narrative*, vol. I, 11–12, Robert Jordan, "Time and Contingency in St. Augustine," *Review of Metaphysics* 8 (1955), 394–417, see 398–403, and Ronald

It is possible that Augustine never meant to connect the two idioms. Some philosophers have interpreted his appeal to impressions as his argument for time's subjectivity or lack of substantial reality.[31] The thesis of time's subjectivity is roughly the claim that we perceive the world erroneously as temporal, for the world is in fact timeless.[32] Augustine seems to subscribe to this thesis in the sense that he begins with doubts about time's existence and ends with an account of measuring time which confirms rather than dispels the doubts. He reduces the temporal present to an instant bounded by a nonexistent past and future. In measuring time, his mind does not move outside the bounds of this instant. If we are to take Augustine's remarks about the nonexistence of the past and future literally, a temporal present having neither a before nor an after is, strictly speaking, an atemporal present. Time's unreality carries into his mind's atemporal apprehension of its impression of time. But his mind is, in fact, impressed with nothing. Its experience of time is an illusion. On this reading of Augustine, he resolves the paradox of time's measurement by discrediting the intuition that gave rise to the paradox in the first place. The intuition that when we measure time, we measure something does not hold up under scrutiny.

Let us suppose for a moment that this reading of Augustine is correct and that he intended to reduce alleged perceptions of time's passage to his mind's atemporal apprehension of its own impressions. Augustine's argument for time's nonexistence, based on his eliminative analysis of time's measurement, is

Suter, "Augustine on Time with some Criticisms from Wittgenstein," *Revue internationale de philosophie* 16 (1962), 378–394, see 391–92.

[31] For the most notorious example of this way of reading Augustine, see Bertrand Russell, *Human Knowledge: Its Scope and Limits* (New York: Simon and Schuster, 1948), 212. More cautious readings along the same lines include those of Suter, "Augustine on Time," 378–94, C. W. K. Mundle, "Augustine's Pervasive Error Concerning Time," *Philosophy* 41 (1966), 165–68, and Hugh M. Lacey, "Empiricism and Augustine's Problems about Time," *Review of Metaphysics* 22 (1968), 219–45.

[32] Note that this thesis is not quite what Kant had in mind when he spoke of time as an intuition. Although Kant believed that the mind did not discover temporality in the world but rather imposed it on the world, he suspended judgment on what the world was like in itself. Hence he would have been disinclined to speak of time as an illusion. For a modern defense of time's subjectivity, in keeping with how I have defined the thesis, see John McTaggart, *The Nature of Existence*, vol. II (Cambridge: Cambridge University Press, 1927), 9–31.

curiously self-defeating. What is it that accounts for his misperception here, given that it certainly seems to him that time passes? If time does not exist and the illusion of time has its source in an atemporal mental act, then how does his timeless perception in a timeless world yield the appearance of a world in time? Since Augustine has advanced his mind's timeless perception of its impressions as the only basis for his awareness of time's passage, we are left to conclude that inadequate attention to his mental contents has left him with the false impression that things are in time. In other words, he is struck with time's passage to the extent that his mind has failed in its activity of ordering times – past, present, and future – in its atemporal present. It should be obvious now why his alleged argument for time's unreality is self-defeating. If his mind can change in its relation to its mental contents, so as to decrease the order of its impressions through inattention, then the illusion of time is based on activity (a change in attention) that is itself subject to temporal placement and measure. Faced once again with the task of accounting for the accessibility of temporal relations, this time among mental events, Augustine will have succeeded only in replicating the paradox of time's measurement for mental activity.[33]

At this point we have come to the critical juncture in our analysis of Augustine's investigation of time. Either we say that his investigation closes on an argument that, though not without philosophical interest, fails; or we say that our analysis remains unfinished until we have considered what role the surrounding meditations on eternity may have to play in the investigation of time proper, as Meijering tells us we must. Philosophers who have chosen to read closure into Augustine's remarks on time have generally taken him to be arguing for the subjectivity of time. For at least two reasons this interpretation of Augustine's intentions is implausible. First, we have no reason for thinking

---

[33] Suter, "Augustine on Time," 392 believes that Augustine is caught in his own paradox because he mistakenly views time in quasi-spatial terms: "Thus we see that, preoccupied with time as length, Augustine internalizes time along with its mental and immaterial measuring-stick. But such a measuring stick ceases to measure." For an able response to this sort of Wittgensteinian deflation of Augustine's concerns, see James McEvoy, "St. Augustine's Account of Time and Wittgenstein's Criticisms," *Review of Metaphysics* 38 (1984), 547–77.

that Augustine had any antecedent interest in the question of time's subjectivity, and it is odd to suppose that he would have developed such an interest having concluded earlier that time forms part of what God has created.[34] Second, there is no textual evidence to suggest that Augustine considered time unreal following his putative "solution" to the paradox of measuring what has no reality.

Witness Augustine's self-description in the first chapter to follow his remarks on time proper:

Now my years are spent in lamentation, and you, Lord, my eternal Father, are my only solace. I have broken up into times, whose order I know not, and in tumultuous changes my recollections, the innermost sinews of my soul, are being torn apart, until I should flow together again in you, purified and melted in the fire of your love.[35]

This is not the description of someone who has managed to contain "time" in the stability of an atemporal present. Instead Augustine seems to be describing his inability to recollect himself *out* of time. His recollections (*cogitationes*) recede from his attention and fall into times whose order he no longer knows.[36] We could attribute his experience of temporal disorder partly to his failure to meet his own condition for measuring time. His

---

[34] *Conf.* 11.13.16 (CCSL 27, 202, 26–7): "Omnia tempora tu fecisti et ante omnia tempora tu es, nec aliquo tempore non erat tempus." ("All times you have made and before all times you abide, and there was not a time in which time was not.") The issue motivating this declaration is whether God acts in time in order to create. Augustine concludes that God creates time in acting and that temporal categories have no application apart from the created order.

[35] *Conf.* 11.29.39 (CCSL 27, 215, 10–14): "Nunc uero anni mei in gemitibus, et tu solacium meum, domine, pater meus aeternus es; at ego in tempora dissilui, quorum ordinem nescio, et tumultuosis uarietatibus dilaniantur cogitationes meae, intima uiscera animae meae, donec in te confluam purgatus et liquidus igne amoris tui."

[36] Normally it would be reading too much into the word *cogitatio* to translate it as "recollection." The verb *cogito* is the iterative form of *cogo* (to collect or bring together), though its usual translation as "to think, or to consider" loses the iterative sense of *cogo* as a repeated or constant collecting, a recollecting. Augustine wished to retain the iterative sense of *cogito*, for he believed that all thinking was at heart a recollecting. See *Conf.* 10.11.18 (CCSL 27, 164, 14–17): "Nam cogo et cogito sic est, ut ago et agito, facio et factito. Verum tamen sibi animus hoc uerbum proprie uindicauit, ut non quod alibi, sed quod in animo conligitur, id est cogitur, cogitari proprie iam dicatur." ("For *cogo* stands to *cogito* just as *ago* stands to *agito* and *facio* to *factito*. But the mind has nevertheless claimed this word [*cogitare*] as proper to itself, so that it is not proper to speak of as cogitated what has not been assembled or collected in the mind.")

mind does not "distend" to embrace in its present the sum of his temporal experience. But notice that his mind's failure has as its effect not merely his perception of his life as being in time, but his perception of his life as coming apart in time. The latter is a *non sequitur* if to this point he has been arguing for time's subjectivity. To make any sense of the above citation, we need to return Augustine's remarks on time to their context as part of a confession.

No reinterpretation of his argument will be possible, however, unless we first take account of certain revisions he makes in his terminology. At the start of chapter 29 Augustine gives a name to the life that is coming apart in time. He calls it a *distentio*.[37] This should come as a surprise. Augustine has earlier invoked the idea of *distentio* to represent his mind's control over time. Now, in a complicated word play, he reverses the import of the term. He extends the basic meaning of *distentio* as a "stretching out" to the extreme of a "sundering or pulling apart." On the basis of a morphological pun, a life pulled apart in *distentio* becomes as well a life held apart in *distentio*. Etymologically *distentio* connects with the verb *distendo* (to stretch out), but its morphology suggests an additional connection to the verb *distineo* (to hold apart), in that each verb shares *distentus* as the form of its past participle. As a life sundered and held apart in time, *distentio* carries the force of both verbs.[38]

Augustine does not shift the ground under *distentio* without also introducing distinctions designed to track the resulting reverberations. He remarks that in so far as his mind manages to order its temporal experience, it is said to be extended (*extentus*) rather than distended (*distentus*). *Extensio* should not be taken to carry the original import of *distentio*. When his mind gains some mastery over time (i.e., orders time), it not only extends itself *over* time but also *out* of time. Given the context of confession, what Augustine evidently means is that his mind extends in some way towards God, who as sovereign over time holds out his

[37] *Conf.* 11.29.39 (CCSL 27, 214, 2): "ecce distentio est uita mea."
[38] For a brief but illuminating history of the term prior to Augustine's usage, see Gerard O'Daly, "Time as *distentio* and St. Augustine's Exegesis of *Philippians* 3:12–14," *Revue des études augustiniennes* 23 (1977), 266–68. Note also O'Daly's comments in *Augustine's Philosophy of Mind* (Berkeley: University of California Press, 1987), 153–54.

mind's only hope of recovering lost times. The nuance added to *extensio* carries over into the meaning of *intentio*, or concentration of attention. When Augustine attends to his experience of the present, he does not restrict his attention solely to his impressions. He refers them to their source, so that time may become his opportunity to recall his life in God. The net effect of Augustine's new terminology is to build within the language of time and time's measurement implicit references to eternity.[39]

Time's ties to eternity have in fact been implicit in Augustine's investigation of how time is measured, but it is only in retrospect, after *distentio* has changed its import, that the nature of the connection becomes clear. As a representation of his mind's control over time, *distentio* refers to his recollection of his past. Through memory his past (in the form of impressions) remains accessible to his present. Remembered time can be attended to, measured, and ordered. As a representation of time's control over his mind, *distentio* refers to his failure to recollect his past. In *Confessiones* x, Augustine ponders the impenetrable depths of his memory and proclaims with finality, "I cannot take in all that I am."[40] The impossibility of self-encompassment leads him in book xi to pronounce his life a *distentio*, a scattering over time. To capture the intent of Augustine's investigation of time, it is crucial that the extended sense of *distentio* as a scattering should not be understood to replace the *distentio* of measured time. Augustine never claims that we cannot measure time. His point is that even when our minds bind up time in recollection and measurement, we remain bound by time. The dual aspect of *distentio* has its source in a contrast between the temporal present and the eternal present. In the eternal present God binds up time without being bound by time. In the temporal present, we can recollect time, but moments of recollection pass and our recollections dissipate.[41] To the extent that we can hold the past in the present and thereby gain a measure of control over time,

---

[39] *Conf.* 11.29.39. Ricœur, *Time and Narrative*, vol. I, 27–28 observes that as of chapter 29, Augustine's appeal to the mind's *distentio* moves out of "the speculative context of aporia and inquiry" and into "the dialectic of praise and lamentation." For all its subtlety, Ricœur's description of the shift from speculation back to confession fails to clarify why Augustine changes contexts so suddenly in his meditation on time.

[40] *Conf.* 10.8.15 (CCSL 27, 162, 60–61): "nec ego ipse capio totum, quod sum."

[41] *Conf.* 11.11.13.

we approximate in very imperfect fashion God's secure sovereignty over time.[42] It is therefore in the *distentio* of measured time that time finds its tie to eternity. But because of the tenuous nature of the connection, the *distentio* of measurement trades off with the *distentio* of entropy.

Augustine's remarks on time proper form an integral part of his confession to God. They establish the tension between recollection of time and dissolution in time, which a creator God, being sovereign over time, could resolve in Augustine's favor. His placement of these remarks in the midst of a meditation on creation has as its intended effect not the isolation of the creature's time from the creator's eternity, but rather the heightening of their contrast. Augustine's failure to master time reflects his lack of self-mastery, the breach in his self-encompassment. As his memory expands, so does the gulf between his mind's occasional hold on time and God's eternal hold. Left to its own devices, his mind moves over time towards increasing entropy. His recognition of this inevitability disposes him to petition God for solace.

In an ingenious way, Augustine has used the skeptical paradox of time's measurement to dramatize the problem of self-integrity of time. Time turns out not to lack reality but ultimacy. As a *distentio*, the temporal present orders time in itself and mimics the eternal present, of which it is an imperfect manifestation. Time's imperfection carries into his mind's efforts at self-definition. Measuring time involves his attempt to recollect himself. But he cannot through his own efforts bring himself to completion in eternity. His failure to master his life in time ensures his mortality.

SIN AND ENTROPY

In *Time and Narrative*, a work much inspired by Augustine, Paul Ricœur speaks of a certain immemorial wisdom which resists philosophical clarity: "immemorial wisdom seems to perceive a hidden collusion between change that destroys – forgetting, aging, death – and time that simply passes."[43] The shift in the

---

[42] *Ibid.*, 11.31.41.   [43] Ricœur, *Time and Narrative*, vol. III, 18.

meaning of *distentio* in *Confessiones* xi illustrates superbly just this sort of collusion. Augustine marks time in his mind's distension throughout most of the book, but towards the end of his meditation, he describes himself as distended and rent over time, disordered beyond his powers of recognition. The passing of time has shifted over, in some mysterious manner, into destructive change. If we try to find the answer to this mystery, the "hidden collusion," within the confines of book xi, we are likely to indict time itself. Augustine tells us there that when we represent time, we bring the past into view by recollecting it in memory. This enables us to "see" things in time. Acts of recollection, though they bring unity to temporally dispersed realities and in that sense "suspend" time, nevertheless take place in time. We never cease to be in time even as we represent it to ourselves, and inevitably there comes a time when the extent of our temporal dispersion outruns our powers of recollection – hence the shift in *distentio*. We lose ourselves to the past as time passes.

This turns out, however, not to be a very satisfactory answer to the mystery. If time's passage and human finitude combine to deform human beings, then Augustine will have committed himself to the theologically disastrous view that God has created deformed creatures. Human deformation would reflect especially badly on the creator, in that we have been made in God's image. The suggestion, then, that time colludes with human finitude to bring dissolution and death, cannot be entertained if we are to stay within the bounds of Augustine's doctrine of creation. And it seems that we should stay within those bounds, at least for the reason that his remarks on time form part of his extended meditation on creation in *Confessiones* xi–xiii. But I would not, on the other hand, commend us to Augustine's dogmatic agenda without also having us consider its underlying philosophical rationale. So what if Augustine is committed by dogma to affirming the essential goodness of time-bound existence? We cannot simply dismiss the possibility that he may have missed the inconsistency between his lament over the entropy of his finite life and his commitment to the integrity and value of his life *qua* created. Nor can we, in any case, rest content with only a negative answer to the mystery of collusion between time and dissolution. If time itself is not at the source of entropy, what is?

There is, in point of fact, no inconsistency between his doctrine of creation and his conception of our deleterious *distentio* over time, and once we return his doctrine to the context of his Platonism, the appearance of inconsistency vanishes and we move closer to the philosophical clarity Ricœur despairs of having. The problem that Augustine introduces near the end of his meditation on time is best characterized as his problem of self-representation or self-knowledge. He suffers in *distentio* the effects of having an inadequate representation of himself. But when we speak of adequacy in self-representation, we invoke the need for a standard or paradigmatic representation of selfhood. Let us suppose for a moment that at the root of inadequate self-representation we find limitations of memory, in particular our inability to remember everything that has happened to us over the course of our lives. If that is the problem of self-representation, then we imply the paradigm of a human mind able to recall the totality of its encounters with the world in a single representation. This falls well short of a serviceable paradigm of selfhood. Simply to have the totality of our experience available to memory is not to have before us an *intelligible* representation of ourselves. More likely it is to have before us a blooming, buzzing confusion. But Augustine never identifies the unity of his self-representation with the simple *distentio* of having his past available to mind. He recognizes that the intelligibility of his life depends on whether he can see himself as unified under the aspect of the good. His memory of things in time, of himself in time, gives him his sense of his temporal situation, as living over time among things in time, but it does not (by itself) reveal to him the significance of his time-bound life. Such is the difference between sensible and intelligible self-representation. For the latter Augustine needs to see in his life over time the unity God sees when God looks at the world *sub specie aeternitatis* and proclaims it good.

Now let us return Augustine's doctrine of creation to the context of his Platonism and see whether we can make better

sense of the idea of "paradigmatic self-representation." God
serves, in Augustine's philosophy, as the source and standard of
the good. God is the source of the good in that whatever God
creates is, by virtue of the creator's art, good; and God is the
standard of goodness in that creation, *as God sees it*, represents
the good. Willing and representing the good are not, in God,
logically independent of one another. God cannot be understood first to have represented the good and then willed it, for
that would make the good conceptually and temporally prior to
what God wills. Instead Augustine envisions God as having
comprehended all of the created order, in its temporal and
spatial dispersion, unified into one atemporal and immutable
representation[44] (i.e., what God sees when God sees that
creation is good), and this representation renders in cognitive
form the wisdom of God's creative act. Because the representation leaves out no aspect of time's unfolding, there is no
past or future to frame God's act of creating, and so there is no
intelligible way to situate it in time. Not being bound in time,
God can supply the standard of intelligibility for beings who are
so bound. Augustine in God's mind is represented eternally as
an integrated unity, and because it is *God's* mind doing the
representing, the unity has normative significance – it establishes Augustine's particular value as part of the created order.
From his time-bound point of view, Augustine can in recollection begin to approximate the unity of his paradigmatic
self-representation in God. To whatever extent he falls short in
his approximations, he fails to be intelligible to himself.

If Augustine seems in *Confessiones* xi to suggest a hidden
collusion between unintelligibility of this sort and time's
passage, it is only because he has in this book left the source of
the unintelligibility out of his account and moved on to explore
contributory causes and symptoms. Having abandoned God as
his principle of intelligibility, he will over time become
increasingly unintelligible to himself. There will be more of his
experience to make sense of and no good way for him to make
sense of it, having rejected "the most fundamental ordering

---

[44] *De civ. Dei* 11.21 and *Conf.* 11.31.41.

principle" in him.[45] Sin brings entropy in its wake, and that is what Augustine describes as the deleterious *distentio* of his life. His perspective in book XI is not inconsistent. It is incomplete. We must look elsewhere for his abandonment of God and its significance for his self-knowledge.

The narrative of Augustine's conversion in *Confessiones* I–IX offers us the most detailed account of his own struggle with sin and its outcome. But of more use to us for now is the schematic account of sin he offers in book X of *De Trinitate*, written over ten years later.[46] There Augustine outlines the pathology of a mind having turned from God to seek intelligibility within itself and the world. Of the turn itself, he will note that this mind begins by enjoying its inner beauties (*intrinsecus pulchra*) as they have been given to it by God, but soon succumbs to the temptation to ascribe them to itself ("*volens ea sibi tribuere*"), and the trouble begins.[47] There is no basis for inner beauties or discoverable values of any sort other than in relation to the eternal will of their creator, and if the human mind overlooks this relation in its perception of itself and its world, it fatally undermines its ability to make evaluative judgments. But judge it must, and so the mind seeks the touchstone of its judgments in the changeable world, becoming ever more frantic in its attachments, hoping to impose by will the stability it lost when it gave up God. The imposition is futile, however, and the mind loses nearly all ability to understand its own nature. Finding itself in a world stripped of inherent value – a world of blind matter in motion – it represents itself as part of such a world and so supposes itself to be a body, a thing ("*corpus esse se putat*").[48] At this stage the mind's pathology has advanced it to the brink of spiritual death. No longer can it view itself in isolation from

---

[45] The phrase comes from Charles Taylor, *Sources of the Self: The Making of the Modern Identity* (Cambridge: Harvard University Press, 1989), 136: "God can be thought of as the most fundamental ordering principle in me. As the soul animates the body, so does God the soul. He vivifies it." I am indebted to Taylor's intelligent discussion of interiority in Augustine and its basis in knowledge of God. See chapter 7, "In Interiore Homine."

[46] Augustine completed the *Confessiones* circa 400. *De Trinitate* x falls between the years 413 and 416. See the Chronological Table of Augustine's Works, in Eugene TeSelle, *Augustine the Theologian* (New York: Herder and Herder, 1970).

[47] *De Trin.* 10.5.7.　　　　　　　　[48] *Ibid.*, 10.6.9.

the fragmentation and dissolution of what it has come to love without measure.[49] Its body has become its tomb.

It is not easy to determine from Augustine's schema whether he has sorted out the cause of sin from its symptoms, but of the pathology as a whole he does have this to say: "Often under the influence of depraved desire the mind acts as if it has forgotten itself."[50] I doubt whether he meant in this remark to identify sin's cause with depraved desire, for that would only have raised a further question about depravity. He seems instead to have intended to identify inadequate self-knowledge (a failure of intelligibility) with depraved desire (a failure of will or attention). Consider in this light the mind's confusion of itself with the corporeal content of its sensible representations of the world. Augustine's critique of this confusion is not aimed at materialism per se, as if the worst ravages of sin were to be found in having a materialist philosophy of mind. It is aimed at the supposition that the world has no value apart from what the human mind chooses to accord it. In reality the world derives its value from having been approved of by God. When the human mind looks for the source of value elsewhere, it turns to itself and supposes its own approval to be creative of value. The world then becomes to this mind the totality of things, and things it represents to itself sensibly, in corporeal imagery. As for the world's significance, there is nothing to represent. Values are imposed externally, via the mind's act of evaluating, and so they are not *in* the world to be represented. There is a disastrous irony in having a mutable mind represent the good as whatever it wills to be good. Since this mind is part of the world upon which it bestows value, it cannot but represent itself as having no inherent value, unless, of course, it presumes itself to be God. If so, time will give the lie to its presumption, for no mutable mind can serve as the standard for value, even its own. The materialism of Augustine's censure robs the world of its true standard of value, replaces it with a human standard, and thereby renders values "unreadable." Having been divested of its intelligibility, the world retains in representation only its

---

[49] *Ibid.*, 10.8.11.
[50] *Ibid.*, 10.5.7 (CCSL 50, 320, 5–6): "Multa enim per cupiditatem prauam tamquam sui sit oblita sic agit."

sensibility. The mind that would be God's must represent itself to be a thing of no discernible value. It acts as if it has forgotten itself, and in a real sense, it has.

In Augustine's Platonic theism, beings made in God's image have the capacity to see themselves as God sees them – not as insignificant assemblages of particulars in space and time, whose value must be arbitrarily assigned, but as animated expressions of divine wisdom. If they can no longer see themselves this way, it is because they have fallen away from the requisite habits of attention. *De Trinitate* x describes in brief the pathology of inattention, and the mind Augustine speaks of there as having fallen refers to his own mind and, by extension, to any human mind having difficulty discerning the good in itself or in the world. But the difficulty, it must be emphasized, cannot be ascribed to simple ignorance or human finitude. There is, on the contrary, something willful about failures of moral vision.

We can with profit take this Augustinian insight back to the scene of Augustine's lament in *Confessiones* xi. He sees himself disfigured over time because he lacks the unified view God has of him in eternity. When God sees Augustine, God represents him as perfected, and if Augustine could see himself through God's eyes, he would have no difficulty making his life out to be significant and intelligible. Here I think we might be tempted to conclude that the discrepancy between Augustine's representation of himself and God's paradigmatic representation of him indicates that he is simply not as good as God makes him out to be. But this could not be Augustine's conclusion. God sets the standard for intelligibility, and so if anyone is mistaken, it is Augustine, not God. It must be the case that Augustine *is in reality* what God represents him to be.

Admittedly this is a curious and at first sight unreasonable position to attribute to Augustine, for it has him reduce evil to an illusion, and surely evil is anything but an illusion. It does seem to me that he commits himself to some form of this reduction, if only in the sense that willing evil and misrepresenting the good have for him the same necessity in their conjunction in humans as willing and representing the good have in God. We set the *standard* for evil, in other words, for whenever we act on a standard of value of our own making, we will "evil" into existence. This is ironic creation, in that we never act intentionally except under the representation of the end of our action as good. We do not, then, will evil *qua* evil, but as evil under some misrepresentation of the good. In the analysis of sin's origination, it will be impossible for Augustine to sort out bad willing from faulty seeing; one cannot go before the other as cause goes before effect. If this commits him to basing evil on an illusion or error (a misrepresentation), it is nevertheless far from clear what his commitment implies. We are apt in the abstract to be misled into supposing that he denies the reality of evil. But if we look carefully at what he means by the rectification of sin and (by the same token) the recovery of self-knowledge, we will have to conclude otherwise.

Confessiones xi, reread in light of *De Trinitate* x, suggests that Augustine's self-forgetfulness, or his inability to recollect himself intelligibly, has its source in his having forgotten God. It stands to reason that if he is ever to recover himself, he must remember God. But here we have a philosophical puzzle. Self-knowledge is not implausibly thought of as a form of recollection, but it is very difficult to cast knowledge of God in the same mold. God does not subsist in time and so does not interact with us on the model of other things in time. There can be no particular time for God to enter into human memory, and when Augustine attempts in his own case to recollect a time of entry, he labors in vain to fix one.[51] Yet if God does not, in some intelligible manner, enter into memory, how could God be *in* memory and hence a subject for recollection? Much depends on the answer to this question – knowledge of God, self-knowledge, the intelligibility of value, the nature of sin, free will. Fortunately Augustine does not leave us without direction. He submits that in seeking God he seeks the happy life (*uita beata*).[52] If the nature of the former kind of seeking seems impenetrable, perhaps the nature of the latter will prove more tractable.

---

[51] *Conf.* 10.25.36.   [52] *Ibid.*, 10.20.29.

CHAPTER 2

The discipline of virtue

In *De Trinitate* Augustine observes that "all who are happy have what they want." Even so, he continues, "not all who have what they want are for that reason happy."[1] We can be wretched in one of two ways. We can either lack what we want or we can have what we ought not to have wanted. His two conditions for happiness, then, are that we have what we want and that we want nothing inappropriate or evil. Modern habits of thought might incline us to take the former condition as establishing the context for the latter, in which case having to limit our desires would diminish our prospects for having all that we want. But Augustine would have us reverse our perspective. Consider the desires that those tutored in wisdom would have, and then impose the condition that for happiness, they must be able to attain all they desire. Underlying his characterization of happiness is his assumption that we could never be happy and vicious. Happiness coincides with virtue. For purposes of clarity, I will refer to virtue-based happiness as *beatitude*.

It may strike us as arbitrary to restrict happiness to beatitude. Individuals do, after all, seem to find happiness in a multitude of satisfactions, not all of which are virtuous or honorable. To prejudice happiness in favor of virtuous pursuits is simply to confuse happiness with virtue. It seems obvious that the two cannot be equated, since we are presented all too frequently with examples of virtuous, unhappy people and vicious, happy

---

[1] *De Trin.* 13.5.8 (CCSL 50, 392–93, 33–37): "Omnes autem beati habent quod uolunt, quamuis non omnes qui habent quod uolunt continuo sint beati; continuo autem miseri qui uel non habent quod uolunt uel id habent quod non recte uolunt."

people. Augustine was, of course, aware that there were wicked people who thought that they were happy. But to his mind there were objective conditions for happiness, and we could be wrong about whether they were met either in our own case or in that of others.

It is an objective feature of happiness to have a good will, because having an evil will subjects our happiness to adventitious loss. Augustine's reasoning, in brief, is this. If we wish to gratify evil desires, we are evaluating as good what is in fact evil. We are disposed to make such an evaluation only if we have abandoned the fixed standard for the good (in God) and substituted in its place some mutable standard. Judging by a mutable standard of value threatens our happiness with instability. The good can change as our standard of evaluation changes, leaving our desires in a state of confusion, and the object of our desires, or what we temporarily judge to be good, can be taken away from us without our consent. Augustine contends that so vulnerable an ideal of happiness is hardly worthy of the name.

His alternative, however, is not obvious. Many goods fall outside our control whose loss would nevertheless seem to diminish our happiness. Some of them are natural endowments, such as health, beauty, and strength, while others are aspects of communal life, such as wealth, friendship, family ties, and citizenship. Although the disposition of natural and social goods is not independent of what individuals will, their presence or absence is to a degree external to what anyone wills. Natural and social goods are temporal goods, subject to the vagaries of time and circumstance, and consequently their loss can be suffered unwillingly. Should we conclude from this, then, that beatitude requires us to reject all our commitments to temporal things?

Such a strategy would inevitably end in self-defeat, since we happen to live in time. But even in his earlier works, where he has yet to accommodate his Platonism to his doctrine of creation, he never demands that we abandon the temporal world of flesh to attain the eternal world of spirit.[2] Instead, he

---

[2] Asceticism was, however, appealing to him. See Peter Brown, *Augustine of Hippo: A Biography* (Berkeley: University of California Press, 1967), 142: "Occasionally, as

insists that virtue should be allowed to guarantee happiness
without requiring the impossible, that we cease to exist in time.
We are to enjoy temporal goods under the discipline of virtue,
and thereby extend our control over ourselves to control over
our enjoyment of temporal goods.

This prescription for happiness does not indicate how we are
supposed to disdain temporal things sufficiently to protect
beatitude from our vulnerable commitments, yet affirm them
sufficiently to rejoin beatitude with the human world of time
and space. On this issue, Augustine had help from Hellenistic
philosophy. The Stoics, above all others, were master strategists
in the struggle to maintain the uneasy alliance between
beatitude and temporal commitments. Their strategy, which
Augustine could have gleaned easily from his reading of Cicero,[3]
was to secure first the invulnerability of beatitude to time and
circumstance, then introduce a separate scale of value for
vulnerable temporal commitments. Virtue, the only uncon-
ditional good, fell wholly under the province of will. As for the
considerable amount of things that remained outside our full
control, they were not goods at all, strictly speaking, for their
loss detracted neither from virtue nor beatitude. Yet they might
be considered to have selective value depending on the
circumstances. If virtue were in no way abdicated or willingly
compromised, the benefits of fortune, such as nature and society
provided, could be preferred (*praeposita*) rather than shunned
(*reiecta*), and the blows of misfortune shunned rather than
preferred. In this way beatitude could be secured without resort
to a Cynic asceticism.

The other Hellenistic paradigm for beatitude available to
Augustine was the Stoicized Aristotelianism of Antiochus of
Ascalon, the reviver of the Old Academy. Augustine would
have found a presentation of his ethics in book v of Cicero's *De*

when he preaches on marriage, Augustine strikes a chill note that would remind his
delighted audience that their priest was also a Neo-Platonist, who lived among
monks; and who could seriously expect them to love the sexuality of their wives and
the physical bonds of their families only as a Christian must love his enemies." His
ambivalence towards the value of sensible, physical, fleshly things derived in part
from Platonism itself, as Hilary Armstrong reminds us in his masterful essay,
"Neoplatonic Valuations of Nature, Body and Intellect," *Augustinian Studies* 3
(1972), 35–59.

[3] See especially book III, *De finibus bonorum et malorum* and book v, *Tusculanae disputationes*.

finibus. He could also have found the views of Antiochus in
Varro. The first three sections of book XIX of *De civitate Dei*,
which Augustine says are based Varro's *De philosophia* (not
extant), culminate in the syncretism characteristic of Old
Academy ethics: Virtue establishes happiness, but happiness
may be augmented by external blessings. Following Varro,
Augustine elaborates this teaching in terms of three distinct
grades of beatitude.[4] In the blessed (*beata*) life we enjoy sufficient
natural and social endowments to make pursuit of virtue
possible, in the more blessed (*beatior*) life we enjoy an excess of
these endowments, over and above the minimum needed for
virtue, and in the most blessed (*beatissima*) life our virtue is
crowned with the highest degree of external blessings, so that we
lack for no significant natural or social good. This graded view
of beatitude is Stoic in founding happiness on virtue, but
Peripatetic in its refusal to exclude external goods from the
definition of happiness. Happiness remains an ethical ideal, in
that when virtue is present, happiness is present, but the
availability of external goods (i.e., goods not wholly under our
control) may influence how well the ideal is realized. In that
respect, beatitude incorporates an element of fortune.

When Augustine applied this syncretic view of beatitude to
pagan philosophy, he was under the impression that nothing of
importance distinguished the ethics of Stoics from those of
Peripatetics or Platonists. Back in book IX of *De civitate Dei*, he
had fully endorsed Cicero's assessment in *De finibus* of the
disagreement among the schools over the importance of external
goods to beatitude.[5] Cicero claimed that whether we refused, in
concert with the Stoics, to designate material benefits (*commoda*)
as goods (*bona*) in addition to virtue, or we accepted the
designation, as did both Peripatetics and Platonists, the
substance of beatitude remained the same. Virtue is always
assumed to predominate in beatitude, though a virtuous life
with external blessings is preferable to one without them. Stoics
may wish to call these blessings something other than goods, but
even Stoics seek to minimize threats to their material well-
being.

---

[4] *De civ. Dei* 19.3.   [5] *Ibid.*, 9.4.

Cicero's syncretism mutates Stoicism into the Stoicized Aristotelianism of the Old Academy. In following Cicero's lead, Augustine reduces philosophy's pretensions to secure beatitude to a single strategy: Secure virtue, then under the auspices of virtue supplement beatitude with the enjoyment of what the world has to offer. Two other options, aside from Stoicism, never gain a hearing. Neither the ethics of Epicurus nor those of Aristotle were in contention for the proper view of beatitude.

Augustine was aware of the Epicurean understanding of happiness, but he failed to take it very seriously. In *De Trinitate* he supplies us with the potted description of Epicurus as the advocate of an unprincipled life of pleasure (*voluptas*).[6] This is followed closely by a citation from Cicero, who sententiously declares that "to want what is unseemly is itself the most wretched thing, nor is it as wretched not to attain what you want as it is to want to attain what is improper."[7] Epicurus was not known in the ancient world for personal licentiousness, but the reputation of his ethics as hedonistic kept Augustine from giving much if any credibility to the Epicurean point of view. Epicurus identified happiness with the serene enjoyment of pleasure, and although virtue, especially prudence, played an important managerial role in the regulation of pleasure, virtue itself did not constitute happiness. Pleasure did.[8] Since Augustine associated virtue with self-determination and self-determination with happiness, he would have understood Epicurus to have been advocating an overly vulnerable view of happiness. Displace virtue from the center of beatitude, and happiness (i.e., attaining what you want) becomes too much an accident of fortune.

---

[6] *De Trin.* 13.5.8.

[7] *Ibid.* 13.5.8 (CCSL 50, 392, 14–16): "Velle enim quod non deceat id est ipsum miserrimum, nec tam miserum est non adipisci quod uelis quam adipisci uelle quod non oporteat." The citation apparently comes from the *Hortensius*. See Maurice Testard, *Saint Augustin et Cicéron*, vol. II, *Répertoire des textes* (Paris: Etudes augustiniennes, 1958), 30.

[8] For the fundamentals of Epicurean ethics, see A. A. Long and D. N. Sedley, *The Hellenistic Philosophers*, vol. I, *Translations of the Principal Sources with Philosophical Commentary* (Cambridge: Cambridge University Press, 1987), 102–57. I do not claim that Augustine's crude portrayal of Epicurus is fair to Epicurean philosophy. For a sympathetic and exacting interpretation of the latter, see Phillip Mitsis, *Epicurus' Ethical Theory: The Pleasures of Invulnerability* (Ithaca: Cornell University Press, 1988).

Augustine never encountered Aristotle's ethics without Stoic mediation. It is doubtful that he would have found it a very congenial alternative if he had. Although Aristotle, like Antiochus much later, insisted that virtue is the dominant component of happiness, he never would have claimed that virtue alone guarantees happiness.[9] Nothing in Aristotle's ethical writings suggests that beatitude is invulnerable to misfortune. A virtuous person may avoid a certain kind of misery by maintaining his or her virtue in the midst of prolonged strife, but it would not be correct to call that person happy simply because of virtue.[10] Aristotle would agree that virtue is a necessary condition for beatitude, but he would not advance virtue as a sufficient condition, as did Antiochus and the Stoics. For Augustine, Aristotle would fall under the same censure as Epicurus. Both contaminate beatitude with fortune. They remove beatitude from the province of virtuous self-determination.

This brings me to the point of my brief excursion into Hellenistic ethical theory. Augustine's sensibilities in ethics are fundamentally Stoic.[11] He refuses to accept the intrusion of fortune into the ideal of beatitude. Admittedly that refusal seems oddly out of keeping with his willingness to accept Cicero's assimilation of Stoicism to Peripatetic philosophy, where fortune does have a limited role to play in the attainment of beatitude. But the motivation behind his acceptance of assimilated Stoicism becomes clear in book XIX, where he launches into his famous denunciation of the tempered optimism of the Old Academy. The Old Academy's graded view of

[9] The difference between Aristotle and the Aristotelianism of Antiochus is discussed in John M. Cooper, "Aristotle on the Goods of Fortune," *Philosophical Review* 94 (1985), 173–96, see 176 n. 7, and Ragnar Holte, *Béatitude et sagesse : Saint Augustin et le problème de la fin de l'homme dans la philosophie ancienne* (Paris: Etudes augustiniennes, 1962), 38. For an excellent discussion of how Aristotle would have responded to the Stoics, see T. H. Irwin, "Stoic and Aristotelian Conceptions of Happiness," in *The Norms of Nature: Studies in Hellenistic Ethics*, ed. Malcolm Schofield and Gisela Striker (Cambridge: Cambridge University Press, 1986).

[10] See *Nicomachean Ethics* 1.8.

[11] See G. Scott Davis, "The Structure and Function of the Virtues in the Moral Theology of St. Augustine," in *Congresso internazionale su S. Agostino nel XVI centenario della conversione*, vol. III (Rome: Institutum Patristicum Augustinianum, 1987), 9–18. Davis contrasts Augustinian with Aristotelian virtues and concludes that Augustine is closer to the Stoic paradigm.

beatitude gives way in Augustine's rhetoric to the intrusions of a hostile world – hostile to the cultivation of virtue and hostile to the enjoyment of external goods. His litany of misfortune lists disease, age, deformity, insanity, deprivation, war, treachery, injustice, temptation, deception, and loss of friends as just some of the possible defeaters of pagan beatitude.[12]

Although it is usual to take Augustine's rhetorical flourishes in book XIX as his farewell to philosophy and its hopes for securing human perfection in time, his profoundest break from the company of the philosophers has already been registered in book IX. By obscuring the distinction between Stoics and Peripatetics on the importance of vulnerable goods to happiness, he leaves both schools with a common moral psychology, wherein reason claims mastery over the passions. The Stoics, Augustine notes, contend that their sages never have the placidity of their reason disturbed by involuntary passions, as in fits of fear or anxiety.[13] By contrast, other philosophers, such as the Peripatetics, are content to claim that no involuntary experience of passion can overthrow the wisdom of the sage. Augustine denies Stoicism its distinctiveness when he argues that the Stoics mean to claim no more than what the Peripatetics claim. Stoic sages, regardless of their rhetoric, enjoy no immunity to the disruptive force of passion. As evidence for this reading of Stoicism, Augustine cites the anecdotal case of the Stoic sage on board a ship at sea, who when faced with the prospect of drowning in a storm, turns pale with fear. According to the recorder of the story, Aulus Gellius in *Attic Nights*, the sage later explains to his inquisitive fellow passengers that his fear had its source in his involuntary apprehensions of imminent grief. Such apprehensions, referred to by Stoics as "phantasms" (*phantasiae*), suggesting their illusory quality, occur in situations of extreme distress and fall outside the sage's power to avoid. Augustine accepts this diagnosis of how the Stoic sage comes to experience fear, and he accepts at least provisionally the further

[12] *De civ. Dei* 19.4–10.
[13] Augustine employs a relatively elaborate lexicon of Latin terms to correspond to the Greek concept *pathē* – *perturbationes*, *passiones*, *affectiones*, *affectus*. Cicero's term, *perturbatio*, is probably the most descriptive way of capturing the phenomenon of interest to Augustine: that is, the way in which emotions can disorder the rational operations of the human mind.

Stoic claim, reported in Gellius, that phantasms vanish upon rational deliberation. Nevertheless, he reads the sage's self-report to illustrate how Stoics dissemble over the supposed constancy of their happiness over changing circumstances. "For, to be sure," Augustine observes, "if this philosopher were setting at nothing the value of what he thought he was about to lose in the shipwreck, such as his life and his health, he would not have been so shaken by the danger as to have the testimony of his pallor betray his fear."[14]

Augustine offers his redescription of the Stoic view of passion as an alternative to the verbal dispute (*uerborum certamen*) between Stoics and Peripatetics over whether threats to material well-being ought to be termed unfavorable or simply evil. The reluctance of Stoics to describe threats to material endowments as evils (*mala*) which jeopardize goods (*bona*) stems from their desire to preserve virtue as the sovereign and sufficient endowment of beatitude. In taking the case of the shipboard Stoic as representative of the inner life of the Stoic sage under adverse conditions, Augustine in effect discounts Stoicism's commitment to the sufficiency of virtue for happiness. For the force of his observation about the sage's fear is that the very experience of the disruptive emotion presupposes that to some significant degree the sage values material well-being and so fears its loss. Unless some judgment of this sort were tied up in the experience of fear, there would be no fear. As Augustine suggests, we do not fear the loss of what means nothing to us. On the other hand, Augustine concedes to Stoics and to other philosophers as well that reason may retain its sovereignty over the involuntary passion. In a moment of reflection, the sage can act to overrule the standard of value embedded in his passion and protect virtue from compromise. Neither Peripatetics nor Stoics would be forced to admit that their sages could be threatened or shaken into trading virtue for vice.

On the issue of the sovereignty of reason and virtue over the passions, Augustine could afford to be generous to his pagan

---

[14] *De civ. Dei* 9.4 (CCSL 47, 253, 81–84): "Nam profecto si nihili penderet eas res ille philosophus, quas amissurum se naufragio sentiebat, sicuti est uita ista salusque corporis: non ita illud periculum perhorresceret, ut palloris etiam testimonio proderetur."

antagonists. Having relieved Stoicism of its pretensions to virtuous self-sufficiency, he offered it back to pagan philosophy much in the way that the Greeks offered Troy the gift of a wooden horse. The moral psychology that he leaves to the philosophers, the basis on which they must move beatitude under rational self-determination, has been fatally compromised by his description of how passion disrupts the peace of wisdom. The image of reason as deflecting passion or emotion in the manner of a fortress wall deflecting an outside enemy no longer captures the quality of the assault. For if Augustine is right to suggest that disruptive passion reveals what the sage values, at least in so far as the passion is itself an expression of some judgment of value, then reason is implicated in the experience and the enemy is within the gates. Even should the sage act against the dictates of passion, that very dissent would indicate an opposition within reason itself, not a conflict between rational and blindly irrational sources of motivation. Passions may implicate judgments of value that the sage would disown or disavow on reflection, but the fact remains that they implicate some kind of judgment and so are never blind. The scene of the confrontation between reason and passion has been altered subtlely to taint the victory of reason with a measure of self-alienation.

Augustine's seemingly innocuous consolidation of pagan views on the passions to a single moral psychology introduces a fatal contradiction into pagan philosophy's attempt to secure beatitude on the strength of virtue. The blessed life is humanly possible only if reason can retain its mastery over passions. This mastery would, moreover, have to correspond to the achievement of self-determination, or it could not be said that virtue and the blessed life converge in human autonomy. Yet this picture of beatitude requires that passion count as an external threat to reason which, when repelled, leaves reason undiminished in its integrity. Augustine's characterization of passion pits one form of judgment against another, leaving reason decimated in its losses and diminished in its victories. Once there is an internal connection between judgment and affection, a breach opens between virtue and self-determination – the very vulnerability Stoic moral psychology had been designed to avoid. In book XIX Augustine exploits the vulnerability to expose pagan philosophy's inability to meet its own ideal, for he has assumed that pagan philosophers have no choice but to accept his description of what a passion is and in so doing work with a moral psychology that is profoundly at odds with their ideal of beatitude.

The development of Augustine's moral psychology, which I will elaborate over the next four chapters, is a fascinating story of his own ambivalence towards Stoic ambitions for invulnerability in ethics. And here I refer to Stoicism not as it existed as a set of doctrines, among which he could pick and choose as he pleased, but as a sensibility that shaped and reshaped his fundamental intuitions about the possibility of beatitude in the *saeculum*, the world of time and change. His early writings display a Stoic confidence that the war of virtue against all manner of external assault could be won on the ground of human self-determination. By book IX of the *De civitate Dei*, a work of his maturity, he no longer believes that the dangerous threats to virtue are the external ones, and his old Stoic confidence in the power of rational self-determination seems to have been eroded away entirely. It would be misleading, however, to take Augustine's interpretation of anecdotal evidence as his dismissal, much less his refutation, of Stoicism. His polemical treatment of pagan moral psychology in book IX represents the outcome of a long internal dialectic in his own thought between his desire to explicate evil and his confidence in the power of knowledge to motivate. Out of this dialectic he fashions a moral psychology with only superficial resemblance to his inherited philosophical wisdom. In suggesting that Stoics can lay claim only to this moral psychology and no other, he replaces rather than refutes traditional Stoic moral psychology.

Foisting an alien view on to one's opponents and forcing them to claim it as their own may sound very much like a dismissal of their genuine views. But there is a sense, a crucial sense, in which Augustine never gives up Stoic ethical sensibilities. His evolving reflections on the ties between reason and affection are bound up with his intuition that the blessed life must in some way be expressed in virtue and self-determination. Although he comes to the very unstoic conclusion that virtue and beatitude never coincide in the *saeculum*, he also refuses, in a very Stoic way, to admit that virtue and beatitude could ever accidentally coincide. To get virtue and beatitude reunited again, divine agency rather than fortune must on his view serve as the impetus for reunion. He would never want to introduce chance or fortune as having to play a constitutive role in whether we manage to attain some degree of beatitude.

Augustine's most intriguing response to pagan philosophy lies in his attempt to define human self-determination, and by extension beatitude, in reference to grace. It is very difficult to formulate his response, however, unless we first consider the manner in which the Stoic convergence of virtue, self-determination, and happiness supplied him with his ideal in philosophy. This ideal survives his theological critique of pagan wisdom. So the place to begin, if we are interested in understanding the connection between grace and autonomy, is with the internal dialectic that ultimately led Augustine to bid farewell to pagan philosophy.

VIRTUE AND EXTERNAL GOODS

In this section I intend to distill the Stoic strategy for securing beatitude from two of Augustine's early works: *De beata vita*, a study of the blessed life in dialogue form, and the first book of *De libero arbitrio*, also in dialogue form, but concerned chiefly with the nature of sin and the corruption of the blessed life. *De beata vita* came out of Augustine's retreat at Cassiciacum, a time of philosophical reflection and leisure shortly before his baptism into the Christian faith in 387. Augustine completed book 1 of *De libero arbitrio* during his brief stay in Rome after his mother's death and just prior to his return to North Africa in late 388.

I have chosen to discuss these particular works in part because they were written during the period when Augustine's enthusiasm for Hellenistic conceptions of wisdom and virtue colored profoundly his understanding of Christian beatitude. Both works lend support to Augustine's short-lived conviction that philosophical wisdom affords human beings a safe haven from the trials and misfortunes of a world in flux. But even more importantly, each of these works reveals the Stoic dimension of Augustine's appropriation of Hellenistic moral psychology. In *De beata vita*, he seeks to secure beatitude against the adventitious loss of things of value, that large class of goods that can be taken away from us without our consent and are therefore considered to be external to us. In *De libero arbitrio*, he probes the nature of moral corruption and concludes that virtue, unlike an external good, never falls outside our control. Beatitude in the mind of the young Augustine remains invulnerable to external challenges of any sort. *De beata vita* and *De libero arbitrio* collectively present this very Stoic frame of mind in its least adulterated form.[15]

In order to fill out this frame of mind, we need to know how Augustine in his early writings proposes to limit the vulnerability of beatitude. This is primarily a question of tactics rather than of doctrine. From the point of view of my analysis, what makes Augustine relevantly Stoic is not that he accepts specific Stoic doctrines,[16] but that he adopts the objective of Stoic ethics in his own articulation of ideal beatitude: that is, he tries to describe beatitude in such a way that it remains fully under human control and fully complete. This goal will encounter opposition on two fronts. First, there is the dilemma posed by our involvement with external goods. How can we

[15] On the matter of Stoicism's influence on Augustine's ethics, particularly in his early works, see the excellent discussions of Robert J. O'Connell, *St. Augustine's Early Theory of Man, A.D. 386–391* (Cambridge: Harvard University Press, 1968), 193–96 and his " *De libero arbitrio I*: Stoicism Revisited," *Augustinian Studies* 1 (1970), 49–68, Marcia Colish, *The Stoic Tradition from Antiquity to the Early Middle Ages*, vol. II (Leiden: E. J. Brill, 1985), 213–20, John Burnaby, *Amor Dei: A Study of the Religion of St. Augustine* (London: Hodder & Stoughton, 1938), 45–53, Eugene TeSelle, *Augustine the Theologian* (New York: Herder and Herder, 1970), 61–73, and Holte, *Béatitude*, 195–206. All of these interpretations point out that Augustine's appropriation of Stoicism is mediated by Neoplatonism. I would not disagree with this, but in the area of ethics I think that this mediation is less significant than it is generally made out to be.

[16] Stoic thought was common currency for late antique philosophers, and its influence on individuals might assume diffuse forms whose traces fail to lead back to a discernible source. Much of Augustine's appropriation of Stoicism was of this variety. Stoicism informed his sensibilities without tying him to a particular Stoic tradition. Nevertheless it is possible to identify the appearance of specific Stoic doctrines in his work, some of which he was certainly aware of as Stoic. For a succinct and highly regarded study of the doctrinal influence of Stoicism on Augustine, see Gérard Verbeke, "Augustin et le stoïcisme," *Recherches augustiniennes* 1 (1958), 67–89.

become involved with vulnerable sources of value and not have that vulnerability adversely affect our beatitude? But how can we avoid these sources of value and still have complete beatitude? Second, there is the threat posed by the vulnerability of virtue itself. How can we be sure that virtue, once gained, remains impervious to involuntary corruption and loss? Without that assurance, beatitude rests on a foundation of sand. I want to leave open the possibility that Augustine's attempt to meet these challenges might serve the Stoic objective without staying strictly within the doctrinal framework of Stoicism.

The central theme of *De beata vita* concerns the completeness of beatitude, or the issue of what we need to have to have beatitude in its fullest measure. At an important point in the dialogue, Augustine asks his compatriots, "What must a person take to himself in order to be blessed?"[17] In answer to his own question, he offers that "it must be something ever enduring, that neither hangs on fortune, nor is exposed to any mishaps."[18] This basic definition of beatitude's object excludes the transitory and the perishable as proper objects of beatific concern. His reasoning here is that beatitude should be thought complete only when we have secure access to what we take to be the source of delight and satisfaction. If that source is itself transitory and subject to loss, the condition of completeness cannot be met. We cannot, for instance, place our beatitude in temporal things and still expect to control when and for how long we possess what we desire. Our beatitude will remain imperfect as long as its source of satisfaction remains vulnerable to adventitious loss. Augustine quickly comes to the conclusion, and not surprisingly, that only the person who possesses God enjoys beatitude.[19]

His association of beatitude's completeness with its invulnerability does not pass without challenge from the gallery. Trygetius, one of Augustine's more spirited interlocutors, points out that "there are many favored by fortune who possess abundantly and fully the things that are enjoyable for this life, even if these are vulnerable and exposed to mishaps, nor are any

---

[17] *De beata vita* 2.11 (CCSL 29, 71, 118): "Quid ergo sibi homo conparare debet, ut beatus sit?"
[18] *De beata vita* 2.11 (CCSL 29, 71, 122): "Id ergo, inquam, semper manens nec ex fortuna pendulum nec ullis subiectum casibus esse debet."
[19] *De beata vita* 2.11 (CCSL 29, 72, 149): "Deum igitur, inquam, qui habet, beatus est."

of those things which they desire lacking to them."[20] The force
of this challenge is its suggestion that the basic condition for
completeness – complete access to whatever gives satisfaction –
can be met by accident. To appreciate this suggestion, we need
to reject the picture of monsters of selfishness gorging themselves
on the fat of fortune. We would do better to picture virtuous
people whose continued enjoyment of fortune contributes
materially to their beatitude. Trygetius can be taken to suggest
that temporal advantages, although they are not utterly at our
disposal, may enter into the constitution of beatitude. If we find
examples of lives lived well under the boon of good fortune, why
not say that the beatitude of these lives depends at least in part
on the availability of good fortune?

Augustine's immediate response to Trygetius is to insist on
the incompatibility of beatitude and fear. "It does not seem to
you, does it, that the one who fears is happy?" Dutifully
Trygetius answers that it does not. "Therefore," Augustine
continues, "if someone can lose what he loves, he cannot but
fear, can he?"[21] The moral of these questions is evident. No one
whose beatitude depends on the enjoyment of transient things
can avoid the prospect of losing what he or she loves. The
prospect of loss occasions fear, and fear mars beatitude's
completeness. The line of thought advanced against Trygetius is
indicative of how far Augustine is willing to allow the
desideratum of stability to set the boundaries of beatitude's
completeness. If we enjoy all manner of temporal advantage,
yet fear for the loss of external goods, it would seem that we lack
only the assurance that fortune will continue. This assurance,
however, is impossible, since in this case we do not have full
control over our access to the source of beatitude.

Trygetius gives no rejoinder to Augustine, but we might
prosecute his case a little further on his behalf. Suppose that the
recipient of continued good fortune simply fails to entertain the
fear of its suspension and that in fact fortune never turns ugly,

---

[20] *De beata vita* 2.11 (CCSL 29, 71, 126–29): "Sunt, inquit, multi fortunati, qui eas ipsas
res fragiles casibusque subiectas tamen iucundas pro hac uita cumulate largeque
possideant nec quicquam illis eorum quae uolunt desit."
[21] *De beata vita* 2.11 (CCSL 29, 71, 129–31): "Cui ego: Qui timet, inquam, uideturne
tibi beatus esse? – Non uidetur, inquit. – Ergo quod amat quisque si amittere potest,
potestne non timere?"

thereby giving retrospective justification to the recipient's lack of fear. How could this case of beatitude be disqualified for incompleteness? Before we can suggest what Augustine's likely response would have been, we must establish the intelligibility of the following claim, whose truth is crucial to the argument of *De beata vita*: The one who places beatitude in temporal things, yet fails to fear their loss, lacks wisdom, but the one who possesses wisdom fails to fear the loss of temporal things.

Augustine defines wisdom in *De beata vita* as the measure of the mind (*modus animi*).[22] The function of this measure is to regulate our possession and use of temporal goods, such that we neither enjoy them immoderately when they are available, nor grieve for them when they are lost. The application of measure moves us beyond vulnerability to the fortunes of temporal advantages, which immoderate and foolish persons experience as abundance in one moment, poverty in the next. For those whose desires are measured by wisdom, the experiences of want (*egestas*) and excess (*redundantia*) are fundamentally alien, since these experiences proceed from a lack of measure.[23] In wisdom we are able to order our desires to the situation at hand. In that way none of our desires will go unsatisfied, and beatitude will be both complete and under our control.

Complete beatitude, or beatitude that owns the plenitude (*plenitudo*) of having all desires met, takes its measure from the supreme measure, the Logos and wisdom of God.[24] To possess God is to have adopted the standard of eternal wisdom in our conduct. In *De beata vita*, however, the content of this eternal wisdom does not extend much beyond the pithy wisdom of Terence, whom Augustine cites approvingly for guidance in the use of temporal things: "Since what you want cannot be done, want what you can do."[25] This unabashedly Stoic counsel captures the essence of the Stoic strategy for handling external goods. Desires are measured to reality, rather than reality to the desires. Since the virtuous, being temperate, have control over their own desires, no adverse changes in fortune can ever disturb their beatitude, nor can favorable shifts in fortune augment its

---

[22] *De beata vita* 4.32.   [23] *Ibid.*, 4.32.   [24] *Ibid.*, 4.34–35.

[25] *Ibid.*, 4.25 (CCSL 29, 79, 55): "Quoniam non potest id fieri, quod uis, id uelis, quod possis." The citation comes from Terence, *Andria* 2.1.

plenitude. Wisdom and virtue perfect us from within. Augustine has harnessed the eternal Logos to the service of Stoic autarky. The Christian saint and the Stoic sage are indistinguishable ideals in *De beata vita*.

It should be clear by now why those who possess wisdom never fear the loss of temporal things. It is because they never desire what they do not already possess. But what about the person who counts on fortune for beatitude and yet fails to fear the loss of its favor? In that case lack of fear is itself a gift of fortune. The recipient of continued good fortune, having no control over its continuation, would have to rely on forces outside his or her determination to protect beatitude from both adventitious loss and fear of same. But even were we to stipulate a case of unfailing fortune, we could not fashion from that a case of beatitude that met Augustine's condition of completeness. We appropriate beatitude only through virtue, because virtue is what we are. It is in our power to distinguish ourselves from the world outside of us. "Something has proper being," says Augustine, "if it abides, if it holds together, and if it always retains its own nature, as is so with virtue."[26] We may enjoy all the benefits of fortune we care to imagine; without virtue, it all amounts to the beatitude of a beggar.

Augustine's response to the revised version of the challenge issued by Trygetius would have been, following the logic of the dialogue as it stands, to draw in some way upon the role of self-determination in the appropriation of beatitude. Consider what would make the benefits of fortune part of my beatitude. At this stage in his ethical thought, Augustine must say that they become part of my beatitude only when I use them to determine myself in accordance with virtue and wisdom. Any other kind of use would leave them still tied to fortune, where they would remain external to my will and outside my control. It would not make sense to say, then, that the benefits of fortune affect my beatitude in any way apart from my own virtuous self-determination. Until they are mediated by virtue, they simply

---

[26] *De beata vita* 2.8 (CCSL 29, 70, 66–67): "Est autem aliquid, si manet, si constat, si semper tale est, ut est uirtus." Cf. Colish, *The Stoic Tradition*, 214–15: "Virtue, he concludes, is the only thing in the flux of the temporal order that shares the divine attribute of permanence."

are not *my* benefits. They are "on loan" to me from outside forces, and I may be deprived of their use at any time. Once fortune's gifts have been mediated by virtue, however, they cannot be taken away from me, for they no longer are external to my will. They have become the occasion for my self-determination. This is where I wish to leave *De beata vita*, with its strong intimation of the identity of virtue and self-determination, with its classically humanist opposition between virtue and fortune, and with its very Stoic appreciation for the consummation of beatitude in the autonomy of the good will.

De libero arbitrio also links beatitude to virtue and self-determination, but it develops the obverse perspective on beatitude's attainment. What would it mean for us to give up beatitude, to forgo the path of virtue, and to perpetuate sin? Would such a course of action even be conceivable in those terms? These questions preoccupy Augustine in book 1. They call for an exploration of the nature of moral evil and the vulnerability of virtue to corruption. In framing these issues, Augustine will demonstrate his continued commitment to the ideal of beatitude's invulnerability to adventitious loss. Virtue, if lost, can only have been given up. It cannot have been taken away. Augustine adopts this view of the loss of virtue as the guiding principle for his investigation of the nature of evil. The challenge he faces in *De libero arbitrio* is to produce the definition of evil that matches his belief that virtue remains invulnerable to all manner of seduction and external force.

The immediate context of book 1 is established by Evodius, whose part in the dialogue is generally to listen and then press difficult questions upon the attention of his friend and teacher. The first question that Evodius poses, and the opening of the dialogue, invites Augustine to reflect on evil in the framework of theodicy. "Tell me," he requests of Augustine, "whether God is not the author of evil."[27] Augustine is glad to accept the request, provided that the range of evil under discussion is appropriately partitioned. Not all evils are evils of commission. Some are suffered. This latter class of evils, what Augustine designates as penalties for sin (*poenae peccati*), does not, as far as he is

---

[27] *De lib. arb.* 1.1.1 (CCSL 29, 211, 1–2): "Dic mihi, quaeso te, utrum deus non sit auctor mali."

concerned, prompt the need for theodicy, a need emerging from cases of *prima facie* injustice on God's part. Whatever people suffer – disease, death, pain, victimization at the hands of others – may be viewed as just punishment for the sins that they have themselves committed.[28] For evil suffered, Augustine believes that God is ultimately the author, but authorship in this case does not carry the stigma of injustice or malevolence.[29] The former class of evils, sin in its many manifestations, poses a different order of challenge to the intelligibility of divine justice and benevolence. Sin cannot be attributed to God's authorship without convicting God of wrongful and unjust activity. But, Augustine observes, "if sins originate from the souls that God has created, from souls indeed that originate from God, how is it not a short leap to attributing sins to God?"[30]

It is in Augustine's attempt to block this attribution that we can begin to discern the complementarity of *De libero arbitrio* and *De beata vita*. The two works trace parallel trajectories in their respective efforts to place beatitude at the disposition of the beatified subject. *De beata vita*, with its concern for the acquisition of beatitude, defines the object of beatitude as the virtuous self-definition of the subject.[31] Augustine subtracts

---

28 Notice that the possible penalties for sin extend beyond what we would normally designate as "natural evil." The victimization of one person by another is for Augustine an instance of sin's penalty, but we would hardly be inclined to call this sort of evil "natural." As for the victimizing itself, Augustine's designation of "sin" would correspond to the contemporary theodicist's notion of "moral evil." William Babcock further illuminates the distinction between sin and its penalty in "Augustine on Sin and Moral Agency," *Journal of Religious Ethics* 16 (1988), 28–55, see 31–32, esp. n. 6.

29 *De lib. arb.* 1.1.1. Throughout his career, Augustine would insist on the connection between suffering and punishment whenever divine justice was at issue. He does not commit himself, however, to what this section of *De libero arbitrio* seems to intimate: namely, that all suffering is proportionate to the gravity of the evil punished. In *De ver. rel.* 23.44, he gives succinct expression to the fundamentals of his theodicy of suffering. From the standpoint of divine justice, human suffering takes its justification from the condemnation of sinners ("damnatione peccatorum"), the edification of the just ("exercitatione iustorum"), and the perfection of the blessed ("perfectione beatorum").

30 *De lib. arb.* 1.2.4 (CCSL 29, 213, 15–18): "si peccata ex his animabus sunt quas deus creauit, illae autem animae ex deo, quomodo non paruo interuallo peccata referantur in deum?".

31 The object of beatitude in *De beata vita* is not, strictly speaking, God, but the appropriation of the wisdom of God. This appropriation amounts to the exercise of virtuous self-definition, or conforming ourselves to the measure of all things, the Logos.

from beatitude all that we experience as external to ourselves, and the result is beatitude that coincides with our self-determination. He can then call the coincidence virtue or wisdom. In *De libero arbitrio*, with its focus on the abdication of beatitude, beatitude is still placed at the disposal of the beatific subject, only here the disposition is determined by an exercise in vicious self-definition. Augustine subtracts from beatitude's loss whatever could be considered the penalty of sin – that is, whatever could be attributed to God – and the result is perversity that we will upon ourselves. This isolation of beatitude's loss from external determinants serves the purposes of theodicy at the same time that it reinforces the centrality of self-determination to beatitude. Once Augustine has defined what remains to evil after penalties have been factored out, he will have found sin whose attribution stops with the sinner.

The first step towards definition is to rule out the best candidates for external determinants of sin. When Augustine and Evodius begin to explore in earnest what gives an action its evil character, Augustine leads them both to exclude sources in the law, education, convention, or the examples of individuals.[32] Evil simply cannot have its source in an external authority, whether that authority is civil, social, or personal. Authority enjoys legitimation only to the extent that it remains un-corrupted by evil. Corrupted authority is not communicable because it is not binding. My sin does not, then, have its source in another's sin, unless I allow myself to be corrupted. In that eventuality, however, the actual source of my sin is not external at all, but my own willingness to be corrupted.

One helpful way of looking at this exclusion of outside authority from the sources of personal sin is as a clarification or enlargement of the scope of sin's penalty. Although my sins are sins for me, they are the penalty of sin for another. They become part of the environment of the adversative and potentially corrupting circumstances in which this person must now live. The difference in perspective makes all the difference. First-person sins corrupt, since they are my sins by definition; third-person sins are allowed to corrupt, since they are external to me

---

[32] *De lib. arb.* 1.1.2–1.3.7.

until I choose to give them authority. Augustine neatly slides the most troublesome external sources or evil – the sins of my community, my society, my friends, and my associates – into the category of sin's penalty, at least when those evils are viewed from my perspective. In so far as they are penalties of my sin, they cannot be the source of my sin. God has control over whether I am exposed to the wiles of my corrupted neighbors, but my giving in to corruption has nothing to do with God, who never wills that anyone sin.

Augustine's isolation of the internal source of corruption from its external occasion comes by way of definition rather than argument. But we can certainly understand the point of the exercise. If I should experience another's sin as the source of my own sin, the fragile distinction between what I do and what the world does to me would collapse. God, who has control over the world, would be saddled with responsibility for my sin, and my beatitude, resting on so vulnerable a virtue, would succumb to circumstances beyond my control. God would cease to be an ethical God, and beatitude would cease to be an ethical ideal. If Augustine wishes to avoid these dire consequences, however, he needs to do more than legislate the separation between external and internal sources of evil. He must supply some independent definition for the internal source of sin, the corrupted will. What is the nature of the corruption?

Augustine's first foray in this direction takes him to the notion of lust (*libido*), or inordinate desire.[33] The turn to lust shifts the focus of definition from the outward manifestations of sin to its internal springs, and in that regard the move is an advance. For his part, Evodius is quite prepared to conclude that "lust dominates in every manner of maleficence."[34] Augustine himself is more circumspect, and he comes up with a case of wrongdoing where the appeal to the agent's affective state fails to clarify the nature of the evil perpetrated.[35] Suppose that a slave murders his master out of the fear that his master plans to torture and abuse him. The slave does not act out of an excess of desire for

---

[33] *Ibid.*, 1.3.8. Augustine uses *cupiditas* as a synonym for *libido*.

[34] *De lib. arb.* 1.3.8 (CCSL 29, 215, 56–58): "Clarum est enim iam nihil aliud quam libidinem in toto malefaciendi genere dominari."

[35] For what follows, see *De lib. arb.* 1.4.9–10.

some possession, but pursues the commendable goal of a life without fear. Augustine takes it as given that a slave sins who knowingly and willingly murders his master, regardless of the provocation. Evodius, sharing the prejudice of his teacher, sees the dilemma. Either sin cannot be defined solely in terms of the affective state of the sinner, or many putatively evil deeds are permissible under the right intention.

Both men were more inclined to adjust the definition than call into question the content of conventional moral wisdom.[36] At this point, however, the definition suffers more from vacuity than it does from moral myopia. The hasty turn to the internal springs of evil has isolated evil affections from evil ends. Since the object or end of evil action positively informs the character of evil affection, leaving the end of evil out of evil's definition strips the definition of any recognition of the difference between inordinate and measured desire. The sage's lack of fear will look like the fool's foolhardiness.

Augustine attempts to increase the definition's power of discrimination by restoring its reference to what good and evil respectively seek:

The desire to live without fear is characteristic of all people, not only the good, but also the wicked. But what is of interest is that the good seek this end by averting their love from things that cannot be possessed without danger or loss; the wicked, however, attempt to remove impediments to their secure enjoyment of these things, and on this account they lead a shameful and villainous life, which is better called death.[37]

It is in the nature of an evil affection to seek satisfaction in the possession of external goods. The wicked commit themselves to

---

[36] I have no interest here in passing judgment upon Augustine's personal ethics. Nevertheless it should be noted that he measured the success of different definitions of evil at least partly in terms of their facility to identify as evil what the consensus of his society identified as evil (for example, slaves killing their masters) and to leave as permissible what the consensus left as permissible (for example, killing an enemy in battle).

[37] *De lib. arb.* 1.4.10 (CCSL 29, 216–17, 63–69): "Cupere namque sine metu uiuere non tam bonorum, sed etiam malorum omnium est; uerum hoc interest, quod id boni appetunt auertendo amorem ab his rebus, quae sine amittendi periculo nequeunt haberi; mali autem, ut his fruendis cum securitate incubent, remouere impedimenta conantur et propterea facinorosam sceleratamque uitam, quae mors melius uocatur, gerunt."

transient and insubstantial sources of value, and therein lies the misery of wickedness.

The definition is now closer to what Augustine needs to delineate the internal source of evil in sin, but it requires further precision. If sin were merely a matter of finding satisfaction in temporal pursuits, it would be hard to maintain the legitimacy of ordinary social interaction. The demands of life in a civil society, where citizens are asked to make commitments to the continuing, temporal welfare of the *civitas*, would all seem to be invitations to sin. Evodius observes, for example, that once external goods are established as the objects of inordinate desire, the blessed have no cause either to defend themselves against aggression, or to defend others, as would be called for in war.[38] They could do neither without manifesting some kind of commitment to things capable of being lost. In general, the rule of law, which regulates temporal commitments in an ordered society, would have no application in the lives of the blessed, who could not make use of its permission to pursue satisfaction in temporal things.

Naturally this is not a conclusion that Augustine would relish. He admits that temporal laws have a legitimate and important function. They manage the society's collective pursuit of the pleasures of body and soul – strength, health, and beauty for individuals, liberty, conviviality, and honor for citizens.[39] Neither would Augustine claim that the blessed never partake in the pleasures of the world. The goal of beatitude is not to exclude life's benefits, but to accord them their proper measure. Temporal laws, however, fall short of this measure, and they are not to be relied on for defining either beatitude or sin. Their own limited measure applies to the external peace of those subject to the coercive power of civil authority: "For as long as they fear to lose temporal things, they maintain in their use of these things a certain moderation suited to the continuation of society, such as can be composed of their like."[40] The measure

---

[38] *De lib. arb.* 1.5.11–12.   [39] *Ibid.*, 1.15.32.

[40] *Ibid.*, 1.15.32 (CCSL 29, 233, 70–72): "Dum enim haec amittere timent, tenent in his utendis quendam modum aptum uinculo ciuitatis, qualis ex huiuscemodi hominibus constitui potest."

of beatitude, by contrast, draws from the eternal law, which regulates the internal peace of individuals.

The definition of evil finds its final precision in the measure of beatitude itself. Affections are the internal springs of sin when they move sinners to seek *beatitude* in the possession of external goods. Augustine describes sin as the inverse of virtue: "to pursue temporal things... as if they were great and marvelous, all the while neglecting the eternal things that the mind enjoys and apprehends directly, and loves without possibility of loss."[41] There is only one way to understand this definition and not turn beatitude into an impossible asceticism. Sin accrues to those who evaluate goods without having incorporated in their judgments the eternal measure of goods. Instead they seek their standard for the good from within the world of time and change, and whatever measure they arrive at will unduly magnify for them the importance of possessing particular temporal advantages.

It is noteworthy that Augustine's definition of evil recapitulates his basis for beatitude. Beatitude for the perverse as well as for the virtuous is founded on assured access to the source of beatitude. "Even pride," he notes, "has a certain craving for unity and omnipotence, but in sovereignty over temporal things, all of which pass like shades."[42] In *De beata vita* and *De libero arbitrio* he argues that self-rule is the key to sovereignty over our own happiness. If we determine ourselves virtuously, we live timelessly and our beatitude is invulnerable. Adopt any other basis for happiness, however, and we have to contest with time. The irony of sin is that vicious self-definition ends in self-dissolution, since sin commits our identity and destiny to what must inevitably pass out of existence.

Augustine's early strategy for securing beatitude comes to this: we unite beatitude and self-determination by appropriating the eternal and transcendental standard of evaluating

---

[41] *De lib. arb.* 1.16.34 (CCSL 29, 234–35, 14–20): "Quocirca licet nunc animaduertere et considerare utrum sit aliud male facere quam neglectis rebus aeternis, quibus per se ipsam mens fruitur et per se ipsam percipit et quae amans amittere non potest, temporalia... quasi magna et miranda sectari."

[42] *De ver. rel.* 45.85 (CCSL 32, 243, 26–29): "Habet ergo et superbia quemdam appetitum unitatis et omnipotentiae; sed in rerum temporalium principatu, quae omnia transeunt tanquam umbra."

temporal goods. The standard is transcendental because it sets the conditions for our use of what may be taken away from us. As long as we follow this standard, we never experience the loss of temporal goods as *our* loss. We are defined in God's timeless eternity, and nothing changes if it is timeless. But should we come to represent ourselves other than as God represents us, we become vulnerable to disintegration and loss of self. Odd as it may sound, we enter into this sort of vulnerability voluntarily, at least in so far as *De libero arbitrio* has established evil to have its source in our refusal to appropriate the measure of measures.

THE DISENFRANCHISEMENT OF THE AFFECTIONS

Ragnar Holte, looking at various phases in the evolution of Augustine's understanding of beatitude, notices that two distinct definitions of the good life are accommodated to one another in Augustine's Cassiciacum dialogues.[43] The Stoic emphasis on the ultimacy of virtue at first alternates with the Neoplatonic emphasis on the transport of a mind possessed by transcendent truth. Augustine then combines these views when he suggests that virtue is the form beatitude takes once we have appropriated the measure of wisdom. We know from *De beata vita* that this wisdom has its source in the Logos, the wisdom of God.

One of the great interpreters of Augustine's debt to Neoplatonism, Robert J. O'Connell, admits that *De beata vita* "represents Augustine's brave attempt to convince his readers that Stoicism and Neo-Platonism were in profound agreement on the nature of human happiness."[44] But as far as O'Connell is concerned, the synthesis breaks down beyond hope of repair over the course of the first book of *De libero arbitrio*, where "Stoicism has finally been forced to yield to the Neo-Platonic emphasis on a transcendent object of beatitude, possessed by the contemplative mind."[45] He bases his interpretation on Augustine's invocation of the eternal law to join reward with virtue,

---

[43] Holte, *Béatitude*, 196–97.
[44] O'Connell, "*De libero arbitrio I*," 49. His fuller analysis of *De beata vita* can be found in *St. Augustine's Early Theory of Man*, 193–96.
[45] O'Connell, "*De libero arbitrio I*," 65.

and punishment with vice.[46] That invocation seems to him to indicate that Augustine has departed from Stoicism's insistence on the internal connection between virtue and beatitude. Instead we must look to a source outside the good will for virtue's reconciliation with beatitude. Neoplatonism points the way.

Marcia Colish, arguably the leading authority on Augustine's Stoicism, lends support to O'Connell's thesis. She notes that even in early works, such as *De beata vita* and *De libero arbitrio*, "Augustine observes that the true good is more than the gratification of an autarchic Stoic rationality in a transcendent Neoplatonic *summum bonum*."[47] The virtues are soon eclipsed by the importance of their end and measure. For Colish, Augustine's crucial reformation of beatitude comes in *De moribus ecclesiae*, where he defines the virtues as forms of the love of God.[48] Once he has identified the virtues with devotion to God, his interest in beatitude shifts from the acquisition of virtue to communion with the personal God of truth. Colish detects reverberations of the shift in the second book of *De libero arbitrio*. The virtues have there been demoted to the status of intermediary goods (*media bona*), whose function is to facilitate the end of beatitude, now understood as our reconciliation with God. Stoic ethics have given way to Neoplatonism's transcendent truth, refashioned as the living God.

My purpose in this section is to explore Augustine's understanding of the consequences of our having appropriated the eternal measure of wisdom. I will first characterize how he supposes wisdom to empower us to withstand challenges to our beatitude, and then in a more critical vein, I intend to show that the empowerment he speaks of is ironic, for it describes the power of those who have been removed from the world in which they interact. But since these objectives proceed under the assumption that beatitude remains Stoic, certainly through the first book of *De libero arbitrio* and even most of the second, I need to address the weighty scholarly opinion against this assumption before I can go forward. Colish and O'Connell, because they

[46] *De lib. arb.* 1.14.30. [47] Colish, *The Stoic Tradition*, 216.
[48] *De mor.* 1.15.25.

offer sophisticated readings of Augustine's encounter with Stoic ethics, afford me an excellent opportunity to clarify my own sense of the continuity between Neoplatonic metaphysics and the Stoic ideal of beatitude in the early works. I would not want to claim, any more than they would, that Augustine fails to modify Stoicism at all with his appeal to God as the measure and end of the human quest for beatitude. The modification, however, serves the Stoic end of eliminating the adventitious and the fortuitous from the conditions of beatitude's attainment. Virtue still remains the form of beatitude, if not its end.

For O'Connell, Augustine's Stoicism in book 1 of *De libero arbitrio* has the feel of an experiment. Augustine is testing the waters in order to determine how well Stoic resources can meet the challenge of his post-Manichaean theology. Is Stoicism able in particular to locate the source of sin in the wills of individuals without prejudicing the justice of God? The task of definition, which we have already reviewed in the previous section, must meet the minimal demands of theodicy, namely, that the virtuous find beatitude through their virtue and that the vicious endure in punishment the cost of their iniquities. Stoicism cannot meet these demands except through appeal to an eternal law, a law whose operation somehow manages to supersede the apparent incongruity in the temporal world between justice and the dispensation of material welfare. The eternal law, as O'Connell rightly calls to our attention, serves as the proper object of the contemplative mind.[49] It also plays a vital role in the completion of beatitude. The key question here concerns the nature of that role.

O'Connell muddies the waters when he describes the issue between Stoicism and Neoplatonism as the choice between deontology and eudaimonism in ethics.[50] The opposition between virtue and happiness would have struck the Stoics as perverse, although this is precisely the opposition that deontological ethics entertains. Deontology establishes rules of conduct independently of the ends of action. Beatitude is just such an end of action, and it may arise, within the purview of deontological ethics, that what we must do by moral law conflicts with

---

[49] O'Connell, "*De libero arbitrio I*," 65.   [50] *Ibid.*, 56, 59–61, 63–67.

interests we have in our own happiness. O'Connell seems to think that Stoicism's attempt to bring beatitude under the control of virtue makes its ethics deontological in character. This interpretation illicitly reads a modern theory of moral obligation into the austerity of Stoic beatitude. We can avoid this tempting confusion if we remember that virtue's separation from happiness would have counted as a *refutation* of Stoic ethics, whereas the separation is clearly not threatening to the coherence of deontological ethics. Stoic ethics, for the Stoics and for Augustine, was a theory of beatitude, not a theory of morality.

The confusion skews O'Connell's interpretation of *De libero arbitrio* because it predisposes him to understand Augustine's invocation of the eternal law as an attempt to reconcile the categorical demands of moral imperatives with desires for external goods. When Augustine speaks of the eternal law as establishing that "merit resides in the will, while reward and punishment attend beatitude and wretchedness," O'Connell hears an appeal "strangely Kantian in tone."[51] What he hears is the echo of his own interpretive bias, which begs the question against Stoicism by failing to take seriously its eudaimonistic credentials.

There is no evidence in book 1 that Augustine would have understood the loss or deprivation of external goods to defeat beatitude and leave virtue begging. The deprivation does defeat the *false* ideal of beatitude that vicious people adopt, since that ideal founds happiness upon the enjoyment of temporal things. The punishment of the wicked can therefore take the form of their own frustrated desires for material comfort and security. As for the role of external goods in genuine beatitude, Augustine continues to think in Stoic terms. They are the reward of those who use them properly, and those who use them properly would never suffer their loss. The certainty of virtue's reward does not depend upon the divine dispensation of material benefits. It has its roots in virtue itself, which brings our enjoyment of the world under our control. There is nothing paradoxical in the

---

[51] *Ibid.*, 64. Cf. *De lib. arb.* 1.14.30 (CCSL 29, 231, 21–24): "Hoc enim aeterna lex illa…incommutabili stabilitate firmauit, ut in uoluntate meritum sit, in beatitate autem et miseria praemium atque supplicium."

suggestion that beatitude is both virtue and the reward of virtue. The coincidence of virtue and virtue's reward follows from Stoicism's attempt to tailor beatitude to fit virtuous self-determination.[52] Augustine still finds this strategy highly seductive at this point in the evolution of his thought.

Colish's attempt to divorce Augustine from Stoic ethics is also premature. The novelty of *De moribus ecclesiae*, a work nearly contemporaneous with book I of *De libero arbitrio*, can easily be overdramatized. Although it is certainly important that Augustine has reformulated the virtues in the language of love for God, he has yet to suggest that the ground of the virtues is ultimately God's love for us. The reversal of perspective that introduces divine agency into the very heart of human willing is still years away. Colish surely overstates her case when she claims that the source of the virtues in *De moribus* serves as "a well-spring that combines the divine initiative with the human response."[53] The mere invocation of love does not compromise Stoic autarky with divine initiative.

It is nevertheless in *De moribus* that cardinal virtues are defined in reference to God. Fortitude, justice, temperance, and prudence take their measure and end no longer from the love of generic eternal objects or the love of an impersonal eternal law, but from love of God, who has a personal identity as the God of Abraham, Isaac, and Jacob. This precision is a rhetorical advance over *De libero arbitrio*, but not necessarily a substantive one. The language of love evokes the importance of the affections to beatitude and suggests the personal quality of human interest in God, but Augustine's actual description of the consummation of virtuous love is coolly intellectual. When love attains its beloved, the result is illumination. We border the divine presence, "touching upon God in an extraordinary manner, beyond the senses," and we are left "enveloped by God's holiness and inwardly enlightened by his truth."[54] If

---

[52] It would be a mistake to describe this coincidence as the *formal* identity of happiness with virtue. It trivializes Stoic ethics to take its destination as its point of departure. The Stoics did not merely presuppose virtue's identity with happiness. They argued for this conclusion based on certain desiderata for happiness.

[53] Colish, *The Stoic Tradition*, 217.

[54] *De mor.* 1.11.18 (OSA 1, 48): "At eum sequimur diligendo, consequimur non cum hoc omnino efficimur quod est ipse, sed ei proximi, eumque mirifico et intellegibili

affections are important at all here, it is because they are receptacles of illumination. It is hard to imagine that love of God in *De moribus* sets the fuse for the explosion of affections in the *Confessiones*. Several years after his conversion, Augustine continues to worship the God of Abraham at the altar of the philosophers.

The one solid piece of textual evidence that Colish offers to displace Stoic autarky from the ethical vision of *De libero arbitrio* is taken from book II, where Augustine supposedly describes virtues as intermediary goods. If that were true, it would suggest that our beatitude transcends our virtue as soon as we find satisfaction in the love of God. Augustine will have departed significantly from Stoic ethical sensibilities. Colish, however, misreads the passage she cites. It reads as follows:

> The virtues, through which we live rightly, are therefore great goods [*magna bona*]; but the sort of bodily things, without which we can live rightly, are the least of goods [*minima bona*]. The powers of the mind, without which we cannot live rightly, are in fact intermediary goods [*media bona*]. No one misuses the virtues, but as for the other goods – that is, the least and intermediary ones – each person can use them not only well but also badly.[55]

Virtues are not themselves intermediary goods because, as Augustine himself indicates, they constitute the form of the good will, or the will ordered to God's eternal law. Their status as "great goods" emerges from their regulative function over the other kinds of goods. When the virtues are present, we use external goods (*minima bona*) in the manner proper to our self-determination for beatitude. Virtue establishes simultaneously the ideal form of our self-determination and the ideal form of our enjoyment of external goods.

Colish's designation of the virtues as *media bona* confuses our ability to determine ourselves either virtuously or viciously with

---

modo contingentes, eiusque ueritate et sanctitate penitus illustrati atque comprehensi."

[55] *De lib. arb.* 2.19.50 (CCSL 29, 271, 5–10): "Virtutes igitur quibus recte uiuitur magna bona sunt; species autem quorumlibet corporum, sine quibus recte uiui potest, minima bona sunt; potentiae uero animi, sine quibus recte uiui non potest, media bona sunt. Virtutibus nemo male utitur; ceteris autem bonis, id est mediis et minimis, non solum bene sed etiam male quisque uti potest."

the form of self-determination that remains definitive for beatitude. In the wake of the confusion, we are left with the deceptive impression that beatitude must be "more" than what our virtues afford us. But since Augustine has heretofore never beatified self-determination apart from its measure in wisdom and virtue, he can hardly be read as demoting the beatific status of self-determination in *De libero arbitrio*.[56] It is because we may err in our pursuit of beatitude that our untutored power of self-determination is only an intermediary good. The ideal of beatitude nevertheless remains that of *virtuous* self-determination, or the autarky of wisdom. The accent of Augustinian ethics is still recognizably Stoic late in book II of *De libero arbitrio*.

My disagreement with Colish and O'Connell does not extend beyond their exaggerated assessments of Neoplatonism's impact upon Augustine's Stoicism in his early writings. It is no exaggeration, however, to notice that Augustine's philosophical moves in both *De beata vita* and *De libero arbitrio* swerve from the narrow paths of Stoicism, generally to follow routes opened up by Neoplatonic metaphysics. His appeal to the Logos or the eternal law takes the measure of virtue beyond the Stoic *ratio* of nature and into the eternal realm of transcendent spirit. This striking divergence from the wisdom of Stoicism has its source in Augustine's profound conviction that the mind cannot find its principle of self-ordering within the world of time and change. If the rules of the virtues (*regulae virtutum*) were not themselves eternal and changeless, neither virtue nor wisdom could protect us from temporal subversion and dissolution.[57] The stability of beatitude in the *saeculum* is possible only when we have some purchase on eternity. Otherwise we are overwhelmed in time, our integrity undone and energy spent.

---

[56] After Colish, *The Stoic Tradition*, 216, has identified the virtues in *De libero arbitrio* as the "means to the end of man's possession of perfect wisdom and truth in God Himself," she has this to say about free will: "It is not an end in itself, an observation which pointedly criticizes the autarchy of the Stoic sage as a form of idolatry and as an absolutizing of man's own power of self-determination." If Augustine were to criticize Stoic autarky at this early stage in his theology, he would be not inclined, I think, to prosecute their emphasis on self-determination, given that the autarky of the sage is informed by the sage's virtue and wisdom. Instead he would focus on the deficiency of the Stoic source of wisdom, which fails to draw from the eternal measure of God's wisdom. That is a very different line of criticism from the one Colish would attribute to Augustine.   [57] *De lib. arb.* 2.10.28–29.

Since the resources of Stoicism fail to transcend nature, Augustine must look outside Stoicism for the vantage of eternity. But his own adaptation of Neoplatonism's contrast between the sensible, changing world of time and the intelligible, stable world of eternity has as its object not the evasion of temporal nature, but its reorganization. "The one who lives justly and in holiness is indeed," Augustine submits, "the unimpaired assessor of things."[58] The things to be assessed are the temporal goods on which our lives depend. How can these goods be managed, integrated within our beatitude, without impairing our integrity? The question begs for a Stoic answer, but without access to the superior perspective of eternity, Stoicism lacks the epistemic credentials it would need to supply a response. When Augustine opens up eternity to the contemplative mind, he perches us between time and eternity, where we may assess and mediate our involvement with temporal things in an ordered and knowledgeable manner.

From Neoplatonism, Augustine has gained the epistemic authority he needs for carrying out the Stoic assimilation of virtue and beatitude. Once ordered to the eternal measure of God's wisdom, virtue loses its vulnerability to temporal dislocation. Its "eternal" constitution gives it this immunity. Virtue in turn regulates our enjoyment of external goods. As long as our most vulnerable source of temporal involvement – desires for the possession of external goods – remains under the control of virtue, time loses its power over us.

Augustine does not take our dependence upon the eternal law for beatitude to compromise our freedom. One temporal item that we must evaluate and order from an eternal vantage is our own life in time. This internal act of self-ordering, which gives our life in time its integrity, is precisely what he would have understood as self-determination. It is a kind of self-definition, out of which come distinct boundaries between us and the world about us. We might wonder, however, why merely epistemic authority gives us power over our affections and desires. It does not follow, except on special assumptions, that superior knowledge automatically results in superior self-control. More than

---

[58] *De doct. chr.* 1.27.28 (CCSL 32, 22, 1–2): "Ille autem iuste et sancte uiuit, qui rerum integer aestimator est."

the basic distinctions of Neoplatonism needs to be deployed to secure the Stoic invulnerability of beatitude.

Augustine does in fact invoke some unusual assumptions about the nature of power. In book I of *De libero arbitrio*, he insists that lust (*cupiditas*), a disordered state of desire, can never overpower the rule of wisdom. He supports his conclusion with the observation that "it would not be consistent with the condition of greatest order, if less powerful things should rule over more powerful things."[59] Apparently Augustine is quite willing to guarantee the invulnerability of beatitude by defining power exclusively in normative terms. The affections whose origins can be traced to our prereflective encounter with temporal things are disenfranchised from the rule of wisdom. They become the mind's irrational motions (*irrationales animi motus*), subject to the dictatorial authority of wisdom.[60] These affections have no power to disrupt beatitude, because they have no right or authority to do so. The norm, "order must subordinate disorder", serves as well for the principle of power.

If wisdom can determine who we are without having to come to terms with our affections, then Augustine has brought invulnerability to beatitude with a vengeance. We are invulnerable to corruption from within and from without. One could be forgiven, perhaps, for thinking that in this case his strategy has worked rather too well. The evil will has not been excluded merely from wisdom: it has been excluded from the world. For it cannot originate in a world where power is always the power to respond to the good. The good will seems similarly dislocated. With its affections for temporal goods disenfranchised, it submits passively to the validity of eternal judgments. It has the same hollow ring as the evil will.

VOLUNTARY SIN

The cost of Augustine's strategy for securing beatitude in time becomes painfully evident over the course of his attempt to resurrect some distinction between the natural (*naturalis*) and

---

[59] *De lib. arb.* 1.10.20 (CCSL 29, 224, 6–7): "Neque enim esset ordinatissimum, ut impotentiora potentioribus imperarent." [60] *De lib. arb.* 1.8.18.

the voluntary (*voluntarius*) in book III of *De libero arbitrio*. Evodius suspects with uncharacteristic perception that Augustine has inadvertently assimilated voluntary movements in and away from beatitude to natural movements, whose descriptions would require no reference to the will.[61] Augustine seeks to allay the suspicion by means of an illustration.

He asks Evodius to consider a stone's downward turn and descent in free fall after having reached its apex in an upward throw, and compare it to a soul's turn away from eternal wisdom and its entanglement in inordinate temporal satis-factions.[62] The two cases are alike, Augustine supposes, because in each case the origin of motion can be attributed properly to the moving subject. The stone is not moved by an external force in its downward flight; hence its movement originates with it. The soul is in no way compelled or coerced to seek its beatitude in temporal things; hence its movement is similarly a self-movement. The cases differ, however, in that the soul alone has the capacity to arrest its motion. Whereas the stone necessarily moves downward in a free fall, the soul can resist whatever attraction draws it towards inferior satisfactions. This ability of the soul to control its own movement establishes the crucial difference between the voluntary self-movement of a rational being and the natural self-movement of a stone.

It is not hard to quibble with the precision of Augustine's contrast. We can (anachronistically) complain that natural self-movement fails to take into account the nexus of causes that enmesh all motions in the natural order. The stone does not move itself, as if it were the cause of its own motion. It is moved by a cause external to it, in this case the attractive force of gravity. Though valid, the objection does not detract from the central feature of Augustine's contrast. Whether a stone is said to move itself downward or be moved downward by the force of gravity, the motion is still relevantly natural, as long as we cannot expect the stone to decide against moving downward and act on its wish.

A more serious objection, however, concerns the character of

---

[61] *Ibid.*, 3.1.1.   [62] *Ibid.*, 3.1.2.

the soul's voluntary motion. If the soul's progress towards the eternal good of wisdom proceeds on the assumption that conditions of greater order always supersede conditions of less order, it is difficult to fathom what resisting (*cohibere motum*) the seductions of disorder could possibly mean. What power could the seduction have over the soul's own internal order? Certainly not a power for disorder. If the soul voluntarily gives in to inferior seductions, it violates the principle that order defeats disorder. That cannot happen given the strictures of *De libero arbitrio*. Voluntary sin is simply not intelligible when our power to act has no independence from the objective norms that inform our conduct.

Perhaps we should say, in Augustine's defense, that the norm of order's dominance over disorder becomes powerful only when those voluntarily seeking their own beatitude *recognize* what the condition of greater order is. The defense falters, however, in as much as ignorance tends to vitiate the voluntary character of an action. If I am unaware of some aspect or import of my action, it is usually not correct to describe what I did voluntarily under a description that would have been unavailable to me at the time of my action. For example, if in seeking happiness I set out on a life of debauchery, not knowing that debauchery ends in misery, it would be odd to say that I voluntarily set out to make myself miserable.

Augustine embroils himself in such oddities when he tries to explain how the universal human desire for happiness fails to come to fruition for many, even though, on the assumptions of *De libero arbitrio*, happiness should be readily available to anyone who desires it.[63] In his effort to solve this puzzle, he invokes the unhappiness that must attend the absence of virtue. Without virtue, we are subject both to the anxiety that accompanies our dependence on temporal goods for happiness and to divinely sanctioned punishment, visited upon anyone who abandons the path of virtue. The law of God, the eternal law, stipulates that those who put their faith in temporal things will most suffer the loss of them – a case of the punishment fitting the anxiety.[64] The necessary connection between vice

---

[63] *Ibid.*, 1.14.30.   [64] See *De lib. arb.* 1.14.30 and 3.15.44.

and unhappiness leads Augustine to conclude that "when we say that people are voluntarily wretched, we do not say this because they themselves want to be wretched, but because their wills are such as to make wretchedness follow necessarily, even involuntarily."[65]

As an attempt to address the intelligibility of a voluntary departure from the good life, Augustine's efforts at precision amount to no more than masterful equivocation. If the acquisition of beatitude is under our control, it stands to reason that the departure from the good life is voluntary for those who are wretched. But Augustine also assumes that the pursuit of wretchedness is not plausible as a motivation for voluntary action. Where does that leave the voluntary status of acting contrary to wisdom, when that act is described *as* a turning away from the good? Apparently somewhere in between voluntary and involuntary.

Later on in *De libero arbitrio*, principally in the final sections of book III, Augustine describes the conditions of human moral agency before and after a primal fall from divine favor.[66] It is in the context of this discussion that he seeks to lend more plausibility to the idea that human beings habitually and voluntarily act contrary to their own interests as rational creatures. Original moral agency, that enjoyed by Adam and Eve in the garden, starts from a condition of rationality, but not wisdom. Our original parents knew enough to accept the precept of God as a commandment that ought to be obeyed, but their knowledge did not fortify them against the malicious seduction of Satan's tempting lies. Had they resisted the seduction, they would have attained wisdom and moved beyond the vulnerability of a rationality untutored in wisdom. Instead, Eve gave in to Satan, and Adam to Eve, thereby forging the first links of a mortal chain that continues into each successive generation. The generations after the fall, in assuming the burden of this chain, begin their quest for beatitude with handicapped moral agency. Instead of the condition of original

---

[65] *Ibid.*, 1.14.30 (CCSL 29, 231–32, 24–27): "Itaque cum dicimus uoluntate homines miseros esse, non ideo dicimus quod esse miseri uelint, sed quod in ea uoluntate sunt, quam etiam his inuitis miseria sequatur necesse est."

[66] *De lib. arb.* 3.18.52–3.25.77.

moral agency, they inherit fallen agency, which involves a greater ignorance of where wisdom lies and a diminished capacity to act on what knowledge remains. Under such conditions, voluntary errings off the path of beatitude are to be expected.

The contrast between original and fallen moral agency is fundamental to the evolution of Augustine's theology of grace, although the description of the contrast itself undergoes change and reformulation, as does the intended import of the fall for the life of virtue. In retrospect, the presentation in *De libero arbitrio* may be seen as exceptional. Not only is there a sharper contrast between the two conditions of agency in subsequent writings, but the motivation there for drawing the contrast is primarily to circumvent Pelagian and pagan hopes for keeping the good life accessible to human moral striving. *De libero arbitrio*, written before the emergence of Pelagianism in North Africa, never addresses the possibility that virtue may fail to issue in beatitude. Having started with assumptions that wed virtue and beatitude together in acts of human self-determination, Augustine instead faces the puzzle that virtue, once gained, seems to move beyond our power to lose. The contrast in conditions of moral agency before and after the fall is intended to suggest, in a rather circuitous manner, the possibility of moral decline, or a turn away from a position of moral strength (original moral agency) to one of moral weakness (fallen moral agency). The story of the fall in book III presents itself, then, as a meditation on the intelligibility of a voluntary turn away from the source of the good life (God). At stake here is the plausibility of Augustine's early ideal of beatitude.

The strategy Augustine employs to meet the challenge of voluntary sin fails because it folds before the demands of the question. The issue of intelligibility emerges most sharply when we ask how someone possessing wisdom could act contrary to the interests a wise person would have. Augustine would respond by denying that anyone has ever been wise. Original moral agency held the best possibility for attaining wisdom, but our primeval forebears failed to realize the possibility. Fallen moral agents lack the wisdom their original parents forfeited through disobedience, and by virtue of an essentially mysterious transmission of the effects of moral failure over generations, they are not likely to gain wisdom through their own efforts. Ignorance and weakness of will handicap each successive generation in its pursuit of beatitude. Given such a diagnosis of the state and subsequent fate of human moral agency, Augustine would seem to deny that the question of a fall from wisdom can be appropriately posed. As long as moral agency never begins in wisdom, he can postpone indefinitely the demand that he explain how a fall from wisdom is possible. Under the rule of an *ad hoc* cynicism, no moral backslider need ever be identified as a backslider from wisdom.

This sort of retreat, however, is not far from surrender. Since his own understanding of sin rests on the notion of perverse preference, our subordination of eternal beatitude with God to transient satisfactions of worldly attachments, Augustine does not leave himself with any way to account for how perverse preference could be *voluntary* once he has banished wisdom from the arena of ordinary moral striving. If he is to postpone the issue of the intelligibility of voluntary sin indefinitely, he must reserve the attainment of wisdom for the eschatological end of moral striving, when the possibility of moral decline is ruled out as a matter of definition. As for the rest of the moral life, with its customary moral declines and advances in pursuit of beatitude, that will have to be relegated to a liminal status of moral quality, partaking neither in wisdom nor in folly, but falling in some indeterminate way between the two:

Apparently there exists some intermediary transition, wherein wisdom turns to folly, which can be described neither as having acted foolishly nor as having acted wisely, and which is not given to persons living in this life to understand except in terms of its contrast with these.[67]

Augustine writes as if this new category for evaluating ethical transitions were an important discovery for our understanding of beatitude and its attainment. In fact, all that he has managed

---

[67] *Ibid.*, 3.24.73 (CCSL 29, 319, 79–82): "apparet esse quiddam medium quo ad stultitiam a sapientia transitur, quod neque stulte neque sapienter factum dici potest, quod ab hominibus in hac uita constitutis non nisi ex contrario datur intellegi."

to accomplish is a polarization of the ethical life into the static extremes of pure wisdom and pure foolishness, with all movement in between cast into mystification. His introduction of the mediating category between wisdom and foolishness has as its sole *raison d'être* the indeterminate status of the beatific knowledge involved in moral declines and advances. As an independent designation it does no real work, except perhaps to expose the nakedness of Augustine's dilemma.[68]

We return again to the nagging problem of how volition and knowledge of the good can in any way come together in an act of voluntary sin. If there is no knowledge of the good involved in a turn away from the good, how can the turn ever count as a voluntary lapse, an act of moral evil? If there is knowledge of good involved, why would a responsible human agent ever willingly contravene this knowledge? Moral evil is no more intelligible for the introduction of a designation that obscures the very point at issue – the status of the knowledge motivating sinful acts.

Within the framework of *De libero arbitrio*, Augustine can do little more to increase the intelligibility of voluntary sin than appeal to the intuitive plausibility of an analogy. He observes that the transition between wisdom and folly is akin to the transition between being awake and being asleep.[69] We could not equate falling asleep with being asleep any more than we could equate departing from wisdom to being without wisdom. That much similarity between the two kinds of transition is enough, Augustine feels, to warrant his talk of an intermediate state of beatific knowledge for moral transitions, a *quiddam medium*. On the other hand, he does not fail to note what makes the two transitions different in kind. The transition between waking and sleeping takes place for the most part without the involvement of a person's will ("sine voluntate plerumque"). Certainly the onset of drowsiness, which marks the transition, does not fall under our direct control. The transition from wisdom to folly, however, is always willed ("numquam nisi per

---

[68] For a critique of this designation along somewhat different lines, see Babcock, "Augustine on Sin," 40, who emphasizes its intractability for the project of theodicy.
[69] *De lib. arb.* 3.24.74.

voluntatem"); otherwise the transition would fail to be one for which we could justly be held responsible.

The comparison between falling asleep and losing wisdom, coming at the dénouement of book III, recalls the earlier comparison in the book between the falling stone and the delinquent soul.[70] Both illustrations are attempts by Augustine to tie the language of moral responsibility, with its invocation of sin, to the language of volition, with its invocation of will. But we may wonder whether any of the difficulties in delineating the voluntary from the natural have been resolved in between.

Falling stones are supposed to be different from falling souls because only souls can stop their own fall. Yet this intuitively plausible distinction encounters difficulties in the face of the assumptions that have framed Augustine's investigation of sin in book I of *De libero arbitrio*. There knowledge is always ordered to the eternal standard of God's order, and our power for self-determination emerges in tandem with our acknowledgment of this standard. These internal connections between knowledge, power, and order leave Augustine with a notion of the voluntary that is either superfluous or unintelligible, depending on the orientation of voluntary movement. If our perception of order "seduces" us in the direction of increasing virtue and wisdom, it is hard to see in what way volition qualifies our natural tendency to conform ourselves to eternal order. If we are moved contrary to wisdom, towards disorder and dissolution, it is even harder to find an intelligible way to describe that movement as voluntary.

The analogy between falling asleep and losing wisdom finds Augustine no closer to an illumination of the voluntary. He has reasserted the importance of will for characterizing the moral life, but without significantly clarifying what individuates operations of will from other movements within the natural order. The power of abstention, invoked in the earlier contrast between the respective movements of souls and stones, does, however, undergo a more precise reformulation.[71] Whereas Augustine's earlier appeal to the power of the soul over its own

---

[70] *Ibid.*, 3.1.2. [71] *Ibid.*, 3.25.74.

movement came without analysis, he now supplies us with a cursory psychology of self-control. No voluntary movement ever takes place in absence of an intentional object ("aliquod visum"), which entices ("allicit") us to possess or effect it. We have no control over what presents itself to us, but we are free nevertheless to accept or reject its impetus to action. When we willingly subordinate superior objects of pursuit to inferior ones, our consent to our inferior perceptions of value ("inferioribus visis") constitutes both our freedom of choice and our degree of culpability.

This psychology, cursory as it is, establishes one of the most important principles of Augustine's philosophy of mind: namely, that we always act in response to what attracts us (even if we should have to act in response to what repels us least). One tempting understanding of free will, that we are self-movers, is consequently ruled out of court. We have no motives for acting independently of what we perceive to be the good in acting. Voluntary movement ties us to the world of our perception. We are moved by its value.

What import this analysis of agency is ultimately to have for Augustine depends, of course, on a whole host of other assumptions about the will, the world, and their interconnection. One striking consequence of his position in *De libero arbitrio* is that he commits himself to an internal connection between the objective order of values and the sources of our motivation to act. It is internal because motivation makes no sense apart from the context of the objective order. If we were able to generate our principles of motivation independently of whatever values there were to be discerned in our situation, we could never be said to act in response to our situation, and our actions would degenerate into meaningless self-movements. Augustine never relinquishes the connection between responding to the good and being motivated to act, and it becomes utterly central to his understanding of free will. Nevertheless, *De libero arbitrio* represents only an early and imperfect stage of its elaboration. In this important but fatally flawed work, he has the objective order of values determine motivation in far too direct and immediate a manner. Volitions are as of yet barely distinguishable from cognitions of order, and consequently voluntary movement tends to fade into the natural movements of the created order.

Augustine's early ideal of beatitude, which I have identified as essentially Stoic in inspiration, brings happiness under the discipline of virtue. We have found the basis of this discipline to be his willingness to reduce volitions to perceptions of order. If we can as a matter of course order ourselves to our perceptions of order, as he implies, then our beatitude is free from all manner of external frustration. The natural order never intrudes upon our happiness, because in retrospect we dissociate ourselves from whatever we have lost over time. Augustine has given us the invulnerability of shadows.

CHAPTER 3

Wisdom's grief

After Augustine's vain efforts in *De libero arbitrio* to establish a foothold for the voluntary in the natural order, the fate of the voluntary/natural distinction in his thought hangs on whether he can bring human willing down to earth. To be more precise, he must do what the classicist Albrecht Dihle credits him for having done: that is, develop some conception of the will (*voluntas*) that no longer presupposes classical psychology's distinction between the rational decisions of the mind and the irrational impulses of the emotions or appetites.[1] Were he to integrate cognitive and affective sources of motivation into his conception of willing, Augustine would potentially have the resources for explaining how a vicious volition could be other than an inexplicable aberration of rational agency and how a virtuous volition could be other than an insubstantial shade of some mind's perception of order.

Augustine's first decisive steps towards articulating this new conception were taken, curiously enough, during the hiatus between the composition of the first book and a half of *De libero arbitrio* in Rome in late 388 and the completion of the rest of the work in Hippo Regius sometime before the end of 395, not long before his ascent to the episcopate. His intervening writings continue to pursue anti-Manichaean themes, especially the

---

[1] Albrecht Dihle, *The Theory of Will in Classical Antiquity* (Berkeley: University of California Press, 1982), 123–44. For other views of Augustine's conceptual innovation, see Neal W. Gilbert, "The Concept of Will in Early Latin Philosophy," *Journal of the History of Philosophy* 1 (1963), 17–35, Charles H. Kahn, "Discovering the Will: From Aristotle to Augustine," in *The Question of "Eclecticism": Studies in Later Greek Philosophy*, ed. Dillon and Long (Berkeley: University of California Press, 1988), 234–59, and Hannah Arendt, *The Life of the Mind*, vol. II (New York: Harcourt, Brace, Jovanovich, 1978), 84–110.

theme of sin as a voluntary act of will, though the polemical intent of the discussions is generally more explicit than it had been in *De libero arbitrio*. But more than a change of tone can be discerned. Peter Brown observes that as a young priest writing against the Manichees over the years between 392 and 394, "Augustine came to appreciate the sheer difficulty of achieving an ideal life."[2] There is little in book I of *De libero arbitrio* to suggest that this difficulty could involve limitations upon our power to will the good.[3] But by book III, Augustine, obviously under the influence of a new sensibility, considers it unexceptional ("nec mirandum est") that our power to will the good can be diminished by our indulgence in carnal satisfactions, even to the point where we will have become incapable of acting upon what we know to be good.[4]

If book III presupposes the perspective of book I (not an unreasonable assumption), Augustine's late invocation of the obstruction of habit to our appropriation of beatific knowledge is anomalous and adventitious. The anomaly has less to do with the peculiar nature of the obstruction than with its placement in a world where our power to conform ourselves to superior objects of attraction has been part of what it means to have a will. What Augustine wishes to introduce in book III, as one of the penalties of sin, is the familiar difficulty of weakness of will, a condition in which the legacy of habitual behavior inhibits us from acting in accordance with what we judge to be in our best interests.[5] As an incapacity to act, it derives from a failure not of

---

[2] Peter Brown, *Augustine of Hippo: A Biography* (Berkeley: University of California Press, 1967), 148.

[3] There is, however, a dramatic passage (1.11.22) in this book describing the penal state of a lapsed soul as one involving the tyrannical reign of the passions (*cupiditates*) over the mind. We would have to admit, certainly, that when we are subject to blind passions, our autonomy diminishes. On the other hand, the context of the passage indicates that Augustine's interests here center on the confusion suffered by those having rejected wisdom, not on the difficulty faced by those attempting to regain wisdom. He never claims that misbegotten affections hinder us from acting on beatific knowledge. He indicates only that the turmoil in our affections is the penalty for our forfeiture of wisdom. The explicit conjunction of having beatific knowledge and not being able to act on it must wait until book III. See William Babcock, "Augustine on Sin and Moral Agency," *Journal of Religious Ethics* 16 (1988), 38–39, for more on the significance of 1.11.22.   [4] *De lib. arb.* 3.18.52.

[5] Although Augustine makes use of our familiar concept of weakness of will, he also wishes to extend its application in an unusual way. We generally hold that in cases of weakness of will, the characteristic inhibition must have its source in the legacy of

knowledge, but of motivation. Since Augustine's earlier assimilation of motivation to cognition in *De libero arbitrio* disallows any handicapping of willing other than by ignorance, there is no way even to formulate weakness of will for the *voluntas* of book I.

The arrival of weakness of will in book III does not, then, take its point of departure from book I and the line of thought initiated there. It in fact emerges from the hiatus in the composition of *De libero arbitrio*. This puts the interpreter of Augustine in the peculiar position of having to read the anti-Manichaean works of the early 390s as departing significantly from the views of *De libero arbitrio*, even though they antedate the completion of that work. The adventitious element in book III will turn out to be, in this case anyway, not unaccountable inconsistency on Augustine's part, but the untidy influence of an alternative line of thought.

INVOLUNTARY SIN

Augustine's critique of Manichaean philosophy, occupying a substantial portion of his early writings, displays all the stridency and attention to detail that one would have expected from a former devotee.[6] For our purposes, however, we may take a selective view of his polemics, restricting our attention to one, albeit central, source of his dissatisfaction with the Manichees – the Manichaean doctrine of the two souls.

In Manichaean cosmology, the kingdom of light, representing God and all that is good by nature, has been invaded by the forces of the antithetical and adjoining kingdom of darkness, representing all that is evil by nature.[7] The ensuing pitched

the agent's *own* past behavior. Augustine would add to that the supposition that all human beings stand under the legacy of what their original parents did. Somehow Adam and Eve managed to implicate all of their descendants in their disobedience. We feel the effects of their disobedience in our own pursuit of beatitude, just as if we ourselves had disobeyed. By virtue of this rather mysterious extension of the internal effects of agency from them to us, we suffer weakness of will as the penalty of original sin. In *De lib. arb.* 3.20.56.ff., he discusses various theories of how souls originate, largely in an attempt to explain the transmission of original sin, but he opts for no particular theory.

[6] Augustine describes his life as a Manichee in the *Confessiones*, especially books III and V. For a judicious assessment of his attraction to Manichaean religion, see Brown, *Augustine of Hippo*, 46–60.

[7] The basic contours of this cosmology are laid out and criticized by Augustine in his *Contra Epistolam Manichaei quam vocant Fundamenti*.

battle between good and evil, a macrocosmic struggle of the light to free itself from engulfment by the darkness, has an important microcosmic analogue in the lives of each of the Manichaean elect. Two souls vie for dominance in the elect, one having its origin in darkness, the other in light. Being of wholly different origin, these souls do not share a common nature in any regard, and the elect identify themselves only with the good soul. The dark soul resides in the elect as an alien force of occupation. While under its influence the elect live in the diaspora of the kingdom of light, never wholly separate from the light by virtue of their identity as good souls, but not as yet returned home to the state of uncontaminated light and goodness.

Augustine's objection to the Manichaean theory of two souls focuses squarely on its naturalization of evil: that is, on the theory's acceptance of evil as a substance, or that which has its own proper form of being. From a theological point of view, the objectification of evil poses intractable difficulties for the notion of God as the benevolent creator of all that exists. If evil constitutes a type of existence, then God creates evil and must bear the burden of responsibility for it. The Manichaeans themselves were willing to limit the scope of God's creation to the kingdom of light in order to admit a separate ontological space for evil, the kingdom of darkness. That willingness freed them from the burden of theodicy, since evil clearly would not originate from God's creation, but it distanced them permanently from the God of the Hebrew Scriptures. For his part, Augustine would rather take up theodicy than rein in the created order and restrict God to a kingdom of light.

In order to discredit the Manichaean alternative, with its seductive avoidance of the need for theodicy, Augustine will exploit the poverty of Manichaean dualism, which shows up whenever dualism is called upon to make sense of moral struggle. The Manichees, having partitioned the universe into good and evil natures, leave themselves divested of the language of volition and without resources to explicate the nature and significance of moral evil. Manichaean evil fails by its very nature to penetrate or corrupt in any way the integrity of the good soul. The good soul is thereby accorded invulnerability

to corruption by ontological fiat, and the multitude of judgments that ordinarily rest on viewing goodness as an ethical
ideal all seem to lose their foothold. Matters are not made much
clearer if the Manichees should, in a revisionist temper, openly
eschew the language of volition and wholeheartedly embrace a
naturalistic reading of evil's invasion and influence upon the
good. What, after all, would be the sense of evil's *in*vasion and
*in*fluence, if evil remains essentially alien and external to the
good? The ontological partitioning of good and evil makes it
difficult, if not impossible, to comprehend what manner of
struggle the two natures could be involved in, either at the
macroscopic level of the two kingdoms or the microscopic level
of the two souls. And Augustine is quite happy to push the
embarrassing questions.

In *De duabus animabus*, a work finished early in 392, he urges
the Manichees to consider how their naturalistic understanding
of evil undermines the critical ethical distinction between what
happens by nature and what happens by will. Without a clearly
delineated concept of the voluntary, the whole fabric of the
moral order unravels. God cannot judge justly the disposition of
souls who have no power of will, and when the foundations for
divine judgment are undermined, there is a general under-
mining of moral evaluations of any sort. "There is no judgment
of merits and faults, no providence, and the world is governed
by chance instead of reason, or rather it is not governed, since it
is not given to chance to govern."[8]
Augustine assumes that the Manichees, no less than he,
would find a universe stripped of its ethical dimension far from
congenial. Presumably they would admit, as he does, that souls
fall under divine judgment and are punished or rewarded in
accordance with their state of virtue, or their conformity with
the eternal law. But if Manichees are genuinely committed to
the system of divine rule by law, they will need to adopt a
different understanding of evil. Augustine expresses their
dilemma as follows:

---

[8] *De duab. an.* 12.17 (CSEL 25, 73, 12–15): "nullum meritorum iudicium est, nulla
prouidentia, et casu potius quam ratione mundus administratur uel potius non
administratur; non enim administratio casibus danda est."

They and I agree, then, that some souls stand condemned under divine law and judgment. But if these souls are good, what sort of justice is that? If they are evil, is it by nature, or by will? But by nature souls can in no way be evil.[9]

Augustine excludes the possibility of a naturally evil soul by dint of definition. "Sin," he writes, "is the will to retain or pursue what justice forbids, when there is freedom to abstain; although without freedom, there is no will."[10] Exclude the dimension of will, and sin takes its place among the natural movements of the created order. But as a natural movement, sin would cease to have the character of sin. "Natural sin" is incoherent given the way that Augustine has chosen to differentiate the natural from the voluntary. It would be as if we were to speak of involuntary voluntary actions. Augustine charges the Manichees with proliferating this sort of nonsense when they speak of our evil nature or the evil that is part of the order of things.

The voluntary character of sinning is taken for granted in *De duabus animabus*. Augustine's rhetorical posture is that of the defender of what everybody already knows to be the case. And in this case, everybody, except apparently the Manichees, knows that unless evil were a matter of what we did voluntarily, the influence of evil could not be voluntarily undone. Our quest for beatitude, for the progressive elimination of vice and acquisition of virtue, could not even get off the ground. The concept of the voluntary grounds the intelligibility of what Augustine calls the discipline of virtue (*disciplina virtutis*) – our self-determination for beatitude.[11]

There is undoubtedly a certain awkwardness to this rhetorical posture, given that Augustine's attempt to delineate the voluntary from the natural in *De libero arbitrio* ends in abysmal failure. Moreover, the failure is embarrassingly conspicuous in

---

[9] *De duab. an.* 12.17 (CSEL 25, 73, 19–22): "conuenit igitur mihi cum eis aliquas animas diuina lege iudicioque damnari. at hae si bonae sunt, quae illa iustitia est? si malae, natura, an voluntate? sed natura esse malae animae nullo modo queunt."

[10] *De duab. an.* 11.15 (CSEL 25, 70, 15–17): "ergo peccatum est uoluntas retinendi uel consequendi quod iustitia uetat et unde liberum est abstinere. quamquam si liberum non sit, non est uoluntas."

[11] *De duab. an.* 13.21. In the previous chapter, I set out the discipline of virtue as Augustine's Stoic strategy for bringing beatitude under the aegis of self-determination.

the matter of moral evil, where Augustine suffers from a most Manichaean-like inability to make sense of the ordinary intuition that vice is of our own making. It seems disingenuous, then, for him to return to the intuition in *De duabus animabus* in order to indict the Manichees for their inability to incorporate it into their metaphysics. Augustine has not as yet developed his Platonic metaphysics into a viable alternative. He stands as much indicted as they do.

Nevertheless, we misread *De duabus animabus* unless we take into account that Augustine self-consciously brackets his own metaphysical commitments before he introduces his definitions of will and sin. He requests that the recondite distinction between sensible and intelligible things – the Platonic basis for his distinction between eternal and temporal things – be allowed to withdraw for a time ("secedat paulisper").[12] In the interim he will prosecute Manichaean metaphysics using only intuitively acceptable connections between sin, responsibility, and voluntary action.

Ostensibly this choice of argumentative strategy relates to Augustine's desire to appeal to an audience whose intellectual habits were uninformed by the intricacies of Platonic metaphysics. William Babcock, marking the change in idiom from *De libero arbitrio* to *De duabus animabus*, draws the appropriate moral:

Augustine could now make his point without using the Platonic notion of the role of the mind in the rightly ordered self or deploying the Platonic hierarchy of strength and virtue on the graded scale of being. He could put his argument, that is, not just in the language of an intellectual and cultural elite, but also in an idiom of example and counter-example that he could reasonably expect his congregation in Hippo Regius to grasp. But the argument itself seems much the same. It is still the free exercise of will, neither internally nor externally compelled, that makes us moral agents of evil and gives to the evil that we do its character as sin.[13]

One could add that, as a further benefit, Augustine disencumbers himself from the framework that has made the intelligibility of voluntary sin so troubling. His Platonic

---

[12] *De duab. an.* 10.13.   [13] Babcock, "Augustine on Sin," 33.

assumptions in abeyance, nothing remains to vex the common consensus on moral responsibility and the voluntary character of sin.

But has the argument really remained "much the same"? Certainly the motivation of the argument has. Augustine wishes to develop the notion of will in counterpoint to the notion of nature, so that the Christian discipline of virtue gains credibility at the expense of Manichaean metaphysics. The lines of development in *De duabus animabus*, however, run counter to those of *De libero arbitrio*, even if they are supposed eventually to arrive at the same place. In *De libero arbitrio*, Augustine situates us in a created order, whose goods motivate us in accordance with their rank in a hierarchy of objective values. That gets him into trouble because motivation seems overly determined by the objective order of goods. Once we have seen the world aright, we find ourselves being moved in the appropriate way, and there is nothing left for volition to do. In *De duabus animabus*, he speaks of willing as if we were able to motivate ourselves independently of what we perceived to be of value. That strategy errs in the opposite direction. Volitions are so little determined by the order of the world that they cease to be motivated in any intelligible way. Augustine flirts once again with the fiction of volition as absolute self-movement, and in that respect at least, the opposite tacks of the two works land him in the same place.

The source of Augustine's difficulty is his tendency to oppose the voluntary and the natural, making volition into a power to abstain from natural movement. When this power is not exercised, and we consent to natural movement, voluntary movement becomes indistinguishable from natural movement. In his discussion of virtue in book I of *De libero arbitrio*, his distinction between natural and voluntary movement is so underdeveloped that he cannot speak of us as acting in nature without implying that our actions are determined by natural forces of attraction. When he tries to "denaturalize" sin and virtue in *De duabus animabus*, he adds to our nature the *sui generis* power of volition and threatens to sever our actions from their motivations. Having defined volition against the involuntary attractions which motivate it, he will find it hard to distinguish involuntary actions from natural movements.

It is not until the final sections of *De duabus animabus* that Augustine shows signs of moving in an altogether different direction. In chapter 13 the distinction between temporal and eternal things, so far in abeyance, returns to the scene in order to supply volitions with their appropriate natural context. This time, however, the distinction is innocent of the Platonic assumptions that had been deployed in *De libero arbitrio* to guarantee the ascendency of eternal order in the life of the virtuous soul. Augustine refashions the distinction as the more familiar (*familiarius*) one between the spirit and the flesh.[14] These two sources of motivation are often antagonistic, and hence we are inclined to act consistently only when one is subordinated to the other. But *De duabus animabus* gives us no reason to suppose that proper subordination, that of flesh to spirit, is the sole accomplishment of beatific knowledge. Even someone knowledgeable might still feel the seduction of the flesh and succumb to its dominance. Greater order and greater power are no longer assumed to coalesce.

Augustine breaks from the stranglehold of his earlier position on volition by allowing the motivating power of goods a measure of independence from how they would motivate when viewed *sub specie aeternitatis*. This margin prevents how we see goods from being equated with how we are moved by them. Our course of action need not automatically follow the path of our best judgment, and if what moves us to act can be described independently of this judgment, we can experience internal conflict. Augustine submits that whenever we seek to pursue better things (*meliora*), our desires for beatitude always encounter the inertia of past sins and habits of the flesh ("consuetudo facta cum carne").[15]

The history of how we have desired and acted on desire, registered in our present experience as the cumulative force of habit, will have an obstructive influence on our ability to allow new kinds of desires, for example, ones framed by beatific knowledge, to determine our willing. This is the idea that

---

[14] *De duab. an.* 13.19.   [15] *Ibid.*, 13.19.

Augustine makes use of in book III of *De libero arbitrio* to describe the consequences of sin (sin's penalty), but its insertion there is incongruous with the metaphysics of volition developed earlier in book I for explicating sin. Volitions cannot intelligibly be said to accumulate as habits unless volitions have a distinct source of motivation in the temporal, sensible world of nature, quite apart from how that world might be supposed to fit into some timeless and unchanging view of things. In other words, we accumulate habits because we experience the world as distended in time, not as an eternal unity. Augustine in *De duabus animabus* admits this much when he grants a measure of autonomy to the seductive power of temporal goods. When we are drawn to these goods apart from their intelligibility in relation to God, our willing partakes in a time-bound, mutable world.

Augustine suddenly finds himself able to explain why the Manichees are tempted by a metaphysical dualism of souls. They mistake the internal conflicts emerging out of time-bound willing for a battle between a good soul and an alien evil soul. Finding themselves set against themselves, they objectify the opposition and deny all identity with it:

It comes to this, that when habits of the flesh and our sins have begun in some manner to war against us and to make difficulty for us, who are striving for better things, some foolish persons, out of the most obtuse superstition, suspect the existence of another kind of soul, which does not originate from God.[16]

This diagnosis of Manichaean metaphysics, though powerful in itself as a critique, compromises the dominant strategy of *De duabus animabus*. Manichaean metaphysics was supposed to have floundered on its commitment to the incoherent concept of involuntary sin. Augustine took Manichaean belief in evil natures to be indicative of this commitment, for he had been imaging natural movement to be tantamount to involuntary movement; neither were described in reference to the will. But if he holds to his diagnosis of why Manichees commit themselves to dualism, he needs to differentiate involuntary movement

[16] *Ibid.*, 13.19 (CSEL 25, 76, 3–8): "eo contingit, ut cum ad meliora conantibus nobis consuetudo facta cum carne et peccata nostra quodam modo militare contra nos et difficultatem nobis facere coeperint, nonnulli stulti aliud genus animarum, quod non sit ex deo, superstitione obtunsissima suspicentur."

from involuntary action, for he will have granted the possibility of our having to sin involuntarily. The Manichees err not because they believe in involuntary sin, but because they fail to recognize that even involuntary sin originates in volition. One faulty explication of a concept does not by itself, however, impugn a concept's ultimate intelligibility, and Augustine seems now to be claiming that involuntary sin can be explicated both meaningfully and correctly.

The discrepancy between Augustine's two approaches to the Manichaean theory of two souls is an instance of his arguments lagging behind his insights. His appeal to the necessarily voluntary character of sin continues the line of thought on the voluntary that had begun in earnest with *De libero arbitrio*. Having there assimilated voluntary to natural movement, he finds it difficult to preserve the connection between virtue and volition. In *De duabus animabus* he associates volition with the power to abstain from involuntary attractions. But he has yet to distinguish involuntary from natural attractions, and hence he tars natural evil and involuntary sin with the same brush. His appeal near the end of *De duabus animabus* to the constraints of habit upon willing marks the beginning of his new line of thought on the involuntary and by extension the voluntary. This line of thought will contradict and supplant his earlier understanding of involuntary sin and alter the manner of his critique of Manichaeanism.

In the summer of 392, a matter of months after the composition of *De duabus animabus*, Augustine confirmed his acceptance of the idea of involuntary sin in a public debate with the prominent Manichee Fortunatus.[17] At a crucial moment in the proceedings, Fortunatus enlists the weighty authority of Paul to support the Manichaean notion of involuntary sin. When Paul speaks in Romans and Galatians of the opposition of the flesh to the spirit, Fortunatus takes him to be referring to the opposition of the evil soul, which by nature cannot be brought

---

[17] For an account of the debate, its background, and its significance, see Malcolm E. Alflatt, "The Development of the Idea of Involuntary Sin in St. Augustine," *Revue des études augustiniennes* 20 (1974), 113–34, and his further reflections in "The Responsibility for Involuntary Sin in Saint Augustine," *Recherches augustiniennes* 10 (1975), 171–86. For an important qualification of Alflatt's account, see Babcock, "Augustine on Sin," 39 n. 12.

into conformity with the divine law.[18] Augustine responds by invoking an alternative notion of involuntary sin. "After [Adam] sinned of his own free will, we who have descended from him were plunged headlong into necessity."[19] This necessity, claims Augustine, takes the form of our soul's habituation to sin, habituation so profound that "it cannot overcome what by sinning it has wrought for itself."[20]

The debate with Fortunatus puts us on the brink of the period in which Peter Brown has the young priest coming to terms with just how elusive the ideal life really is. In the final moments of *De duabus animabus*, Augustine concedes that our misbegotten habits war against us ("militare contra nos") in our pursuit of beatitude.[21] In public debate, however, he takes the further step of insisting that internal conflicts are never resolved in favor of what we would want for ourselves in light of beatific knowledge. Thrown upon our own efforts, we cannot abstain from pursuing inferior objects of attraction, even when we recognize and condemn how our pursuit violates the order of creation. Involuntary sin becomes the premier symptom of the impotence of knowledge. A more dramatic departure from book I of *De libero arbitrio* could hardly be imagined.

William Babcock observes that as of *Contra Fortunatum*, Augustine "has now restricted the free exercise of will to the first instance, the first sin of the first human being."[22] After Adam, all sins are involuntary in the sense that knowledge of the good life either is lacking through some sort of culpable ignorance or is present but fails to carry the will in tow.[23] Sin is voluntary, in the restricted sense of being avoidable, only for original moral agency.

The connection between Adam's voluntary sin and the involuntary sins of his descendants is admittedly mysterious, and it is difficult to understand how the notion of voluntary sin gains any further clarity by virtue of its restriction to an original agent. Augustine seems to have cut his losses on the problems

---

[18] See Rom. 8:7, 7:23–25; Gal. 5:17, 6:14.
[19] *C. Fortunatum* 22 (CSEL 25, 104, 2–4): "postquam autem libera ipse uoluntate peccauit, nos in necessitatem praecipitati sumus, qui ab eius stirpe descendimus."
[20] *C. Fortunatum* 22 (CSEL 25, 104, 11–12): "uincere non possit, quod sibi ipsa peccando fabricata est."   [21] *De duab. an.* 13.19.
[22] Babcock, "Augustine on Sin," 40.   [23] See *De lib. arb.* 3.18.52.

surrounding voluntary sin by excluding it from the fallen world. This leads him to refocus his attention on involuntary sin and to begin to elaborate his psychology of fallenness. His conception of will emerges out of this psychology, and it departs significantly from his naive conception of the voluntary in his early writings against the Manichees.

THE REHABILITATION OF THE AFFECTIONS

The philosophical fall-out of Augustine's acceptance of not merely the possibility, but the inevitability, of involuntary sin is evident in his critique of pagan philosophy in *De civitate Dei*. As I suggested in my opening remarks to chapter 2, the force of his critique depends on his prior rejection of Stoic moral psychology – in particular, its claim that reason alone determines the quality of human affections. If the Stoics were right to trace all claims upon human desire to the single source of rational judgment, then knowledge of the good would always issue unfailingly in the proper emotional and volitional response. Although Augustine's abiding interest in securing beatitude against adventitious loss predisposed him to conflate motivation and cognition, so that knowledge would always be efficacious, his interests in explicating evil finally forced him to draw some distinction between the two. Faced with Manichaean opponents and with his own odd inability to render voluntary sin intelligible, Augustine turned his attention inward to find in himself more than one source of motivation. Internal conflict, especially of the sort registered in involuntary sin, indicated that desires conforming to moral wisdom had to compete with other kinds of desires, and not always to good effect.

Having accepted the phenomenon of involuntary sin as part of human psychology, Augustine found himself in no position to return to the Stoicized will of the first book of *De libero arbitrio*, where he had assumed far too simple a view of how knowledge of the good is appropriated. One way of viewing the genealogy of Augustine's moral psychology up to this point is to notice that his interests in reclaiming Paul's avowals of internal struggle from Manichaean exegesis worked against his predisposition to put motivational integrity into the very definition of willing. His naive confidence in the power of wisdom to motivate had to give way to a messier but more profound moral psychology that took on the intricacies of moral failure. If we read his critique of pagan moral psychology in *De civitate Dei* in light of how he came to accept the idea of involuntary sin, it becomes apparent why he fails to give any further credence to Stoicism's radical claim that wisdom eliminates disruptive affections altogether. Unitary sources of motivation, such as Stoic wisdom, offer no resources to the psychology of moral struggle. Augustine rejects the idea that wisdom and moral struggle are mutually exclusive (internal struggle is a psychological fact, even for the saints); hence he more than happily reinterprets Stoic psychology to describe the battle between reason and the passions, two distinct and often antagonistic sources of motivation.

Augustine's reinterpretation of Stoicism to have it join Peripatetic psychology is far from innocuous, for in depriving pagan psychology of Stoicism's radical ambition to free us wholly from inner turmoil, Augustine in effect describes philosophy's fall from grace. Pagan philosophers must rejoin virtue and happiness on the basis of a mitigated Stoicism, where wisdom can at best hold the passions at bay. Despite Augustine's pretense of intending only to eliminate an idle distinction among competing schools of philosophy, he does not offer the assimilated version of Stoicism as a substantive advance over the original. Instead he leaves the pagans with a limping Stoicism. The ideal of philosophy remains the Stoic one of having wisdom and virtue free from the influence of disruptive affections, the *perturbationes*, but regardless of this ideal, passions continue to plague the peace of the sage. In order to appreciate the subversive intent of his reinterpretation of Stoicism, we need to recognize that Augustine continues to hold pagan philosophers accountable for Stoicism's shortcomings.

Following his denial in book IX of *De civitate Dei* of the uniqueness of Stoic psychology, Augustine observes that the important question to ask about the affections is not whether (*utrum*) they occur in the life of wisdom and virtue, but why (*quare*).[24] The particular affections he invokes to make his point

---

[24] *De civ. Dei* 9.5.

are those of anger, grief, and fear – emotions all having their source in our perception of a conflict between what we would will to be the case and the way that the world actually is. Grief emerges from our experience of the conflict, fear from its anticipation, anger from either the experience or its anticipation.

Augustine's choice of these affections is aimed specifically at the Stoic claim that a person possessed of wisdom and virtue would never experience a genuine conflict between will and world. Stoic sages avoid the experience of loss and diminished beatitude because they will the world to be as it is. Their reasoning, once under the auspices of wisdom, leaves them committed only to what they can effect without fear of frustration. In practice this restriction leaves them valuing as good only their own consent to what the world presents to them as a *fait accompli*.[25] Under these terms, affections having their source in a putative conflict between will and world must be the product of mistaken reasoning. Unhappy reasoners have erroneously supposed that things should be other than they are, and their unhappiness has its source in the disharmony of their perception. They nevertheless retain their power to disavow the perception, and once informed by wisdom, they can eliminate misbegotten affection in the same manner in which they would rectify an error. They recognize the truth and give their consent to it.

Reason's invulnerability to disruptive affections is, according to Augustine, the issue on which Stoicism finds common cause with the rest of pagan philosophy. All of the schools respect the prerogative of reasoners to disavow affections that they judge to be out of keeping with wisdom, and all seem to be committed to the view that some affections, at least, have no *ratio* of their own. Pagan moral psychology, when interpreted in this ecumenical manner, would allow that disruptive affections are occasionally experienced before reason has delivered its verdict on whether

---

[25] Kahn, "Discovering the Will," 253, reflecting on a passage from Epictetus, describes Stoic practice along similar lines: "The life of the committed Stoic is thus a continual process of self-definition, of identification with the inner world that is 'in our power,' of deliberate detachment from the body and from the external world that lies beyond our control."

the loss of some material advantage would count as the deprivation of a good. But it would insist that we remain free, upon rational deliberation, to disown the involuntary affection.

As long as our power to reason allows us to disown miscreant passions in retrospect, the ideal of philosophical beatitude seems as possible in mitigated Stoicism as in the original, the only difference being that in the original, reason could spare us from having to experience miscreant passions in the first place. Augustine suggests, however, that pagan philosophy's common hope for the sovereignty of reason over passion rests on its misconception of passion. Because reason rules in its own house only when it casts out rebellious passions, pagan philosophers must insist on the distinction between what moves them when they reason and what moves them prior to their having reasoned, and then identify themselves, their *true* motives, only with the former. That way, when they disown some disruptive passion, they reassert the integrity of their power to judge wisely. If, however, their passions should in some way *embody* their power to reason, reason could not cast out rebellious passions without having to divide its own house. Augustine contends that affections must have a *ratio* of their own; otherwise they would never move us. The basis of pagan moral psychology – that of two wholly distinct sources of motivation, only one of which emerges from reason – is therefore corrupt.

Augustine's reformulation of the nature of affect becomes part of his alternative moral psychology in book XIV of *De civitate Dei*, wherein he links affectivity to quality of willing:

It is the quality of human willing that is of interest. For if it is perverse, it will move us to have perverse emotions. But if it is well directed, its emotions will be not only beyond reproach, but worthy of praise. All emotions, certainly, involve the will; in fact they are nothing other than forms of will.[26]

---

[26] *De civ. Dei* 14.6 (CCSL 48, 421, 1–5): "Interest autem qualis sit uoluntas hominis; quia si peruersa est, peruersos habebit hos motus; si autem recta est, non solum inculpabiles, uerum etiam laudabiles erunt. Voluntas est quippe in omnibus; immo omnes nihil aliud quam uoluntates sunt." I follow Babcock, "Augustine on Sin," 43, in my rendering of *uoluntates* as "forms of will." Henry Bettenson (trans.), *City of God* (Penguin, 1972, 555), prefers "acts of will," but that carries too much the suggestion that the affections are voluntarily controlled.

Augustine distinguishes four fundamental forms of will, each form assuming its characteristic quality in relation to an intentional object. Desire and delight correspond respectively to our anticipation and possession of what attracts us; fear and grief to our anticipation and possession of what repulses us. Within this basic framework for affectivity, Augustine pursues the question of the ideal affective state. Which forms of the will can be recognized, albeit in a transformed state, as constitutive of beatitude? He will use the Stoic ideal of dispassionate wisdom as the norm for pagan philosophy, and against it he will mark his own departure from the wisdom of the schools.

Except in his more hyperbolic moments, Augustine does not equate the Stoic ideal of *apatheia* with insensitivity. Even should sages fail to experience the disruptive emotions (*perturbationes*) that afflict those whose reason deviates from wisdom, he would suppose them nevertheless to have affections corresponding to their perfected state of reason. Augustine refers to these affections by the Greek term *eupatheiai*, and by Cicero's Latin coinage, *constantiae*.[27] The Latin term especially suggests the stability of an emotional life under rational control, one where right reason has excluded irrational passions and brought about a state of *apatheia*, fixity and tranquillity of mind. In terms of the fundamental forms of will or affection, the Stoics will preserve three in the transformation from error and ignorance to the beatitude of wisdom. Wisdom turns desire into resolve, delight into well-being, fear into reserve.[28] There is no analogue for grief. No sage could ever experience a diminution of beatitude and still have the credentials of a sage. Grief is not amenable to beatific transformation.

As for what does get transformed, it is perhaps easiest to

---

[27] *De civ. Dei* 14.8 contains a discussion of the nature of the *eupatheiai*, and 14.9 contains two views of *apatheia*, one presupposing its connection with the *eupatheiai*, and one more polemical view establishing it as a condition totally without affect. For commentary on Augustine's treatment of Stoic *apatheia* and *eupatheia*, see the discerning analysis of Marcia Colish, *The Stoic Tradition from Antiquity to the Early Middle Ages*, vol. II (Leiden: E. J. Brill, 1985), 221–25.

[28] The contrasts in the Latin are between *cupiditas* and *voluntas*, *laetitia* and *gaudium*, *metus* and *cautio*. See *De civ. Dei* 14.8 (CCSL 48, 423, 3–4). The members of each of these pairs are closer to one another in common meaning than my translation would suggest. I have deviated somewhat from a literal translation of the second member of each pairing in order to indicate their significance as terms of art.

envision the transformation in terms of a correspondence between a cardinal affection and a cardinal virtue. Well-being springs from delight in justice. It is an affection ordered to the recognition and acceptance of the proper order of the world. Resolve is desire tempered to pursue only the good. Reserve refers to prudent use of material advantages and avoidance of material disadvantages.

While it is not difficult to imagine how justice mediates delight and well-being, and how temperance mediates desire and resolve, prudence does not seem to illuminate the connection between fear and reserve. The difficulty here stems not from the analogy between virtue and affection, however, but from the obscurity of the Stoic distinction between goods (*bona*) and advantages (*commoda*). Fear in its untutored state produces in us affections that are based on our misapprehension of advantages (things having a selective value) as goods (things having a beatific value). In conformity with prudence, reserve produces in us affections that have no part in any misapprehension of the status of material advantages. But since in the case of fear such misapprehension is requisite for having the affection, it is hard to see why reserve would not replace fear altogether rather than transform it.

That the Stoics either flatly refuse or find it difficult to supply eupathetic equivalents for discordant forms of affection is not lost on Augustine. He is sympathetic to their view that right reason results in the right affections, finding in this some recognition of the influence of wisdom on forms of will, but he does not believe that the Stoics capture the right beatific transformations. The perfect state of beatitude would sustain delight and love, the concordant affections, but it would wholly exclude fear and grief, the discordant affections. The perfect state, however, is not humanly possible in the *saeculum*. It must await life in eternity. For those still in the world of time, Augustine insists that life on the road to beatitude must involve a eupathetic transformation of all four forms of cardinal affection. Not only fear, but grief as well, has its appropriate *ratio*.[29]

---

[29] In *De civ. Dei* 14.9, Augustine presents scriptural evidence for the value of discordant affections in the life of virtue and wisdom.

Marcia Colish is right to observe that Augustine's sharpest break from the Stoic ideal of *apatheia* comes with his recognition that virtue and grief are compatible.[30] Often, in fact, grief is the necessary and appropriate affective form of virtue. Augustine is clear in his use of the term "grief" (*tristitia*) that more is at stake than the experience of unpleasant or painful physical sensations. "I have preferred to speak of grief," he notes, "because affliction and pain are more commonly associated with physical distress."[31] He differentiates grief from potential synonyms in pain (*dolor*) and affliction (*aegritudo*) in order to highlight the cognitive component of the affection in question. Grief must incorporate our judgment that something of value to us has been lost. Depending on the nature of our recognition of loss, our grief sometimes modulates into related forms of affection, such as compassion, sympathy, sorrow, anger, and remorse. The life of virtue without this range of affections, without grief in particular, is either blind or insensitive. For the Stoics, such blindness or insensitivity is willful in so far as they refuse to accept transient bearers of value as important to their own beatitude. Augustine has felt the attraction of this stance, with its posture of apparent invulnerability to the ravages of time, but now he finds it reprehensible.

What makes grief commendable, however, is certainly not the discordance of the affection itself. In a perfect world, there would be no need for grief, and wisdom would not suffer for its lack. The need for grief emerges only from within a fallen world, where human willing is often out of joint with the created order of goods. Saints succumb to temptation, sinners harden in perversity, friends falter and betray friendship, neighbors boast of folly and reject the truth. In situations such as these, calling for grief and its related affections, affection must be proportioned to its object and brought under the rule of virtue. Otherwise it partakes of the world's vanity. We could say about grief, the one cardinal affection totally alien to the Stoic sage,

---

[30] Colish, *The Stoic Tradition*, 223–24. She makes her case specifically in reference to Augustine's exegesis of the Gospel of John. The passion of Christ served for Augustine as a very powerful inducement to reject Stoic *apatheia* as the model for Christian sanctity.

[31] *De civ. Dei* 14.7 (CCSL 48, 423, 60–62): "ideo malui tristitiam dicere, quia aegritudo uel dolor usitatius in corporibus dicitur."

that it finds its kindred virtue in fortitude. Fortitude carries with it the conviction that grief is based not on the ultimate condition of things, but on their penultimate condition. Christian wisdom proportions grief to the hope of redemption beyond time, and fortitude prevents the affection from modulating into despair.[32]

The Stoics meet with stern censure in book XIX of *De civitate Dei* for their stiff-necked fortitude. Augustine ridicules them for wanting so much to preserve the blessedness of wisdom without grief that they are driven to assert that a sage who is afflicted with every kind of physical torment and illness is nevertheless happy, even unto suicide.[33] That Stoics could under any circumstances commend the suicide of their sages is for Augustine powerful testimony against their vain efforts to concoct a fully realizable ideal of beatitude in the *saeculum*. His own verdict on their efforts takes the form of a sardonic epigram: "There is great power in those evils that make a murderer of fortitude."[34]

In varying degrees of complicity, all of the schools known to Augustine have participated in the corruption of fortitude. The Stoics are the worst, for they have followed the maxim of Terence with relentless insistence, refusing to admit that the designs of the wise could ever meet with frustration in the world.[35] This strategy leaves fortitude with nothing to do except wait for the moment when the illusion of invulnerability collapses and then play the part of executioner. But even members of less austere schools, such as the syncretists of the Old Academy, attempt to incorporate beatitude into virtue, come what may. Augustine observes that Varro, a student of the Old Academy, believes that suicide in the face of evils is sometimes

---

[32] See *De Trin.* 13.7.10.

[33] *De civ. Dei* 19.4 (CCSL 48, 666, 116–17): "O uitam beatam, quae ut finiatur mortis quaerit auxilium!" ("What a blessed life it is that seeks for its end the aid of death!")

[34] *De civ. Dei* 19.4 (CCSL 48, 668, 161–62): "Magna uis est in eis malis, quae fortitudinem faciunt homicidam."

[35] *De Trin.* 13.7.10 puts forth a critique of Stoicism comparable to that of *De civ. Dei* 19.4. In *De Trinitate*, Augustine cites Terence's maxim as the epitome of pagan wisdom: "Since what you want cannot be done, want what you can do." He then disparages this wisdom as pathetic "counsel given to the wretched, lest the wretched be more wretched" ("consilium est datum misero ne esset miserior," CCSL 50, 396, 60–61). Recall that in *De beata vita*, an early work, Augustine is disposed to accept Terence's advice.

appropriate for the virtuous and, *ex hypothesi*, blessed person.[36] Either this belief involves a massive equivocation on the meaning of beatitude, or it is a betrayal of the virtue of fortitude. In either case, Augustine associates the spirit of the pagan schools of philosophy with the sin of Stoicism – its attempt to found a delusive view of beatitude upon a fraudulent view of virtue: "And these philosophers, since they will not believe in the beatitude they do not see, contrive to make for themselves in its place an utterly false beatitude, based on virtue as mendacious as it is arrogant."[37]

Because throughout much of book xix[38] Augustine seems at least rhetorically fixated on the ills of mortal life, it is tempting to read his farewell to pagan philosophy as an exercise in pessimism and cynicism. Philosophy seeks to admit a judicious measure of material well-being into the definition of beatitude, and Augustine responds by dwelling on all the occasions when we would need to rely on fortitude to ward off despair. The moral seems to be that there is no counting on even a modicum of material well-being in this life of sorrow. Philosophy seeks to found beatitude on the achievements of virtue, and Augustine responds by depicting the life of virtue as a continual and often ineffectual struggle against temptation and vice. Here the moral seems to be that the very need for virtue bears witness to the misery of the human condition. When Augustine weds pessimism about material well-being to cynicism about the satisfactions of virtue, he appears to discount possibilities for beatitude in the *saeculum* in order to introduce the need for an otherworldly alternative to philosophy's broken promises. If this were all there were to his dissatisfaction with pagan philosophy, he could offer his educated pagan readers no more than the suggestion that their philosophical wisdom will fail to protect them from misery. His appeal to otherworldly beatitude is idle. It merely restates his verdict against philosophy.

One good reason for rejecting this reading of Augustine's

---

[36] *De civ. Dei* 19.4.

[37] *Ibid.*, 19.4 (CCSL 48, 669, 200–202): "Quam beatitudinem isti philosophi, quoniam non uidentes nolunt credere, hic sibi conantur falsissimam fabricare, quanto superbiore, tanto mendaciore uirtute."

[38] See, for instance, *De civ. Dei* 19.4–10.

critique of philosophy is that it gives him no credit for understanding his opponents. Certainly pagan philosophers would not be surprised to hear that the virtuous person must cope with external difficulties, often of a sort markedly disadvantageous to beatitude. It is due to the very unreliability of material good fortune that virtue and the wisdom it represents must hold the center of the good life. Augustine will convince no one of the poverty of philosophy merely by insisting that its wisdom falls short of happiness. But despite his rhetoric of pessimism, Augustine has in mind the reformulation of virtue and wisdom for life in this world, not the otherworldly transplantation of pagan wisdom to more favorable material conditions. Taken out of context, his devaluation of worldly fortune obscures the nature of his critique against pagan wisdom and makes him seem unfairly dismissive of philosophy's claim to have brought beatitude under the care of virtue.

A rather different view of Augustine's critique emerges once we set it in the context of the moral psychology he has developed in opposition to the schools. We may pass quickly over his critique of beatitude based on material well-being. Augustine was not under the mistaken impression that philosophers equate beatitude with uninterrupted enjoyment of material goods, such as bodily integrity and health. Most philosophers would admit, however, that the loss or lack of material good fortune can diminish the quality of human beatitude. Even the Stoics, who claim that goods of fortune have no beatific value, experience involuntary passions of anxiety and fear when their material well-being comes under threat. In emphasizing the vulnerability of human life to material loss and pain, Augustine underscores the vulnerability of philosophical beatitude to the disorder of passion, the sort of passion that binds reason involuntarily to the perishable world. Pagan philosophy's best and only answer to passion's intrusion upon the peace of reason is, as far as Augustine is concerned, mitigated Stoicism, or faith in reason's sovereignty over disordered (unreasoned) affection.

Virtue expresses the sovereignty of reason over passion, of order over disorder, and the force of Augustine's critique of pagan wisdom centers on whether pagan virtue can lay claim to this power of sovereignty. His contention that it cannot, that it will instead fail miserably, has everything to do with his own understanding of the nature of passion. It is on the basis of his moral psychology, which he expounds mainly in books IX and XIV, that he dismisses pagan virtue as fraudulent in book XIX. The involvement of his earlier analysis of the nature of passion is evident, for instance, in his critique of the pagan virtue of temperance. Augustine describes virtue in general as the summit of human goods ("bonorum culmen humanorum"), a status virtue enjoys because of its regulation of the use and enjoyment of material goods. Challenges to virtue's regulatory function come from vices (*uitia*). The virtue of *temperantia*, Augustine's Latin rendering of the Greek virtue of *sóphrosyné*, bears witness to virtue's continual struggle against vice not as an external threat, but one internal to virtue – "vices not alien, but clearly ours, our very own."[39] Augustine's critique of pagan temperance comes precisely in his redescription of *sóphrosyné* as *temperantia*. He denies the philosophers the purity of their practical reason. Temperance delimits an internal struggle of desire against desire, and reason cannot disown the "irrational" desire as having its source of motivation external to reason. The desires motivating a vicious or disordered passion are our own, and since passion embodies judgment, as we learned in book IX, our reason is implicated in our vices. Once redescribed in terms of Augustine's moral psychology, pagan philosophy's attempt to preserve virtue's innocence from worldly compromise seems either fraudulent or self-deceived.

I do not think, however, that the bare invocation of an alternative psychology of the passions, in which reason mixes with affect, can save Augustine's critique of pagan philosophy from the charge of dogmatic otherworldliness. For if he locates the failure of pagan virtue in reason's passionate ties to temporal goods, he leaves to philosophy the impossible task of removing reason from all its attachments to temporal goods. But he could not possibly endorse this view of philosophy, since it would commit philosophy, whether pagan or Christian, to realizing the radical ideal of Stoicism, whose psychology promised falsely

---

[39] *De civ. Dei* 19.4 (CCSL 48, 665, 65–66): "uitiis...nec alienis, sed plane nostris et propriis."

to banish discordant affections from the experience of wisdom. In point of fact, Augustine does not need to endorse so radical an ambition, even as an ideal, for his goal in philosophy is not to eliminate disruptive affections but to rehabilitate them. We see him stuck in an impossible otherworldliness only because we have yet to offer the full context of his moral psychology to his critique of pagan virtue.

In book XIV, in his sharpest departure from Stoicism, Augustine admits grief into the perspective of Christian wisdom. The Stoics deny that the sage, who through wisdom and virtue enjoys beatitude, can be affected by grief. Why does one sort of wisdom exclude grief and the other embrace it? A correct but misleading answer would be to say that Augustine has given up the possibility of perfect beatitude for this life, and so a grieving wisdom would not mar the perfection of Christian beatitude as it would Stoic beatitude. The answer misleads because it fails to address the source of wisdom's grief and so offers only a superficial understanding of Augustine's divergence from pagan philosophy. When the Christian saint grieves, it is not for the loss of material well-being, but for personal failures of vision and love, for having robbed creation of its creator, for having usurped God's dominion. In short, the Christian saint laments failures of virtue. For the Stoic sage, such grief would be misplaced. Once wisdom is attained, the imperfections of virtue belong solely to the past, and the sage enters the invulnerable present of perfected virtue. From the perspective of *apatheia*, the sage's past history of unmeasured passion and imperfect virtue may as well belong to someone else. The past exerts no limiting influence over the achievements of wisdom.

When Augustine insists that Christian saints retain grief within wisdom, he is not claiming that virtue is weaker than the Stoics supposed. He is pointing out that wisdom's immunity from grief rests on the illusion that knowledge can somehow remove the sage from time. To have a past is not only to admit grief into wisdom, it is to face the inevitability of involuntary sin. Pagan philosophers have given reason extraordinary powers over passion because they have failed to see how passion carries reason's past into its present, often in disruptive fashion. Involuntary sin emerges out of the conflict of reason against itself on the field of memory. Because our lives extend over time, our willing bears the impress of what we have been. Perceiving and willing are for Augustine both achievements of temporal synthesis, and just as we can fail in recollection to represent ourselves intelligibly, so we can fail in willing to integrate our desires. Lack of integration in willing gives the past the power to disrupt the present, as if over time we have become estranged from ourselves. Wisdom must sometimes mourn the triumph of time over knowledge, or in Peter Brown's memorable words, "Augustine has been forced to consider the mysterious manner in which he could create his own tomb in his memory."[40]

Set within the fuller context of his moral psychology, Augustine's critique of pagan virtue can be seen to have pagan otherworldliness as its target. On his reading of Stoic psychology, Stoics try to protect virtue and beatitude from temporal dissolution by seeming to situate subjects of virtue and beatitude out of time's influence. Other pagan philosophers, he observes, give a grudging admission to the persistence of passion, but they nevertheless express Stoicism's pious hope that wisdom will remove reason's vulnerability to misguided desire. Augustine's objection to pagan philosophical piety is not so much that it has the wrong view of wisdom but that it has an unrealistic way of understanding how wisdom is appropriated. Temporal beings do not exit from time when they have appropriated wisdom and gained in virtue. Pagan philosophy has based its hopes on a premature restoration of God's image in humans. Having come to see this hope as a fraud, Augustine redirects his attention to the intricacies of time-bound willing.

The sweeping scope of Augustine's criticism of philosophy is a measure of his own confidence in having found an alternative to its piety. If his critique of pagan philosophical aspirations to beatitude were merely destructive, he could hardly be said to have freed himself from the seductions of Stoic invulnerability. He will not, in other words, have developed a real alternative to pagan philosophy if his moral psychology leaves only a vacuum in the wake of pagan virtue. But he claims to be able to redeem

---

[40] Brown, *Augustine of Hippo*, 159. The image of the tomb comes from Augustine himself in *De sermone Domini* 1.12.35, where he likens the soul under the burden of habit to Lazarus in the grave. Brown illuminates the image by connecting habit to memory.

virtue (and by extension philosophy) if virtue is referred to God.[41] It is on the basis of this claim that Augustine frees himself from the need of a Stoic ethical paradigm and occasions a profound break with his own philosophical inheritance. The nature of his appeal to God and its significance to philosophy are large questions requiring extended consideration. They are the subject of my remaining two chapters.

[41] *De civ. Dei* 19.25.

CHAPTER 4

Grace and conversion

Augustine looked for wisdom beyond what he could find in the pagan philosophy of antiquity, whose principal luminaries have given philosophy its venerable, if remote, parentage. When seen through the prism of his theology of grace, this parentage is difficult for us to make out, for it has been transfigured by interests that seem alien to its origins. We are less sure of Augustine's midwifery in philosophy than we are of his paternity in theology. For the young man who read Cicero's *Hortensius* and burned with enthusiasm for philosophy defended, as an old bishop, a wisdom remarkably different from the one Cicero sought to impart to Latin culture.[1] Augustine's break with ancient philosophy earned him his undisputed place at the foundations of medieval theology and culture, but it also roused the suspicion that his rejection of classical learning in favor of the revealed order of Scripture indicated a break from philosophy itself.

There have been few willing to accept Augustine's development of his doctrine of sin and grace as commensurable with the philosophical investigations of the pagan schools of antiquity. The various schools that come under fire in *De civitate Dei* – the Platonists, Peripatetics, Stoics, and Skeptics (*novi Academici*) – all depend on reason for illumination. Augustine, for his part, darkens reason with sin and insists on tying the human quest for knowledge to the influence of divine power upon human willing. It would seem, then, that if grace and sin

[1] The standard account of Augustine's education in the classical arts of rhetoric and philosophy and his eventual transformation of them is Henri Irénée Marrou, *Saint Augustin et la fin de la culture antique* (Paris: E. De Boccard, 1938), which should be read in conjunction with his later *Retractatio* (1949).

are to be elements in a critique of pagan philosophy, they are so only as part of faith's internal purge of reason's pretensions. Once faith has secured its own authority, Augustine's theological disenfranchisement of pagan beatitude will then appear alien or hostile to philosophy, either as an exclusion of philosophy altogether or as an attempt to minimize its influence in matters of ultimate human import.

Interpretations of this sort appeal most to those who find a veritable chasm between faith and reason and who tend to view the history of philosophy between late antiquity and the Renaissance as a gloomy time. Although I do not happen to share this outlook, it does seem to me that the gravitation of beatitude, virtue, and freedom towards their common source in divine agency poses a difficult problem for those, like myself, who look for the threads of a common debate between Augustine's thought and philosophies without theistic assumptions. The issue here is only indirectly the question of influence. We might say, with some justice, that some amalgam of Stoic ethics and Platonic metaphysics continues to inform the expression of Augustine's theology of grace, even when that theology starts to draw its primary sustenance from the Pauline epistles. But if the terrain of Augustine's thought takes its ultimate shape from theistic assumptions, traces of some recognizably classical concerns and forms of expression in his more mature writings might not lead anywhere. In light of this possibility, the nature of Augustine's response to his philosophical inheritance becomes of paramount interest. Does he theologize philosophy only to abandon it, or can there be such a thing as a theological philosophy?

In the opinion of the great historian and student of the classical world, Charles Norris Cochrane, the theological transformation of philosophy under Christianity's influence saved philosophical investigation from shipwreck upon a series of untenable oppositions pitting humanity against nature, virtue against fortune, freedom against necessity, science against self-knowledge. These oppositions were symptomatic of classical philosophy's desperate attempt to define the power of human self-determination in opposition to the power of nature, a strategy destined to leave "mankind a stranger in his own household."[2]

Augustine enters Cochrane's magisterial narrative, *Christianity and Classical Culture*, as the principal architect of the doctrine of sin and grace. This doctrine, Cochrane contends, "marks, in its most acute form, the breach between Classicism and Christianity."[3] On one side of the breach, we have classical philosophy, with its naive faith in reason's ability either to design or discipline desire in light of beatific knowledge, and on the other, we have Augustine, who both accuses and redeems philosophy on the basis of another kind of faith:

> To Augustine...there was no such folly among the many follies of philosophy as to suppose that mankind, by reason of any capacity inherent in himself, possessed the ability to discover a good independent of that which was intrinsic to him as a created being, much less to generate within himself the impulse needed for its realization. Thus, for him, the classical ideal of perfectibility through knowledge or enlightenment was wholly illusory; and, for the aberrations of humanity, he saw no remedy through education, whether conceived as intellectual discipline or moral habituation or both, *apart from* a recognition of the creative truth in the light of which alone these processes might properly be understood.[4]

Cochrane reads Augustine's doctrine of sin and grace as an essential corollary to his doctrine of creation. The created order offers human creatures access to the goods that will provide their activity with its proper orientation and end; grace and sin designate sufficient and deficient ways in which these goods can be recognized, pursued, and used. By restoring nature to creation, Augustine placed both humanity and the world under the embrace of God's providential order.

Cochrane takes this restoration to be of enormous import for philosophy. He credits Augustine for having rescued philosophers from the fruitless labor of having to cull values from a play of blind forces. In themselves movements in nature mean nothing; only under the aspect of creation can they signify the good. Philosophy's quest for wisdom in an order bereft of God's presence invariably degenerates into Promethean self-assertion

[2] Charles Norris Cochrane, *Christianity and Classical Culture: A Study of Thought and Action from Augustus to Augustine*, rev. ed. (New York: Oxford University Press, 1944), 411.
[3] *Ibid.*, 451.   [4] *Ibid.*, 451–52. Italics in the original.

in the face of fate or fortune. But with the reintroduction of the divine hand, the quest for wisdom becomes intelligible in light of the wisdom animating all things. We can come to know and love the good because God has supplied us with both the source and impetus of the quest. Augustine does not abandon philosophy: he makes it possible.

So sweeping a dependence of philosophy upon theological assumptions is, I think, nearly impossible to sustain as a general thesis. Nor are Cochrane's historical speculations altogether plausible, since he tends to burden exceedingly broad categories, such as "Classicism" and "Christianity," with the communication of enormous complexity.[5] But there is something to be admired in his reading of Augustine, for he gets to the heart of Augustine's quarrel with the wisdom of the schools. Christian commitment does not induce Augustine to reject pagan ideals of virtue and beatitude. He rejects them because they are inadequate in themselves. They promise what they cannot deliver. That much Cochrane makes clear. The other side of the story – the alternative to these ideals – is more difficult to make out. Why should the fact that values have been divinely created have any bearing on the success or failure of philosophical investigation? Even were we to stipulate that Augustine's creator God has etched wisdom into the face of nature, we would still need to know how we manage as part of nature to recognize the wisdom we represent. Invoking providence does not help much here. The bare fact that those who have wisdom are the ones led by God to have it may be of great theological interest, but it seems adventitious to philosophy itself. We need an account of grace that is a real alternative to the classical pursuit of wisdom and not just the miraculous resuscitation of philosophy's corpse.

Cochrane's narrative, though wildly ambitious in its scope and claims, points the way here. Augustine's theology of grace should be understood as his answer to inadequacies in pagan prescriptions for wisdom and beatitude. In order to qualify as an answer, however, his theology must have been in some important way addressing the same question as the philosophies

[5] See Paul Oskar Kristeller's review of Cochrane in *Journal of Philosophy* 41 (1944), 576–81.

it purported to replace. If we formulate the question appropriately, we will have the thread of continuity between the virtues of pagan philosophy and Augustine's redescription of its virtues in relation to God.

First we need to consider Augustine's manner of address to philosophy. Book XIX of *De civitate Dei* is his most sustained explication and critique of his philosophical inheritance. Using Varro's book on philosophy as a guide, Augustine begins his own book with his attempt to disassemble the variety of Hellenistic schools (*sectae*) into their basic elements. Out of these elements he begins to piece together what he will offer as the most representative construct of pagan wisdom. His efforts to this end are guided by his conviction that the highest good (*summum bonum*) is the defining element of any philosophical school. It takes him all of three sections to come up with the composite of pagan wisdom. Beatitude follows upon the guidance of virtue, ill fortune notwithstanding, and may be augmented with the virtuous enjoyment of good fortune. This composite, which represented Varro's preference, mediated Stoic and Epicurean extremes on virtue's role in the good life. Virtue was to have pride of place in happiness, but without having exclusive rights to its content. Augustine notes near the end of section 19.3 that Cicero and Varro differed on whether such a doctrine could be ascribed to the Old Academy of Antiochus, but it is clear that his own interests are not in questions of history. If anything else is clear from this exercise in definition, it is that Augustine's access to the richness and complexity of classical thought was very limited. To read him as addressing the essence of ancient philosophy in his criticisms of the Hellenistic schools, we would have to believe, as Augustine seemed to, that the diversity of historical options in philosophy served to elaborate a few paradigms of the highest good, the best or most representative of which could identified by a process of abstraction.[6]

---

[6] In 19.1–2, Augustine describes Varro as having partitioned philosophical schools into three basic types. There were those which placed the highest good in the soul, those which placed it in the body, and those which acknowledged that both body and soul would have to play a role in its make-up. The Stoics comprised the first group, since they admitted only virtue into the content of happiness; the Epicureans

For Augustine, pagan philosophy in its representative form embodied the common hope of the schools, the hope that time would harbor the peace of eternity if the power of reason and virtue were set against the chaos of change. To entertain this kind of hope was to wage an infinite war with finite resources. Among individual schools, there might exist variations in exactly where the battle lines were drawn between happiness and fortune (i.e., the question of whether external goods could augment happiness), but the nature of the war was everywhere the same. The philosophers pitted human powers of self-determination against the powers driving the cosmos. Virtue gave them their only hope of controlling or disarming fortune, which conveyed the effects of whatever they experienced as an alien power. This abstract, highly simplified, and idealized portrait of the multiform schools of pagan philosophy in book XIX of *De civitate Dei* is not far from what Cochrane presents under the rubric of Classicism. In both cases there is reason to suspect that the interpreter has not allowed the historical schools a fair hearing.

In Cochrane's case, certainly, this is problematic, since he identifies himself as a student of history at the outset of his study.[7] Persuasive historiography requires careful attention to

represented the second, since they subordinated virtue to the cultivation of pleasure; and the Old Academy more or less fitted the last, since Varro understood Antiochus to allow some independent place for pleasure in happiness, provided that virtue suffered no compromise as a result of pleasure-seeking. These basic types admitted subdivisions in matters having nothing to do with the identification of the highest good, such as whether the doctrines of a particular school were held by its members as certain or merely probable. Varro multiplies the three basic positions on the highest good by the number of possible positions on ancillary matters, and he comes up with 288 schools, "not the ones which were then in existence, but the ones which could have existed" ("non quae iam essent, sed quae esse possent" [CCSL 48, 657, 30]). After having summarized Varro's tedious process of subdivision, Augustine joins with Varro in dismissing the subdivisions as irrelevant, seeing that philosophy's true concern is with the nature of the highest good. That leaves ancient ethics reduced to stock portraits of Stoicism, Epicureanism, and Old Academy syncretism.

[7] Cochrane's declaration of intent appears in his preface to *Christianity and Classical Culture*, vi: "It is none of my business as an historian to pronounce upon the ultimate validity of Christian claims as opposed to those of Classicism. My task is simply to record those claims as an essential part of the historical movement which I have attempted to describe. This I have done to the best of my ability by letting the protagonists on either side speak, so far as possible, for themselves." Kristeller (review, 580) doubts that Cochrane has abided by his own restrictions. Instead, "he

the complexity of motivation and aim in historical subjects, and it is very difficult to do that when so many characters are made to speak under one roof. But in Augustine's case, the simplifications of the historical record are less obviously lapses in historiography. One who in looking at the legacy of philosophical thought on the good life puts more weight on what the true view of the good life is ("de rebus ipsis") than on what the members and interpreters of the various schools actually thought or said ("de hominibus quid quisque senserit scire") is not likely to be writing history in any conventional sense of the discipline.[8] In fact, very little of *De civitate Dei* allows the pagan world to speak with its own voice and through its own purposes and intentions, since the "history" Augustine proposes to render of this world is of how its own self-understanding has been made to serve an alternative set of purposes, ones which it could have recognized only dimly by the light of Platonic philosophy. The distinctiveness of the human voices in his narrative of the earthly city (*civitas terrena*), to which the pagans have been consigned, is continually muffled by the superimposition of providential design. Augustine recounts pagan Roman history, as well as the history of ancient Israel, as part of the universal history of Christian redemption. Pagans enter this history ironically. Divine design rather than their own understanding of purpose frames the intelligibility of their contributions to philosophy and civilization. Pagan wisdom becomes an imperfectly understood or incomplete Christian wisdom. Just as such anachronism and apologetics make it difficult to call *De civitate Dei* a work of history, they make it hard for a modern interpreter to determine which representatives of ancient

has written a book on ancient history in which the present day contrast between Christianity and modern science, as he sees it, is read into the contrast between Christianity and ancient philosophy."

[8] Augustine displays remarkably little interest in the historical positions of the schools. He notes, for example, that Cicero and Varro differed in their assessments of what Antiochus and the Old Academy taught on the matter of the good life. Since these two interpreters supply him with his primary access to ancient ethical thought, we might suppose him to take more than a casual interest in the nature of their disagreement. His reaction is telling: "But what is that to us, we who should judge things as they are rather than account it of great import what anyone supposed to know concerning the opinions of men?" ("Sed quid ad nos, qui potius de rebus ipsis iudicare debemus, quam pro magno de hominibus quid quisque senserit scire?" De div. Dei 19.3 [CCSL 48, 663–64, 76–78]).

philosophy retain enough of their appearance in Augustine's composite portrait to stand in any meaningful way under his address.

In my own analysis of Augustine's rejection of pagan beatitude, I have reconstructed his target as the Stoic ideal of invulnerability in ethics, buttressed with the resources of Platonic metaphysics and epistemology. Stoicism insists on the sufficiency of virtue for happiness, and Platonism supplies virtue with the knowledge needed to complete the equation. A thumbnail sketch of the symbiosis of these two schools of thought would render Augustine's understanding of pagan philosophy in representative form. Stoic virtue defeats the powers of fortune by conforming action to the knowledge that Platonism supplies of an eternal order. This strategy works, however, only if we are able to identify wholeheartedly with the eternal content of our knowledge. Augustine's growing recognition of the time-bound nature of human willing led him to doubt the simple dominance of reason for defining virtue and happiness. In book xix of *De civitate Dei*, he concludes that the pagans have betrayed their own ideal by saddling it with a false understanding of the virtues. Pagan virtues are insufficient where sufficiency counts for all, and this makes them illusory. If this verdict is to carry against the pagan schools of philosophy, Augustine must at least be right to suppose that they share a common psychology. "There is little or no difference," he contends, "between what Stoics and other philosophers think regarding passions which disrupt our minds; for both sides exempt the mind and reason of the sage from being subject to them."[9]

But even if Augustine were right about the guiding assumption of pagan moral psychology, there would still be the matter of the use to which the psychology is put. Does the ideal of ethical invulnerability, appearing as a hybrid of Stoicism and Platonism, have any interesting connection to the historical positions of the schools? I believe that it does, which is why I

---

[9] *De civ. Dei* 9.4 (CCSL 47, 253, 72–75): "aut nihil aut paene nihil distat inter Stoicorum aliorumque philosophorum opinionem de passionibus et perturbationibus animorum; utrique enim mentem rationemque sapientis ab earum dominatione defendunt."

have bothered with labels like "Stoic" and "Platonic," but a certain futility will accompany too much interest in the question. The access that we have to Augustine's theology of grace, in so far as the theology represents something more than a blind appeal to God to supply what philosophy could not, depends on whether philosophy manages to survive its move from a pagan to a Christian regime. The lines of continuity will emerge, if they emerge at all, out of Augustine's attempt to unite the schools in a common enterprise. The minute we seek to replace that enterprise with the multiplicity of historical voices, we consign Augustine to do battle with ancient philosophy in limited engagements, where the stakes are too low to call for a theological revolution of perspective. Augustine understood his theology of grace to reformulate the very foundations of philosophy, even as it respected philosophy's most cherished aspirations. We must try as well to understand it that way, or risk failing to understand it at all.

If we accept Augustine's composite portrait of pagan wisdom, however, we must be more temperate than Cochrane was in our assessment of whether the portrait captures the essence of its subject. I do not suppose that we can seriously entertain the idea that Augustine manages to address the entire antique heritage of philosophy in its incarnation as the spirit of some Classicism. It is almost better to embrace the opposite extreme and accept Augustine's interpretation of the schools solely as a dialectical movement in the internal dialogue of his own thought. At least in that vein we would be encouraged to understand his doctrine of grace as part of the evolution of his own philosophical sensibilities.

My actual procedure over the past two chapters has been to use two of Augustine's early writings to formulate his Stoic ideal of invulnerability in ethics and then to select subsequent writings to suggest how the ideal begins to fall apart. Since the fate of this form of beatitude emerges within the confines of Augustine's own works, I have in practice treated Augustine as his own audience. I have made comparatively little effort to give independent confirmation in the sources that Augustine's early view of beatitude is, in point of fact, Stoic, or that his later rejection of the philosophical schools as a composite is a fair rejection of each individual school. This does not mean that I think Augustine is entirely original in his early work or entirely mistaken about antique philosophy in *De civitate Dei*. I am willing, nevertheless, to accept the implication that on the basis of my use of texts I cannot claim that Augustine's reconstruction of philosophy corresponds to *the* pagan ideal of beatitude, if such a beast really does inhabit the ancient traditions of ethical thought. That much I am happy to give up, since I am skeptical about whether Augustine's composite description of the schools can be counterpoised to a single, dominant way of thinking among the philosophers of antiquity.[10]

Some might argue that I am forced to give up much more in letting Augustine speak for philosophy. In particular, I seem to stifle the conversation between Augustine and pagan philosophers by depriving the latter of their own voice. For without having some independent access to the voices that Augustine describes in his narrative as opposed to his own, it would seem impossible to assess whether his departure from the schools retains some continuity with the philosophical investigations of antiquity. I admit that I run this risk in so far as Augustine could have been utterly misguided in his understanding of philosophical thought, for if he were, his own assessment of what should count as pagan beatitude would be without insight. But the risk is minimal. He gives every indication of being an astute interpreter of the philosophy that came his way, and although we may wish to question the scope or accuracy of particular interpretations, it is fair to assume that his enormous role in the transmission of pagan philosophy, especially Stoic and Platonic elements, rested at least in part on his ability to understand and appropriate philosophical ideas.[11] We may assume, in other

---

[10] The quest for invulnerability or freedom from fortune was, I think, a preoccupation of much of Hellenistic ethical reflection, but there were significant differences in how various schools carried out the quest.

[11] Note, for instance, Peter Brown's assessment in *Augustine of Hippo: A Biography* (Berkeley: University of California Press, 1967) of Augustine's facility with the Platonists, Porphyry, and Plotinus: "He evoked the dilemma of these men in so masterly a fashion, that modern interpretations of the enigmatic Porphyry still gravitate around the tenth book of the *City of God*.".

words, that although Augustine's composite of the schools does not garner the essence or universal form of antique ethical thought, it does take in important features of a cross-section of philosophical options as they were transmitted to him.

The real limitation of my method, as far as I am concerned, is that my perspective must follow Augustine's transformation of philosophy as an internal development of his theology. This puts me in the position of having to use his early works, *De beata vita* and *De libero arbitrio* I, as my source of his Stoic ideal of virtue's invulnerability, even though he has already begun in these works to modify his philosophical inheritance to reflect his own interests. Because an internal perspective can assess external influences only after they have been appropriated, it automatically loses some of the ways in which Augustine leaves his impress on what he inherits. But it would be a tall order for any perspective to supply the whole story.

I have focused thus far on Augustine's change of mind about virtue. The Stoic attempt to use virtue to set absolute limits to human vulnerability to external sources of corruption represents in broad adumbration the intersection of pagan ethical sensibilities and his early theology. Later in his career, when Augustine has become preoccupied with the involvement of grace in human self-determination, he will castigate as pagan or Pelagian (which, for Augustine, came to nearly the same denunciation) the desire to deploy the life of virtue as the reflection of human self-mastery. Virtue ceases to reflect autonomy once sin and grace have obscured the expression of free choice (*liberum arbitrium*) in the universal human quest for happiness. But if virtue's image of self-determination deceives, the older Augustine might well have rebuked his younger self for having been taken in. Both *De beata vita* and *De libero arbitrio* elaborate an ideal of beatitude which would inscribe happiness within virtue and thereby use self-determination to limit vulnerability to misery. For the older Augustine this strategy expressed perfectly the animus of pagan philosophy and Pelagian theology. Nevertheless, in his *retractatio* of *De libero arbitrio* he defends his earlier work from the suggestion coming from Pelagian quarters that his identification of sin as the expression of perverse self-determination implied a complementary identification of virtue as the expression of enlightened self-determination.[12]

Augustine tries to avoid the implication by accusing the Pelagians of reading him in bad faith. They fail to respect the motivation of *De libero arbitrio*, a work which took aim against the Manichaean reification of sin as the expression of evil nature. This motivation clarifies what is said there about sin and, supposedly, what is not said there about grace. Augustine insists that if he had been interested in developing the doctrine of grace in *De libero arbitrio*, he would certainly have done so without restricting the source of virtue to our free and informed choices. "For it is one thing," he notes, "to ask about the source of evil, and quite another to ask about the source of our return to original goodness, or how we become better."[13]

If we allow Augustine the prescience he claims for himself on the matter of grace, then we must grant that neither the pagan attempt to found happiness on virtue nor the Pelagian attempt to found virtue on freedom ever gained a foothold in his thought. Not only would this be a distortion of much of the argument in *De libero arbitrio*, especially in the first book, but it would encourage us to rewrite the history of grace in Augustine's thought as a story of small mistakes marked out along the route of a fundamental, though sometimes unspoken, truth – that our power of self-determination must have its source in God rather than in ourselves. Augustine's *retractatio* invites us to purge the demons from the inner evolution of his theology by recasting them as the enemies of grace, who have forever stood outside the precincts of truth. This is one invitation, I think, we would do well to decline.

The best hope we have for unraveling the intricacies of grace lies in our getting beyond Augustine's polemical relationship to philosophy, whether that relationship takes the form of denunciations of pagan virtue or derisions of Pelagian confidence in the integrity of human willing. One way to this end is to notice

---

[12] *Retrac.* 1.8.

[13] *Retrac.* 1.9.2 (CCSL 57, 24, 29–31): "Aliud est enim quaerere, unde sit malum, et aliud est quaerere, unde redeatur ad pristinum, uel ad maius perueniatur bonum."

that his portrait of pagan beatitude in book XIX of *De civitate Dei* bears a family resemblance to the vision of beatitude espoused in his early theological writings. If we force Augustine to face his own demons, the history of the doctrine of grace is less likely to exclude philosophical concerns, and we are more likely to view the final shape of the grace in terms more illuminating than faith's triumph over reason. Those, at least, were the hopes I harbored when I used Augustine's own writings to resurrect the ideal of invulnerability in ethics, knowing full well that the form of the ideal would then belong as much to Augustine's theology as it did to pagan philosophy. The justification of those hopes rests on whether our access to the doctrine of grace broadens by having placed philosophy on theology's inside track.

I believe, in any case, that we are presented with the right question in Augustine for moving from the regime of nature to the regime of grace in matters philosophical. In what way, that is, does the graced memory facilitate sin's transformation into virtue? This question emerges from the margins of Augustine's aborted attempt to satisfy the ideal of invulnerability in ethics without taking memory seriously into account, especially the way in which memory mixes with desire to form oppositional forces within us and of our own making. The Manichees misidentified these forces and so missed their import, and the pagan philosophers, as far as Augustine is concerned, tried to overlook them, much to their own folly. The followers of Pelagius, he will contend, fail to appreciate the depth of internal conflict, which makes Pelagians on the issue of redemption no better than pagans in Christian dress. Augustine himself, having first identified inner forces of opposition as *consuetudo* (meaning roughly "habit" or "custom"), spends the best part of his remaining career exploring their dissolution in the regenerative furnace of divine agency.

I am suggesting, then, that the ideal of invulnerability in ethics remains the lodestone of Augustine's philosophical interests. He never discards the idea that virtue expresses the *ideal* form of our self-defining activity in the world. What he comes to deny is that virtue reflects resources of power that we alone generate to maintain our integrity – our sense of self – in the world around us, where time and change seem to promise us only entropy and dissolution. That kind of self-generated power is illusory, since to postulate it would require us either to divest ourselves of all of our potentially discomforting desires, so that we would never want what we could not will, or to deny that we are ever motivated independently of the eternal deliverances of wisdom. The first strategy would have us conform wholly to the changing world outside of us, and the second would have us act as if we were not in the world, subject to time and change. Augustine's invocation of grace purports to dissolve the dilemma without eroding the essential connection between virtue and self-determination.

But how is the connection preserved? The short answer is that we appropriate grace in recollection, and through recollection we are able to effect the gradual convergence of virtue and self-determination. I think that commentators on Augustine have failed to entertain the short answer (much less the longer one) because of Augustine's insistence on the necessary involvement of divine agency in human feats of virtue. With God playing so intrusive a role in the life of virtue, it is hard to imagine how virtue can serve in any way as the measure of human autonomy. But in trying to imagine this, we tend to overlook the fact that our lives extend over time. As a result, we look only at discrete moments of divine and human interaction in the hope of determining some degree of compatibility between human freedom and divine grace. This sort of analysis has held center stage in much of the scholarship on Augustine's theology of grace, and it is ultimately a futile exercise.[14] Moments of interaction tell us less than we need to know about the constitution of human self-determination under divine auspices. The bounds or limits of this self-determination emerge clearly only over time.

When Augustine's break with the pagan philosophy of antiquity is interpreted as part of his continuing meditation on

---

[14] Generally interpreters will worry about whether grace is resistible at the moment of its offer. I discuss the scholarship surrounding the seductive but misleading worry about resistibility in the section "Irresistible grace" in chapter 5 (pp. 197–206 below).

virtue's vulnerability to time, his emphasis on grace should be seen not so much to obscure virtue's expression of human self-determination as to complicate the path of transmission in perceptive ways. Virtue cannot be a perfect mirror of autonomy, any more than memory can be a perfect mirror of time. But we can have aspirations to these effects provided that we do not suppose ourselves to be the root cause of our own power. Augustine's theological assumptions obviate the need to locate the origins of human self-determination in expressions of human power. If God's power always lies at the bottom of ours, then we must cease trying to mark self-determination at the point where unadulterated human power begins to assert itself. Instead, Augustine invites us to observe the way in which we can define ourselves without having to appeal to self-generated sources of power. The philosophical interest of grace emerges out of this process of self-definition.

TWO WILLS AT WAR

I want to begin looking at the work of grace at the scene of Augustine's conversion. The dramatic resolution of book VIII of the *Confessiones*, where Augustine finally accepts the full obligations of his Christian calling, follows upon his heightened frustration at not being able to act on his own best judgment. Augustine arrived at the scene of his conversion, the garden of his residence at Milan, already a convinced man. After having taken up the pursuit of wisdom nineteen years previously, spurred on by his reading of Cicero, he had made considerable progress towards his desired end. His Manichaean detour, with its confusing cosmology of warring substances, was over. The books of the Platonists had helped him to comprehend the nature of God's incorporeal and changeless reality.[15] In his subsequent and eager readings of Paul's epistles, he rediscovered what he took to be the essence of Platonic wisdom, though with the added insight that no lasting appropriation of eternal peace and truth could ever be had without first turning humbly to the incarnate God.[16] The way of eternity was open only to those

---

[15] *Conf.* 7.10.   [16] *Ibid.*, 7.21.

who knew how to seize upon the gift of God's spirit, the gift the crucified savior left behind to human seekers of wisdom. Augustine brought to the scene of his conversion a mind tutored in the wisdom of Paul, a heart weary of a life of worldly ambition and longing for Christian beatitude, and a will desirous of translating knowledge and desire into conviction and action. But this was not enough.

The preamble of book VIII consists of a series of conversion stories. They describe persons whose conversion to the Christian life was marked by an obvious renunciation of temporal beatitude. Victorinus, an enormously learned man, enjoyed a great reputation among pagans and Christians alike for his rhetorical skills and his knowledge of literature and philosophy. When he finally decides to make a public profession of his Christian faith, he risks his reputation among his cultured pagan friends, who are likely to ridicule his decision, and forfeits his position as a professor of rhetoric at Rome. Under the reign of Julian the Apostate, Victorinus would have been barred as a Christian from teaching rhetoric and the liberal arts.[17] His act of profession, then, was a clear preference for a new life over an old one. In another conversion story, two well-placed servants of the imperial court come across a book describing the life of Anthony, the father of Egyptian monasticism. One sees in the pages a call to a new life. He convinces his companion to become a friend of God (*amicus dei*) instead of a friend to the emperor. They both renounce their positions in the imperium and take a vow of chastity.[18] Later in book VIII, Augustine tells us that Anthony's life involved no less a radical turn to God. After hearing the words of Matthew 19:21, a call to discipleship and divestment of worldly goods, Anthony takes the Gospel reading as a personal address and decides on the spot to give up his wealth and seek God in the desert.[19]

These conversion stories within a conversion story heighten

---

[17] *Ibid.*, 8.5.10.

[18] *Ibid.*, 8.6.15. Augustine learned of the conversion of these two court officials from Ponticianus, a fellow African. Pierre Courcelle conjectures that Ponticianus was recounting to Augustine the conversion of St. Jerome and a friend. See Courcelle, *Recherches sur les Confessions de saint Augustin*, nouvelle édition augmentée et illustrée (Paris: E. De Boccard, 1968), 181–87.   [19] *Conf.* 8.12.29.

the drama of Augustine's predicament. He is a man who has run out of reasons not to convert to the Christian life, and he has compelling reasons to cross the narrow bridge of will that joins wanting to convert with converting. None the less, his compelling reasons do not compel after all, and his soul suffers the torment of the irony:

> And what reasons did I not use as lashes to scourge my soul, so that it might follow me as I was striving to follow you? But it withstood me, refused to follow, and gave no excuse for its refusal. All of its arguments had been consumed and destroyed – unspoken trepidation remained. For my soul did dread as death itself being held back from the flow of habit in which it languished towards death.[20]

Augustine knew what he should do to promote his own well-being, but his past practices of judgment and action, expressed in his present state of will as the legacy of habit, blocked him from acting on his knowledge. At the limits of persuasion and self-recrimination, his knowledge found a formidable opponent in habit, whose force derived from the volitional inertia of discredited knowledge, the lingering hold of all those reasons for acting once thought to be viable.

The Manichaean Augustine would have understood the opposition between knowing and willing to be a skirmish in the war of two opposing souls, only one of which could be identified with the person experiencing inner turmoil. Warfare imagery, which would have a good soul, full of light and knowledge, do battle against a dark and ignorant evil soul, comforts in so far as it suggests that our inability to act upon knowledge of the good has no bearing on the integrity of our willing. In cases where knowledge seems impotent, the Manichee would have to conclude that knowledge and its opposition cannot have their respective sources in the same soul. The good soul may be prevented from expressing its knowledge of the good as will, but it remains undivided in its approbation of the good. Its power to

---

[20] *Ibid.*, 8.7.18 (CCSL 27, 124–25, 37–42): "Quibus sententiarum uerberibus non flagellaui animam meam, ut sequeretur me conantem post te ire? Et renitebatur, recusabat et non se excusabat. Consumpta erant et conuicta argumenta omnia: remanserat muta trepidatio et quasi mortem reformidabat restringi a fluxu consuetudinis, quo tabescebat in mortem."

will the good has, however, been overwhelmed by an alien power. Once internal obstacles to willing have been rendered into external impediments, the soul has a metaphysical guarantee of integrity. The writer of the *Confessiones*, however, goes out of his way to castigate such metaphysical comfort.[21] Augustine notes that two natures – one good and one evil – hardly do justice to the complexity of internal conflict, "for if there are as many contrary natures as there are wills resisting one another, there will be not only two, but many, contrary natures."[22] As long as one object of desire can be perceived as attractive independently of another object of desire, there is no theoretical limit to the number of different objects that can simultaneously claim our attention. So when they infer the existence of different orders of reality from the experience of internal conflict, the Manichees compromise their own metaphysical dualism with an unwieldy proliferation of natures. There would have to be as many natures as there were conflicts between desires for different goods.

Augustine's case against the Manichees presupposes that perceived goods need not be real goods in order to motivate. Neither attending a Manichaean conventicle nor attending public theater is, for Augustine, a real good, since each inhibits the attendee's cultivation of wisdom. Nevertheless, that each may be perceived as good by the same deluded or perverse mind introduces the possibility that two evil objects of desire may come into conflict. Or, to cast the difficulty for the Manichees a little less tendentiously, Augustine suggests that we consider, from the Manichaean point of view, the choice between attending Catholic services and attending public theater. Since neither is to be considered an appropriate object of desire, the Manichee seems forced to conclude that any conflict between

---

[21] *Conf.* 8.10.22–24, This section interrupts the main interest of book VIII – Augustine's agonized description of his own conflicted will and its ultimate and dramatic resolution – in order to refute the Manichaean theory of two souls. Although the polemical intent of the section is oddly out of keeping with the introspective focus of the rest of book VIII, the placement of this critique does indicate how seductive Augustine must have found the Manichaean rendering of internal conflict.

[22] *Conf.* 8.10.23 (CCSL 27, 127, 21–22): "Nam si tot sunt contrariae naturae, quot uoluntates sibi resistunt, non iam duae, sed plures erunt."

them would have to have its source in two opposing evil natures, even though Manichaean doctrine stipulates that evil has an undivided nature.[23] The moral of this sort of example is that the momentous conflict between past perversity and present calling to renewal is no more amenable to Manichaean metaphysical comfort than less momentous conflicts, where the comfort seems obviously ridiculous. Augustine refuses the temptation to cast the inhibiting force of his past as somehow less a part of his identity than his desperate desire to overcome his past: "While I was deliberating whether to enter at that moment into the service of the Lord, my God, as I had long resolved to do, it was I who was willing and I who was unwilling; I was both willing and unwilling."[24]

Not all forms of internal conflict correspond to a choice between two polarized alternatives, one presumed to be good, the other evil. More generally we experience conflict whenever we are unable to order or exclude competing objects of desire, all of which must be perceived by us to be good in some respect; otherwise their conflict, as well as their status as desiderata, would be unaccountable. One object of desire may, of course, be judged evil relative to another, but we do not pursue what we judge to be good in no respect. The notion of the good that Augustine invokes in his critique of the Manichees keys the good to what human agents suppose it to be. When he moves to the particular case of his being torn between his delight in eternal truth and his habitual pleasures, we can still recognize in his torment the general form of internal conflict. It is the same soul (*eadem anima*), divided in its will, that stands torn between two objects of desire, two perceived goods.[25]

If Augustine is right to reject Manichaean analysis and attribute internal conflict to a conflict between goods rather than to some war between irreconcilable natures, it seems that he has gained insight into his own situation. He cannot avoid identifying himself at least partially with whatever binds him from within. This follows from his critique of the Manichees, but

---

[23] *Conf.* 8.10.23.
[24] *Ibid.*, 8.10.22 (CCSL 27, 127, 13–15): "Ego cum deliberabam, ut iam seruirem domino deo meo, sicut diu disposueram, ego eram, qui uolebam, ego, qui nolebam; ego eram." [25] *Conf.* 8.10.24.

it does not in fact do much to illuminate the nature of his internal turmoil. All we know so far is that he must be attracted to both contestants for his will, for otherwise it would be difficult (if not impossible) to account for how he could experience his conflict as internal rather than as the frustration of his will by external impediments. His conflict is very puzzling, however, once we take into account his judgment that one of the perceived goods unambiguously displaced its contender in value. Augustine relates the contradiction of his situation as follows:

I had thought that I was from day to day putting off the time when I would follow you alone and disdain worldly hope because there appeared to me no certainty upon which I might lay out my course. But the day had come for me to see myself exposed and for my conscience to inveigh against me: "Where is your tongue? Surely it was you who used to say that you were unwilling to cast off the weight of the world's vanity for the sake of an uncertain truth. Look now that the truth is certain and the weight still presses upon you..."[26]

The source of vanity's power over Augustine is obscure. If he *knew* that his Christian vocation was superior to whatever glory the world had to offer him, what continued to attract him to his hollow and discredited life of worldly ambition? The general form of the internal conflict seems not to apply here after all.

The principal shortcoming of Augustine's critique of the Manichaean analysis of internal conflict (or more accurately, the Manichaean deconstruction of internal conflict) is that he fails to distinguish cases of indecision from cases of weakness of will when he attempts to establish a *reductio ad absurdum* of Manichaean assumptions. Simple indecision can result when competing options offer undiscernibly different degrees of pleasure or when some crucial piece of information is lacking which would illuminate the selective value of one object of desire over another. Suppose that a lascivious person has on a particular day the unique opportunity to gratify his vice in conjunction with his neighbor's wife, but to do so he would have

---

[26] *Ibid.*, 8.7.18 (CCSL 27, 124, 27–32): "Et putaueram me propterea differre de die in diem contempta spe saeculi te solum sequi, quia non mihi apparebat certum aliquid, quo dirigerem cursum meum. Et uenerat dies, quo nudarer mihi et increparet in me conscientia mea: 'Vbi est lingua? Nempe tu dicebas propter incertum uerum nolle te abicere sarcinam uanitatis. Ecce iam certum est, et illa te adhuc premit...'"

to forgo the opportunity to rob his other neighbor's house.[27] If this person cannot decide between his lust and his greed because the gratification of each vice gives him equal pleasure, then he is likely to suffer indecision of the first sort. If, however, he finds lust more pleasurable in gratification than greed but is not sure that his neighbor's wife will accommodate him, he will likely suffer indecision of the second sort. Both kinds of indecision are alike, however, in that the person finds himself, given the circumstances, incapable of ranking the value of one object of desire relative to another. Since the perceived goods of the situation nevertheless retain their attractiveness independently of one another, the perceiver's failure to make a judgment of their relative worth results in internal conflict. Now if all internal conflict were of the character of indecision, the Manichaean move to alienate the problematic source of conflict, so that problematic desires were externalized and made alien to the person having them, would indeed seem absurd. Not only would that strategy fail to address multiple sources of conflict, but it would not even handle the simplest case of two competing objects of desire, since in cases of indecision it is the differentiation between external and internal desires that is precisely at issue. If, for instance, our vicious person knew which of his desires were his true desires (those "internal" to him), then he could hardly be said to suffer from indecisiveness. But cases of indecision, despite their ubiquity in human life, do not exhaust the category of internal conflict. Those suffering from weakness of will have the ability to rank competing objects of desire relative to one another. The characteristic incapacity of will associated with weakness is the inability to have one's judgment of the relative worth of the objects count in the determination of one's will. Phenomenologically indecision and weakness of will are quite distinct. We suffer indecision as the pull of (at least) two different sources of attraction, while we experience weakness of will as being held back from what really attracts us.[28]

---

[27] The example is drawn from the more elaborate competition of vices that Augustine describes in *Conf.* 8.10.24.

[28] I realize that the phenomenology advanced here is somewhat crude in that the competition between different sources of attraction, whether it is expressed as indecision or weakness of will, rests on a very loosely defined notion of attraction.

Without a clear distinction between these two types of internal conflict, we miss what makes Manichaean avoidance of internal conflict sometimes tempting. Augustine encourages us to overlook its appeal when he suggests that his counterexamples to Manichaean metaphysics (all cases of indecision) capture the same phenomenology of conflict that is involved in his struggle to overcome his addiction to temporal goods and seek the, satisfaction of eternity.[29] But consider some of the basic features of Augustine's divided will. The choice between temporal goods and eternity is not the sort of choice that translates into the simple selection of one object of desire over another. Eternity is not an object that a temporal chooser can select, as if the chooser had the option not to live in time. To the extent that there are two objects of desire at war over Augustine's will, they are two different paradigms of the good life. One paradigm is to enjoy temporal goods without recognizing or acknowledging their connection to God's creative activity; the other to embrace temporal goods under a comprehensive enjoyment of God. In wanting to opt for eternity, Augustine is committing himself to a profound reevaluation of how he has lived and how he will continue to live in time. We should expect, in light of the comprehensive scope of the choice he faces, that his resolution will involve a change in self-understanding as much as it does any particular course of action. But it would seem, on the other hand, that choosing is not a sufficient cause either for ushering in new self-understanding or for quickening the will. By the beginning of book VIII, Augustine has already ranked the wisdom of the world relative to the promise of eternal life. When measured in relation to eternal wisdom, the worldly strategy of confining the search for beatitude to temporal resources simply has no redeeming features. It is futile, self-destructive, and in its

---

Certainly we can be indecisive between two very unpleasant yet unavoidable options; nevertheless I would want to describe that as being pulled between two sources of attraction. For my immediate purposes, the basic contrast between indecision and weakness of will is more important than a precise characterization of the possible ways in which each might be experienced. It is clear from even my coarse distinction that Augustine's experience of internal division partakes of the phenomenology of weakness of will, not the phenomenology of indecision. See, for example, *Conf.* 8.5.10.   [29] *Conf.* 8.10.24.

contempt of God's dominion over time, sinful. Augustine's judgment favored his Christian vocation in the strongest possible terms.

Faced with this description of Augustine's situation, where neither his judgment, his reason, nor his desire seems to stand in the way of his vocation, it is not so easy to identify the source of his internal conflict. His choices have come down to two alternatives, one he knows to be good, the other evil. If he cannot put aside evil to pursue the good, evil would appear to constrain him, and we are returned to the Manichaean analysis he deplores. The Manichees would have him externalize the source of constraint, leaving him to struggle against power alien to his own. Although this kind of analysis falls flat when it is made to serve as a general description of internal conflict, it has a certain appeal in cases where internal impediments to willing have no apparent connection to what the agent would represent as good. In Augustine's experience of internal conflict, his knowledge and his desire have lined up against the pattern of his past life, which in light of his knowledge should have no further power to attract. Nevertheless, the past constrains. Where does the power to constrain come from? If we assume in the spirit of Manichaean analysis that any constraint upon us must originate from outside of us, internal conflict in the form of weakness of will is not really possible. We cannot will against ourselves. This deconstruction of internal conflict is plausible, I think, in so far as the phenomenology of volitional paralysis can be allowed to suggest the causal origin of the power obstructing willing. Our experience of being constrained (as opposed to the experience of being attracted) would always be taken to imply the presence of power alien to our own.

Augustine's alternative is at least partly to deny the obvious. It may seem obvious that in the extremity of volitional paralysis, we evaluate without effect only one course of action as worthy of pursuit. It may seem equally obvious that our affections rally around this same course of action equally without effect. It may seem to us as we undergo this experience that our insides are being held hostage by an alien force of occupation. All of these appearances, however, are from an Augustinian point of view profoundly misleading. In particular, our experience of being constrained from within masks the one condition necessary for the possibility of internal conflict of any sort – that two or more competing objects of desire contend for our attention. We are led to believe in taking the experience of constraint as a guide that the discredited way of life, the path we would like not to continue, holds no attraction for us by way of either judgment or desire. Well, it does not relative to our present judgments and desires, but it does relative to our past. Our present state of will, however, includes its past states in the form of habit, and therefore the discrepancy between our past practices of willing and our present willingness for change can be expressed as volitional paralysis, or our experience of being constrained from within. This experience of constraint reflects upon analysis two conflicting sources of attraction. The trick is to recognize that one source shows up only when we accord ourselves temporal extension.

Our banal concept of habit, with its connotations of gum chewing and cigarette smoking, fails to do justice to the soul-splitting torment that Augustine associates with *consuetudo*. Even so, "habit" is not a bad translation, since the difference between habit and *consuetudo* is more a matter of degree than of kind.[30] Both concepts invoke the peculiar way in which the judgments of the past can continue to vie with the judgments of the present long after those past judgments have been discredited by new knowledge and different interests. To appreciate the flavor of *consuetudo* under the designation of "habit," we need to bear in mind that even our modest concept of habit invites us to entertain the immodest suggestion that weakness of will results from the obstructive agency of a past self. Our state of will at critical junctures of decision presents itself either as a synthesis or as a discontinuity of the past and the present. Discontinuity emerges from the conflict between rationalized

---

[30] We need to be somewhat circumspect here. Habitual action is generally thought of as unreflective activity. *Consuetudo* can be unreflective, but in order to follow the way in which it might obstruct a change of heart, it is important to remember that *consuetudo* does not begin as mindless activity. It has its source in the coordination of judgment and desire that enables us to act intentionally. The same point could be made of habit, provided that habits were distinguished from simple tics of behavior.

desire of the past and rationalized desire of the present. We say that habit holds us. Synthesis represents whatever is involved in our ability to translate judgment and desire into self-knowledge and intentional action. Conversion is an example of synthesis, but as yet we have no account of conversion.

Augustine's appeal to *consuetudo* to explicate internal conflict raises too many puzzles of its own to have triumphed unambiguously over Manichaean sensibilities. Instead of rendering internal opposition as the encounter of two different natures and inheriting the problem of accounting for their interaction (the notorious difficulty of metaphysical dualism), Augustine renders the opposition as the encounter of two different wills (*duae uoluntates*) and creates a whole new problem of their interaction.[31] Pick your poison. Talk of two wills in the *Confessiones* must, of course, be taken as elliptical for the way in which we can, as temporal creatures, will against ourselves. Augustine is not introducing a new form of dualism. He never speaks of two wills in the same person as two wholly independent, complete items. One will, representing the person's immediately perceived interests, lacks integrity ("tota non est") because it has no command over its counterpart; the other will, representing the person's formerly perceived interests, lacks what its counterpart does have ("hoc adest alteri, quod deest alteri")[32] – a revised understanding of beatitude. The two wills fit together as one will, though the means of their reintegration calls for explanation.

It may be thought that the deeper puzzle of Augustine's position lies in his postulation of a divided will. Does it make sense to suggest that past constellations of judgment and desire could oppose coordination of judgment and desire in the present, as if there were two wills in competition? I frame the question with "judgment" on both sides of the opposition because the language of two wills, however elliptical in intent, suggests that something more is going on in internal conflict than the struggle between reason and desire. Opposed to one another are two distinct apprehensions of the good. One of these

[31] See, for instance, *Conf.* 8.9.21.   [32] *Conf.* 8.9.21.

happens not to find favor in the mind's eye in light of current knowledge, but in some way it continues to influence willing.

If this description strikes us as strange or even incoherent, it is probably because we tend not to give our apprehensions of the good much if any temporal extension. When one apprehension replaces another, we do not expect the superseded apprehension to continue to influence our ability to will. Apprehension aims at knowledge, and knowledge, unlike desire, has no past. We can apprehend the truth and arrive at knowledge at a given moment in time, and that moment can pass, but the knowledge itself is timeless. Only error has a history. Discredited apprehensions belong to the history of error, and since these apprehensions never were what they once seemed to be (i.e., perceptions of truth), we can be left with the impression that, as long as knowledge is apprehended, the errant judgments of the past have no power over the present. Desire, on the other hand, consorts with error as well as knowledge, and it extends into the past to produce the habits that occasionally contest rule by knowledge. The force of habit seems to spring from desire that has lost its *ratio*.

In order to understand how Augustine's portrayal of two opposing wills within a will differs from the more familiar portrayal of desire's assault upon reason, it is important to remember that apprehensions of the good are discredited in retrospect. That is, it is only from the perspective of newly acquired knowledge and greater certainty that judgments once thought to be viable enter into the past as mistakes. In characterizing the obstructive influence of past states of will upon the present, we must be careful not to overlook the role that judgment has had to play in constituting past states of will. Present states of will enter the past as syntheses of desire and judgment. Past states of will are remembered in the present in forms that must represent (if memory serves) both components of the synthesis. Retrospection enables judgments upon the judgments of the past, but it does not in discrediting past judgments set old desires free to disrupt the knowledge of the present. Desire disrupts knowledge not because desire motivates independently of reason (a crypto-Manichaean position), but because the temporal extension of our identities allows desire to follow the lead of discredited judgments.

The possibility of the divided will poses no problem of coherence if we can sometimes understand failures of volition as symptoms of temporal dislocation. Dislocation results from the lack of integration between past states of will and our current self-understanding and knowledge of the good. Ten years or so prior to writing the *Confessiones*, Augustine would have found the idea of temporal dislocation mystifying. In book I of *De libero arbitrio*, he had put to his friend and student Evodius the rhetorical question, "What is as accessible to willing as the will itself?"[33] No reply was solicited, since the question was intended merely to remind Evodius of the obvious fact that no external obstacles block us from ourselves. From that obvious fact, Augustine was to draw an enormous conclusion. Beatitude, which depended on the acquisition of a good will, must be immediately available to us. For unlike the external, corporeal goods (*corporis bona*) whose acquisition preoccupied the deluded, the good of wisdom required only that we take command of ourselves.[34] In book VIII of the *Confessiones*, Augustine finds himself making the uncomfortable observation that he had more control over his bodily movements than he had over his volition.[35] What wonder (*monstrum*) had invaded his interior to stand between him and his volition? There is no paradox here. Only time in the incarnation of habit (*consuetudo*).

FUGITIVE BEGINNINGS

Between *De libero arbitrio* and the *Confessiones*, Augustine had come to recognize that in addition to the way that space housed external impediments to willing, time opened up an interior space for internal obstacles. This recognition was gradual and complex, as I have tried to suggest in previous chapters, but once he had made the fundamental admission, Augustine did not puzzle long over the possibility of internal division. His extended meditation of book VIII of the *Confessiones* on his

---

[33] *De lib. arb.* 1.12.26 (CCSL 29, 228, 54–55): "Quid enim tam in uoluntate quam ipsa uoluntas sita est?"

[34] *De lib. arb.* 1.12.26.   [35] *Conf.* 8.8.20.

divided will is not supposed to leave us wondering over the spectacle of Augustine having to contend against himself. He raises the issue of its cause only to settle it quickly with an appeal to habit.[36] Discontinuity of will is manifest and intelligible to those who live in time. We have more to wonder about in the matter of reintegration. Once we become internally divided, we lose in division the power to reconstitute ourselves. Habit's hold over us will then have defined the internal limit of our self-determination and set the stage for divine entry.[37]

God presumably does intervene at some point in the dénouement of Augustine's extremity. But where exactly is hard to say. Augustine reports hearing the voice of a young boy or girl coming from the neighboring household. In a songful manner ("cum cantu") the voice repeatedly chants the command, "take up and read" ("tolle, lege"). After brief reflection on the possible origin of the words, Augustine decides that they must be interpreted as a divine command for him to open his book and read whatever verse his eyes should first happen to land upon. He recalls how Anthony had been converted after hearing by chance the words of Matthew 19:21 and taking them as a personal admonition to discard his possessions and follow God. With eagerness he returns to the place in the garden where he had departed from his waiting friend, Alypius. There he finds the book of Paul's letters ("codicem apostoli"), which he immediately snatches up and opens. He reads part of Romans 13:13–14, "not in revelry and drunkenness, not in chambering and debauchery, not in vain striving and jealousy, but put on the lord, Jesus Christ, and make no provision for the flesh in your desires." With that admonition taken in, all the shadows of his former irresolution were scattered ("omnes dubitationis tenebrae diffugerunt"). Augustine had traversed the divide of his will.[38]

Much has been made in the scholarship over the accuracy of the "tolle, lege" episode. Some suspect that Augustine has at

---

[36] *Ibid.*, 8.9.21.

[37] Cf. Brown, *Augustine of Hippo*, 175: "Augustine emphasized this experience of the force of habit because he now thought that such an experience proved conclusively that change could only happen through processes entirely outside his control."

[38] See *Conf.* 8.12.29 for his highly compressed description of his conversion.

this point in the *Confessiones* given us literary artifice rather than autobiography.[39] Perhaps he has embellished the plainer facts of his past for dramatic effect, or perhaps he has created a few facts out of whole cloth. But whether his details stand as artifice or reportage, they are situated to meet expectations he has been cultivating in his readers. The past that held him in sin is the same past that led him to the brink of conversion, and that past reaches back into the first seven books of the *Confessiones*. In book VIII, the sin-bound and the God-bound faces of the past meet in a contest of two wills. Knowing as we do that these two wills are aspects of a single life, we do not expect the outcome of their contest to be the simple elimination of one of the wills. Nor do we expect, after having been treated to Augustine's profound diagnosis of his internal division, that heroic effort might eventually tip the balance in favor of his reintegration. On the contrary, God must knit together what time and sin have rent asunder. In short, we expect more than a show of power from above or bravado from below. More than a *deus ex machina*. The divine hand in conversion ought to be light enough to render the sins of Augustine's past transparent to his knowledge under grace.

It is remarkable how thoroughly the "tolle, lege" episode defeats these expectations. The best candidate for the "moment" of conversion is when Augustine finds himself addressed in one of Paul's verses. He finds himself so addressed because he interprets himself as falling clearly under Paul's admonition and because he has encountered this admonition without having intended to do so. This sort of interpretive exercise comes in for censure earlier in the *Confessiones*, when Augustine is criticizing the practitioners of astrology. While he was a young man and still a Manichee, Augustine found the success of astrologers (*mathematici*) at prediction impressive enough to warrant serious attention. The proconsul of North Africa, whom Augustine encountered in Carthage, attempted to convince the young

---

[39] Courcelle's argument for literary artifice (*Recherches*, 188–202) remains at the heart of the debate. For a more recent contribution, including a sympathetic assessment of Courcelle's case, see Leo C. Ferrari, *The Conversions of Saint Augustine* (Villanova: Villanova University Press, 1984), 51–70. Neil Forsyth voices intelligent skepticism about the ultimate interest of the debate in his magnificent study, *The Old Enemy: Satan and the Combat Myth* (Princeton: Princeton University Press, 1987), 409–10.

Manichee that the predictive successes of divination could all be ascribed to chance. Although the argument failed to disabuse him of astrology at the time, Augustine looking back recounts it with approval:

If it should often happen that when someone turns randomly through the pages of a book of poetry, he comes across a verse marvelously in accord with his own interests, even though the poet may have intended to write of something else entirely, it should not then be surprising, he was saying, if out of a human soul, acting on some higher instigation but knowing nothing of what was happening inside itself, there should sound forth an utterance which by coincidence and not because of any practical knowledge fits the interests and doings of the inquirer.[40]

Nothing in this compact argument suggests that the person seeking some form of self-knowledge does not gain from the chance encounter with an appropriate verse or a perceptive voice. We could claim, noting the very forms of encounter involved in Augustine's conversion, that although neither the verse taken from Paul nor the voice heard from the adjoining household originated from minds who knew and intended to address the mind of Augustine, he nevertheless benefited from them no less than if they had come from minds well acquainted with his. But the point of the argument against divination is that we cannot attribute special prescience or knowledge about ourselves to someone else if we have no basis for the attribution other than the mere fact that we have benefited from what the person said or wrote. In the case of singling out a particular verse from a book by chance, it seems clear that if the verse results in self-knowledge for the seeker, it serves as the occasion rather than the source of the knowledge. The situation is exactly parallel in the case of listening to someone who has no particular knowledge of our person or situation. Whatever self-knowledge comes of that comes incidentally, not from the prescience of the speaker. Now return to the scene in the garden. Augustine overhears the voice chanting, "tolle, lege," which leads him to

---

[40] *Conf.* 4.3.5 (CCSL 27, 42, 39–44): "Si enim de paginis poetae cuiuspiam longe aliud canentis atque intendentis, cum forte quis consulit, mirabiliter consonus negotio saepe uersus exiret, mirandum non esse dicebat, si ex anima humana superiore aliquo instinctu nesciente, quid in se fieret, non arte, sed sorte sonaret aliquid, quod interrogantis rebus factisque concineret."

his unforeseen encounter with Romans 13:13–14. What prevents us from applying the argument against divination here?[41]

The uncertain status of the voice should at least make us hesitate. It is not the voice of God, though Augustine is tentative at best about what he will say about it. It sounded as if ("quasi") it belonged to a boy or girl, yet he pleads ignorance ("nescio") as to which it really was. He cannot recall whether he has ever heard the chant, "tolle, lege," in the context of some children's game ("in aliquo genere ludendi"). Nevertheless he decides that its import must be that of a divine injunction to cast his lot upon a randomly selected verse from the book of the apostle. If we are to assume that his interpretation of the chant as divinely inspired is beyond doubt, at least as far as the narrative is concerned, then the hesitations that hedge in the origins of the chant diminish in importance. Augustine may not know who owns the voice, but he does know that the owner expresses (probably unwittingly) the mind of God.

Vindicianus, the old proconsul, would have ventured that the soul of the voice acted on some higher instigation ("superiore aliquo instinctu"), unknown to itself, which coincided with the demands of Augustine's situation. Supposing that were true (and it seems plausible as an interpretation), the design behind the conversion would still not succumb to the argument against divination. Once the "higher instigation" of the voice receives the added specification of being from God, the voice becomes the vehicle for special prescience. God knows Augustine better than Augustine knows himself. If God has "borrowed" the voice to communicate to Augustine, then Augustine is listening to the person who knows him best of all. The point carries over to the reading of the verse. Paul may not have been speaking to Augustine, but God was speaking to Augustine through Paul. The apparent randomness of Augustine's selection of Romans 13:13–14 has the ironic effect of reinforcing the deliberate design of the outcome, only it is not Augustine's design. At the same time that chance seems to exclude his control over his situation, providence allows the book of the apostle to mediate God's response to him.

---

[41] Courcelle (*Recherches*, 200, n. 1) has noted the parallel between *Conf.* 4.3.5 and 8.12.29, but he gives no indication that it poses any special problems of interpretation.

It would hardly be just to accuse Augustine of using a *deus ex machina* to resolve the division of his will. In fact, God's entry into the scene of conversion is so subtly mediated that we tend to lose the thread of the divine presence unless we pay careful attention. The divine hand has a light touch. Still the question remains, Have we learned how Augustine's reintegration has come about? Surely his facts fail to satisfy here. The voice and the verse do not of themselves offer new light on the nature of his impasse. Though marks of God's providence, they reveal little that has not already been seen. We are given no reason to believe that Augustine has misdescribed his internal conflict, and his mediated encounters with the divine seem only to represent under the divine authority the very command that he was unable to give himself. We know very well why he has not been successful in his attempt to give himself the command to follow God. Most of book VIII offers an inside view of his divided will. When in the book's closing moments Augustine reads Paul and hears God reissue the command through Paul, he discovers (mysteriously) that he has already crossed over the divide of his will and no further resolution is necessary. The book closes without ever supplying us with an inside view of his will's synthesis, the expected complement to the view we had been afforded of his will's discontinuity. Augustine seems to have kept his gift of self-knowledge largely to himself. Are we faced here with a failure of his artistry?

The *Confessiones* is such a deliberately written work that it is hard to believe that Augustine's powers as an artist would have failed him by default at the crucial moment in the narrative of his conversion. He does not appear even to attempt to describe the quality of God's influence on his will's division in the "tolle, lege" episode. God merely says the word (through intermediaries), and the word is done. There is, of course, always the possibility that we have missed the import of the mediation. Perhaps the art of divine agency lies in the telling of the human drama. If so, it is not a possibility that is easily tested apart from some mirror for Augustine's conversion – one which would allow us to see his experience reflected in the categories of theology.

Augustine himself suggests Paul as his mirror. One of the key descriptions of the force of habit in book VIII comes laced with references to Romans 7, that chapter of Romans where Paul describes the contest between sin's hold on the flesh and the law's hold on the mind.[42] The contest results in the celebrated Pauline paradox of Romans 7:15, "I do not understand my own actions. For I do not do what I want, but I do the very thing I hate." Augustine evidently saw in his own experience of internal conflict an autobiographical gloss on the meaning of Paul's text.[43] He identified the violence perpetrated upon his will by habit (*uiolentia consuetudinis*) with Paul's forced captivity under the law of sin (*lex peccati*).[44] Paul's internal captivity became his, and his became Paul's. The convergence of their maladies suggests a convergence of cures. The resolution to their respective conflicts should be similarly graced.

Romans 7 shows up in some of Augustine's exegetical writings of the period from 394 to 396. From the time of his ordination to the priesthood in 391, he had engaged himself in an intensive study of Scripture in response to his new ecclesiastical responsibilities and his eventual ascendancy to the episcopate of Hippo Regius. Paul grabbed the center of his attention in the few years prior to the composition of the *Confessiones*. In two works focused on Romans – an informal exposition on selected propositions and a more sustained treatment of exegetical difficulties handled only briefly before – we witness a dramatic transformation in Augustine's understanding of the work of grace.[45] The trans-

---

[42] *Conf.* 8.5.10–12. Augustine either cites or alludes to Romans 7:14, 7:16–17, 7:22–23, and 7:24–25.

[43] Augustine's reading of Paul and his reading of his own conversion are mutually dependent in the *Confessiones*. I will suggest something of this interdependency in my analysis, but without indicating where Augustine's interests may have been distorting Paul's self-understanding. For the fuller story, see the rich study of Paula Fredriksen, "Paul and Augustine: Conversion Narratives, Orthodox Traditions, and the Retrospective Self," *Journal of Theological Studies* N.S. 37 (1986), 3–34.

[44] *Conf.* 8.5.12. Cf. Rom. 7:22–23.

[45] The two works I have in mind are *Expositio quarundam propositionum ex epistula ad Romanos* and *De diversis quaestionibus ad Simplicianum*. There were other exegetical works on Paul composed by Augustine in the mid 390s, but they are of less interest for explicating his description of his conversion. The scholarship on this critical period in the evolution of Augustine's theology is remarkably contained, though what exists is of high quality. I owe debts to Brown, *Augustine of Hippo*, 146–57, Eugene TeSelle, *Augustine the Theologian* (New York: Herder and Herder, 1970), 176–82, J. Patout Burns, *The Development of Augustine's Doctrine of Operative Grace* (Paris: Etudes augustiniennes, 1980), 30–49, Paula Fredriksen, "Augustine's Early Interpretation of Paul," Ph.D. dissertation, Princeton University (1979), and

formation is sufficiently profound to be spoken of as a conversion of perspective. Augustine gives to God a role that he had once reserved to the human agent, and nothing remains quite the same in his theology thereafter. The theological conversion sets the stage for the *Confessiones*, where Paul mediates a conversion of a different sort. The conversions mirror one another, perhaps imperfectly, but enough to encourage us to return to the scene of the garden with the Paul of Augustine's immediate past.[46]

In 394 Augustine arranged in manuscript form responses he had given in Carthage to fellow clergymen seeking to understand the intricacies of Paul's letter to the Romans. The resulting *Expositio* preserves the disjointed quality of an exchange with interlocutors. Augustine responds to each verse individually, presenting the verses more or less in their order in the epistle, and although he does not cover every verse (apparently he wasn't asked about every one), he pecks his way through all sixteen chapters. What unity there is to his presentation comes from a schema he sets out early in the *Expositio* for organizing Paul's expansive reflections on the functions of law and grace.[47] The schema can also be taken to represent a morphology of regeneration. Augustine appears to have been reading Romans through the lens of his conversion.

The morphology comprises four stages. Before we have acquired knowledge of what we ought to pursue and what we ought to avoid, we seek to gratify our desires in an indiscriminate manner. Augustine describes this condition as the stage prior to the law (*gradus ante legem*). In this primitive condition, we sin with abandon and approve of what we do: "Prior to the law,

---

William Babcock, "Augustine's Interpretation of Romans (A.D. 394–396)," *Augustinian Studies* 10 (1979), 55–74.

46 When I say "immediate past," I of course mean to imply a time frame relative to Augustine's retrospective description of his conversion, not relative to the supposed time of the conversion (386). I have no stake in the issue of whether the conversion of 386 is accurately described over ten years later in the *Confessiones*. Most formulations of the issue miss the necessarily anachronistic character of conversion and so pose the matter of accuracy in misleading terms. For the corrective, see the analysis in Fredriksen, "Paul and Augustine," 26–34.

47 *Propp.* 13–18. Although I will be citing from Divjak's Corpus Scriptorum edition, I will preserve the chapter divisions of Migne's *Patrologia Latina* in order to facilitate cross-referencing. For a text and translation of the *Expositio* in a convenient edition, see Paula Landes (née Fredriksen), *Augustine on Romans* (Chico: Scholars Press, 1982).

then, we do not fight ourselves, since not only do we covet and sin, but even look favorably upon our sins."[48] Nevertheless, we lack the knowledge of the law that reveals sin as sin. When that knowledge finally emerges, we move into the stage under the law (*gradus sub lege*). The hallmark of this stage is internal conflict: "Under the law we do battle but are vanquished. For we admit that the things we do are evil, and by admitting this we will not wish to do them at all, but since grace is not yet present, we are overcome."[49] New knowledge has enabled us to see our customary objects of desire in an unfavorable light, but old desires live on in habit, and our new will is too puny to wrest determination away from habit. Help comes when from the depths of our infirmity we appeal to the power of the liberator. The spirit of Christ intervenes in the stage under grace (*gradus sub gratia*). We then find ourselves enabled to will the good which we desire under the auspices of knowledge of the law. Habit does not simply disappear, but as long as we remain empowered by the spirit, the legacy of our perverse past expresses itself only as the annoying static of defeated desire: "Even if while we are in this life certain desires of the flesh contend against our spirit to lead it into sin, even so our spirit, because it is fixed upon grace and the love of God, refuses assent and forbears to sin."[50] In the consummation of regeneration, the stage of perfect peace (*gradus in pace*), perverse desire ceases to trouble us in any manner. Under grace we are enabled to withhold our consent to temptation and therefore avoid sin. In peace we have no temptation. Not merely sin but its possibility will have been eradicated. Augustine denies that an embodied soul ever reaches this final stage in this life. Habit is too closely

---

[48] *Propp.* 13–18 (CSEL 84, 7, 3–4): "Ante legem ergo non pugnamus, quia non solum concupiscimus et peccamus, sed etiam approbamus peccata." In order to remain consistent with the remainder of his schema, Augustine would have to modify this description of activity prior to the law. If we fail to have knowledge of sin, we cannot be said to look favorably upon sin *as* sin. What we approve of is the object of our desire, an imagined good that has yet to be recognized by us as sinful.

[49] *Propp.* 13–18 (CSEL 84, 7, 5–7): "Sub lege pugnamus, sed vincimur, fatemur enim mala esse, quae facimus, et fatendo mala esse utique nolumus facere, sed quia nondum est gratia, superamur."

[50] *Propp.* 13–18 (CSEL 84, 7–8, 23–25 and 1): "tametsi desideria quaedam carnis, dum in hac vita sumus, adversus spiritum nostrum pugnant, ut eum ducant in peccatum, non tamen his desideriis consentiens spiritus, quoniam est fixus in gratia et caritate dei, desinit peccare."

tied to mortality for its influence to recede entirely. Only at the resurrection of the body, when the flesh is transformed, will there be the possibility of a perfect peace between the spirit and the flesh. "The peace will be perfect," he notes, "because nothing will resist our not resisting God."[51]

The crucial transition in the morphology of regeneration comes between the stages under the law and under grace, when the spirit of Christ responds to the cry of those in anguish. Their willing acceptance of the spirit marks the moment of their conversion. Yet the nature of conversion remains mysterious until we recognize that Augustine has taken Paul's categories of law and flesh and transformed them into categories of virtue and time. The condition under the law corresponds in Augustine's exegesis to Paul's avowals that he is carnal and sold under sin (7:14), that he does not do what he wants but instead does the very thing he hates (7:15), and that the law of sin, which dwells in his flesh, contends against the law of his mind (7:23).[52] In terms of Augustine's morphology, Paul cannot withhold his consent to the desires that prevent him from acting on his knowledge of the law. The category of law invoked here suggests that what Paul knows is a set of injunctions for behavior. Now he has come to this knowledge, his life is exposed as condemnable under divine judgment. For the law exposes sin as sin, and someone who knowingly sins puts himself under a death sentence. Thus does Paul lament, "For sin, having found opportunity in the commandment, deceived me and through it slew me" (7:11). Augustine attributes the damning knowledge of sin not so much to knowing the content of the law as to knowing that the law, such as it is, is just. "For each person acknowledges that he is dead when he is not able to fulfill that which he admits is justly demanded."[53] The recognition of the

---

[51] *Propp.* 13–18 (CSEL 84, 8, 12–13): "Ideo autem perfecta pax, quia nihil resistet non resistentibus deo."

[52] Although Paul speaks in the first person, Augustine does not in the *Expositio* understand him to be speaking autobiographically. Instead he reads Paul's avowals as an edifying device. Paul illustrates what it means to be under the law by adopting the persona of someone in this condition. The *Expositio*, however, by no means contains Augustine's final assessment of the status of Paul's avowals in Romans 7. See, for instance, *Retrac.* 1.22.1.

[53] *Propp.* 40 (CSEL 84, 18, 1–2): "Tunc enim se mortuum quisque cognoscit, cum illud, quod recte praeceptum esse confitetur, implere non potest."

law's justice already indicates rudiments of the virtue of justice. From there, Augustine moves deftly to insinuate the remainder of the virtues in conversion from death to life and flesh to spirit.

"We know that the law is spiritual" (7:14). What is it that makes us spiritual? Minimally, the status requires that the person can meet the demands of the law. "For each person made spiritual as the law is spiritual readily fulfills its demands and will not be under the law but with it."[54] But mere ability is insufficient, for it sometimes happens that circumstances make external conformity to the law's demands possible for a time. Carnally minded persons, for instance, find conformity to the law convenient when submission favors or at least does not threaten their enjoyment of temporal goods. Obedience under such circumstances fails to count, however, because the persons involved have misunderstood the beatitude that the law measures. They have staked their beatitude on the enjoyment of transient goods, while the law conforms conduct to the enjoyment of eternal goods. The occasional correspondence between the demands of the eternal law and the dictates of worldly wisdom is an accident of situation. Circumstances adverse to the enjoyment of temporal goods would quickly reveal where the heart of the carnal soul really resided.[55] Those brought under the spirit differ from their carnal counterparts in being disposed to follow the law under any circumstances. Augustine completes his basic identification of the *homo spiritualis* by supplying the requisite dispositions behind the ability to obey the law. The one made spiritual as the law is spiritual is also "the one who is not taken in by temporal goods or frightened by temporal evils."[56] In the framework of eternal beatitude, these two dispositions define the virtues of continence and fortitude.[57]

As the virtues work themselves into the morphology of regeneration, Augustine takes the occasion to rework the category of the flesh. His key move is to employ temporal goods (*bona temporalia*) and carnal goods (*bona carnalia*) as equivalent

---

[54] *Propp.* 41 (CSEL 84, 18, 11–12): "Similis enim quisque factus ipsi legi facile implet, quod praecipit, nec erit sub illa sed cum illa."   [55] *Propp.* 48.

[56] *Ibid.*, 41 (CSEL 84, 18, 12–14): "is est autem, qui iam non capitur temporalibus bonis nec terretur temporalibus malis."

[57] Cf. *De moribus ecclesiae* 1.15.25; *De civ. Dei* 19.4.

designations.[58] The assimilation moves flesh and law squarely under the rubric of beatitude and its attendant virtues. Goods are of the flesh not merely because they appeal to the desires of mortal flesh but because they are subject to the sort of change and diminution that mortal flesh is paradigmatically heir to. In relation to beatitude, it is clearly the mutability of the goods rather than the source of their appeal that makes them contemptible. Of themselves goods of the flesh are innocuous. Inordinate desire bears the guilt of their involvement in sin. All of these ideas come together nicely when Augustine explains what Paul means in Romans 8:7 by the "prudence of the flesh" (*prudentia carnis*).[59] Prudence is the virtue of practical reason, for through it we distinguish in individual cases between what should be sought and what should be avoided. If prudence is of the flesh, it means that the mind sorts out objects of desire without having a proper comprehension of the nature of beatitude. It does not mean that the flesh judges instead of the mind. Such a suggestion would come perilously close to the Manichaean dualism of souls. Augustine cautions readers of Paul not to conclude that "some nature, which God did not create, vents hostility against God."[60]

When the conflict between the false prudence of the flesh and the knowledgeable prudence of beatitude emerges in full relief, we will have reached the limit of the stage *sub lege*, where time makes its most dramatic purchase upon the flesh.[61] The purchase takes the form of carnal habit (*carnalis consuetudo*), whose power of constraint emerges out of the discontinuity between past and present practices of judgment. Because Augustine has reworked the law of the flesh as the problem of habit,[62] it is possible to see in the crisis of our condition under the

---

[58] See, for instance, *Propp.* 48, 52.   [59] *Ibid.*, 49.

[60] *Ibid.*, 49 (CSEL 84, 22, 20–21): "aliquam naturam, quam non condidit deus, inimicitias adversus deum exercere." Since God created the flesh, the flesh cannot be the source of evil in disobedience.

[61] We have returned to Augustine's exegesis of Paul's avowals in Romans 7. Note especially his gloss on 7:23 in *Propp.* 45–46, where he connects Paul's law of sin, the law dwelling in his flesh, with carnal habit.

[62] The force of Augustine's own genius is quite evident in the reworking, since Paul could scarcely have meant to characterize the struggle between flesh and spirit as the problem of conversion. Babcock ("Augustine's Interpretation," 60–61) identifies a critical point of incongruity with Paul when he observes that Augustine "drives a

law a failure of the virtues. The obvious candidate for the source of the failure is prudence, since prudence fails to overcome what went for prudence in the past, the wisdom of the flesh. Yet the very fact that the law of sin (*lex peccati*) contends as habit against the law of the mind (*lex mentis*) indicates that prudence has done its job. We have been made aware of what justice demands of our willing. If two wills continue to vie in us for authority to determine our action, the fault belongs to continence. This virtue is supposed to maintain our integrity against the onslaught of perverse desires, whose influence threatens to dismember the unity of action and knowledge of the good. When habit is able to transmit perverse desires across time, so that our past moves out of joint with our present, continence stands indicted. What is remarkable about this impasse in our pursuit of beatitude is not the acute failure of continence, but the relatively strong presence of justice and prudence.[63] These two virtues cannot be applied effectively without continence, but their involvement in precipitating a crisis of continence testifies to their active presence. Augustine has narrowed the gate for divine entry into the will to the single virtue of continence.[64]

If we take Paul from the *Expositio* directly to the scene of Augustine's conversion in the *Confessiones*, we will find that the immediate background to the "tolle, lege" episode describes the crisis of someone burdened under the law. The criteria of the crisis are met figuratively in the narrative. Just prior to his conversion, Augustine engages in bitter self-reproach for being

wedge" between 7:24–25a and 7:25b. The first belongs to the stage under the law, when habit reigns over the law of the mind, and the second belongs to the stage under grace, when the spirit of Christ enables the mind to withhold its consent to the law of sin. See *Propp.* 45–46. Fredriksen ("Paul and Augustine," 27–33) discusses the nature of Augustine's pervasive misreading of Romans 7.

[63] The fourth cardinal virtue, fortitude, is not at issue until after conversion, when temporal evils threaten to subvert the convert's prudent, just, and tempered commitment to the eternal measure of beatitude.

[64] Once the spirit has entered the divided will through the door of continence, it may extend its influence to the virtue of fortitude. In *Propp.* 60, Augustine suggests the extension when he defines the scope of free choice (*liberum arbitrium*) in regeneration. By free choice, the person under the law accepts the gift of the spirit, and no less by free choice he or she remains with the spirit ("in quo permanens, quod nihilominus est in libero arbitrio"). Over time and at our instigation, God's spirit adds fortitude to our continence.

seduced by the voices of his past. These voices he takes to represent vanities of vanities (*uanitates uanitatium*), those empty delights that were his former mistresses (*antiquae amicae*).[65] Though their voices have grown faint in his hearing, they have retained a formidable spokesman in habit. Augustine then envisions the chaste dignity of continence (*casta dignitas continentiae*), who in personified form counsels him to rely on God's strength rather than his own for the resolution of his internal division. He hesitates a moment, with the voices of the vanities still murmuring in his ears, and continence advises him further to grow deaf to the desires of his flesh, since the law of God speaks of different delights: "Block your ears against the unclean obscenities of your earthly members, so that they might be mortified. They tell you of delights, but not of the ones that the law of the lord, your God, tells you."[66] Thrown into a state of deep confusion and inner turmoil, Augustine retires to the shade of a fig tree and addresses his pleas for forgiveness and regeneration to God.[67] The "tolle, lege" episode follows, and he is converted.

Augustine's description of his crisis turns on the figure of continence. She is in personified form external to him, a fair indication that continence is not within him. He is addressed by the very virtue he lacks, and the form of the address emphasizes his own inability to fill the lack himself. Continence tells him, by speaking to him from the outside, that it cannot emerge as a virtue from his inner resources. He has reached an impasse. In the leaner language of the *Expositio*, Augustine has arrived at the limit of the stage under the law, and in order to move under grace, God must intervene to supply what he lacks for further progress in beatitude.

For stage-setting, the *Expositio* seems to work well. But what of the conversion itself? In the morphology of regeneration, the moment of conversion comes when we receive grace in response to our petition for the aid of the spirit. It is unclear from the *Expositio* whether the reception of grace necessarily involves our

---

[65] *Conf.* 8.11.26.
[66] *Ibid.*, 8.11.27 (CCSL 27, 130, 46–48): "Obsurdesce aduersus immunda illa membra tua super terram, ut mortificentur. Narrant tibi delectationes, sed non sicut lex domini dei tui."   [67] *Ibid.*, 8.12.28.

explicit consent to the spirit's influence. Petitioning for aid, a step which is clearly delineated under the law, is not the same activity as accepting aid. If receiving the spirit should be interpreted to require our consent, then from the human side of things two kinds of intentional activity usher in conversion. First there is the petition for divine aid, which marks the end of the stage under the law, and then there is the acceptance of divine aid, which marks the conversion itself, the transition between the stages under the law and under grace. The alternative view would be to cast the reception of grace in terms of divine initiative. The spirit works its influence upon us without waiting for our consent, and we "discover" our conversion in retrospect.

Augustine's remarks in the *Expositio* on election favor viewing the reception of grace as our acceptance of God's offer of renewal. In Romans 9:11–13, Paul brings up Jacob's election over Esau in order to dissociate the basis of election from the accomplishment of good works. Since the younger brother found favor in God's eyes before either brother was born, it cannot be the case that God calls his chosen on the basis of their good works. The chosen are elected because they are called in accordance with God's unmerited mercy. Augustine's interest in this argument of Romans lies in its implications for divine justice. In his exegesis, he agrees with Paul that good works do not precede God's calling. On the other hand, he is unhappy with the idea that election is purely arbitrary, for that would seem to exclude the interests of justice from the process of selection. Augustine arrives at a compromise position when he suggests that God foreknows which people will accept their calling to the life of faith, and so God chooses his elect on the basis of foreknowledge of faith:

If indeed election has no basis in merit, then there is no election. For all are equal prior to their merits, and selection among altogether equal things cannot be called election. Since the holy spirit is given only to believers, God certainly does not elect the works which he himself bestows when he gives the spirit to work good things through love, but nevertheless he does elect faith.[68]

[68] *Propp.* 60 (CSEL 84, 34, 16–21): "Si enim nullo merito non est electio, aequales enim omnes sunt ante meritum nec potest in rebus omnino aequalibus electio nominari.

Good works follow faith as gifts of the spirit. These are also foreknown, but not as conditions of election, since they are present only in someone already converted. In the absence of good works in those yet to be converted, the *ratio* of election requires that the reception of grace coincide with their acceptance of grace. This acceptance is the sort of faith that Augustine insists is a matter of free choice (*liberum arbitrium*).

Although his remarks on election do not establish a direct connection between election and conversion, it is tempting to read one in on the basis of his graded morphology of regeneration. If all souls begin in an unconverted state (i.e., *gradus ante legem*), the number of souls elected from eternity to salvation must correspond at the end of time to the total number of converted souls.[69] The question is then, Where does acceptance of a calling (a necessary condition of election) fit within the broader scheme of regeneration? It must be at the moment of conversion, when we move under grace and receive the spirit. In order for there to be compatibility between Augustine's exegeses of Romans 7 (the divided will) and Romans 9 (election), we have to supplement his account of conversion to reflect his understanding of a calling. Simply put, in anguish under the law we call upon God, God calls us to new life, and if we have been elected, we accept.

The fit between conversion is the *Confessiones* and calling in the *Expositio* is rather poor. If free choice of his calling were the hinge on which his conversion turned, we might have expected Augustine to dramatize the moment of choice. But as the "tolle, lege" episode stands, can we even tell when the moment occurs? It is hard enough deciding at what point an offer of the spirit has been tendered to Augustine. He seems to identify the voice as God's point of entry into the scene, but it is in reading the verse from Paul that his torment ends. He gives no indication, however, that he chose with deliberation to respond to either.

Sed quoniam spiritus sanctus non datur nisi credentibus, non quidem deus elegit opera, quae ipse largitur, cum dat spiritum sanctum, ut per caritatem bona operemur, sed tamen elegit fidem."

[69] The protasis of the conditional assumes that we exclude angels, the virgin Mary, Jesus Christ, and Adam and Eve as special cases. (None of these souls have suffered under the burden of original sin.)

His obedience to the command to take up and read follows as a matter of course from his interpretation of the voice as a personal address. It does not emerge as a discrete moment of decision. When he encounters the book of the apostle, he is all receptivity. He does not have to consent to the spirit's presence, because after he has read the verse, no shadow of hesitation or irresolution remains over his will. This moment of inner clarity and conversion is memorable precisely because it is the moment when Augustine no longer needs to choose.

Despite some promising stage-setting the theological categories of the *Expositio* do not distinguish moments of divine initiative from human response in conversion, and so they do not afford us our desired inside look at the reintegration of Augustine's will. The source of their failure lies in the *Expositio*'s description of a calling, which when woven into the morphology of regeneration encourages us to look to choice for our window on conversion. But choice is so inconspicuous in the episode of Augustine's conversion that we barely notice his responses to divine initiative as matters of will. What stand out instead are the vehicles of the calling, the voice and the verse, and even these hardly enter the scene like a cavalry charge. Discernment of the divine presence is a delicate art.

In between his informal exposition of Romans and the writings of the *Confessiones*, Augustine took the opportunity to extend his meditations on both the divided will and the nature of a calling in yet another work of exegesis on Paul. Simplician, the aged bishop of Milan and successor to Ambrose, had by letter invited Augustine to reflect on some difficult passages in Scripture, among them Romans 7:7–25 and 9:10–29. This was the same Simplician who had in the *Confessiones* commended Augustine to the wisdom of the Platonists and headed him towards his conversion with the story of the conversion of Victorinus, the rhetor.[70] When Augustine found the time to reply to his friend and mentor in late 396, he took up in one of two books familiar themes from Paul. What began as exegetical exercise for the newly installed bishop of Hippo ended in the quiet revolution of his theology. It is appropriate that Simpli-

[70] *Conf.* 8.2.3–5.

cian should have played a role in instigating the conversion of perspective that cast its most evocative reflection in the pages of the *Confessiones*.

The first question of the first book of *Ad Simplicianum* rehearses the *Expositio*'s reading of Romans 7 in greater detail. The essentials remain the same. Augustine still believes that when Paul speaks of his torment under the law of sin, a law set within his flesh, he represents himself as someone under the law of God and in need of grace.[71] Being *sub lege* continues to mean being under the dominion of carnal habit. Out of carnal habit emerges desire (*cupiditas*), whose influence on willing overrides our acknowledgment of the law's disapprobation of sin. The familiar impasse between our knowledge of the good and our disposition defines the boundary between law and grace. In order to cross over from law into grace, we must exercise free choice to invoke the aid of the liberator.[72] Augustine again admits grace into human willing through the gate of continence. The spirit fortifies us from within to resist desire (of the bad sort), and with desire repressed, the way opens for us to translate knowledge into deed: "Grace makes an end to yielding, and strengthens the human mind against desire."[73]

As before with the *Expositio*, Augustine's exegesis of Romans 7 puts us on the threshold of his conversion. If he follows the lead of the *Expositio* on the nature of a calling, we will go no farther than the threshold. In the second question of the first book, where his attention turns to Romans 9 and the basis of God's election, he does carry over from his earlier exegesis the suspicion that election cannot even be called "election" if nothing at all commends one candidate over another.[74] But Augustine's main concern in *Ad Simplicianum* is with Paul's message that "no one should take pride from meritorious works" ("ut de operum meritis nemo glorietur").[75] On this score, the *Expositio* falls short. It attempts to negotiate the narrow route between human pride and divine tyranny by cutting a fine distinction between

---

[71] *Ad Simpl.* 1.1.1. [72] *Ibid.*, 1.1.14.
[73] *Ibid.*, 1.1.9 (CCSL 44, 14–15, 166–68): "Vt autem non cedatur sitque mens hominis aduersus cupiditatem robustior, gratia facit." [74] *Ad Simpl.* 1.2.4.
[75] *Ibid.*, 1.2.2 (CCSL 44, 24, 13–14). Augustine understands that message to be the theme of Paul's entire letter to the Romans ("intentionem apostoli quae per totam epistulam uiget").

two kinds of intentional activity – what we do when we accept our calling and what God does for us afterwards. The first counts as a special use of free choice, when we act to promote our own good in advance of any divine prompting. Because some of us refuse our callings, the faith of those who do accept supplies some basis for their election. The second defines the class of good works, or works whose accomplishment presupposes that the spirit of God has worked through us to good effect. Certainly those under grace can themselves intend to do the good that they do, but divine power and intention always anticipate their own. In *Ad Simplicianum* Augustine refuses to entertain the distinction between faith and works any longer. "If God decides election through foreknowledge, and he foreknew Jacob's faith, how do you show," he asks, "that God still has not elected Jacob from works?"[76] The answer is that you can't. Not, at least, if you believe that the goodness of a work takes its measure from God.

Augustine does not rush to the conclusion that acceptance of a calling, or the act of faith, comes under the umbrella of what is given with the spirit. There are theological costs to this view, of which he is well aware. If, for instance, I have no opportunity to advance my own beatitude in even the most modest manner prior to the influence of grace, then God must elect me from the common mass of sinners (*massa peccati*). No distinctions of merit emerge out of this mass, for under the onus of original sin I am as worthy of damnation as anybody else.[77] There ends Augustine's quest for delicate distinctions that would allow God justly to elect some, reject others. The most he can do to salvage God's justice is to claim that those who are not elected are never passed over unjustly, though even that claim depends on the mystery of inherited guilt. If there is justice in God's mercy to an elect few, then it is justice sublimed in mystery, the operation of "some hidden equity, indiscernible by human measures" ("alicuius occultae atque ab humano modulo inuestigabilis aequitatis").[78]

Augustine's willingness in *Ad Simplicianum* to take a hard line

---

[76] *Ad Simpl.* 1.2.5 (CCSL 44, 29, 145–47): "Si igitur electio per praescientiam, praesciuit autem deus fidem Iacob, unde probas quia non etiam ex operibus elegit eum?"   [77] *Ad Simpl.* 1.2.16.

[78] *Ibid.*, 1.2.16. For more on the fate of God's justice in Augustine's early exegetical writings on Paul, see Babcock, "Augustine's Interpretation," 63–67.

on justice is partly a measure of his commitment to a doctrine of limited atonement. He assumes without question that salvation universally offered in Christ will fail to be universally accepted. Yet in terms of how Augustine comes to run the issue of divine justice into the ground, it is clear that his most jealously guarded commitment rests with restoring the work of redemption wholly to God's initiative. In his reconsideration of Romans 9, he begins to notice how the special status that the *Expositio* had given to our free acceptance of our calling robbed the divine will of some of its integrity. For if it really were within the power of Esau, the representative of the souls passed over, to reject his calling, then human perversity would establish itself as an absolute limit to God's redemptive power. Augustine would rather argue that not all callings are equal. Some aren't intended to be accepted.[79]

The collapse of one delicate distinction in election is going to require the creation of another. In particular, if Augustine wants to build human response to a calling into the divine initiative (thus making faith a gift of grace), he needs to distinguish two modes of calling. One mode fails to elicit faith because the recipient has not been elected. The other mode manages somehow to cause the consent of the recipient to the life of faith. Strictly speaking, the first mode is more a punishment than a calling. The second mode, though a calling in the truest sense, seems to involve a contradiction. Can consent be both voluntary and caused? For Augustine the conjunction must hold. If consent is not voluntary, it is not consent. If consent is not caused, God does not have control over the calling.

Augustine's solution is simple and brilliant. When God calls those who have been elected for redemption, he suits the calling to the needs of their situation. The inevitable result is that they follow: "For the elected are those who were called suitably, while those who neither suited nor obeyed their callings are not elected, since they have not followed when called."[80] In a

---

[79] *Ad Simpl.* 1.2.14.

[80] *Ibid.*, 1.2.13 (CCSL 44, 38, 369–71): "Illi enim electi qui congruenter uocati, illi autem qui non congruebant neque contemperabantur uocationi non electi, quia non secuti quamuis uocati." Burns, *The Development*, 37, describes Augustine's theory of

suitable calling (*vocatio congruens*) the recipient is not forced to consent (a contradiction in terms), but is drawn out in a divinely contrived environment of choice to assent to a new way of life. The efficacy of the suitable calling (its irresistibility) results from the providential coordination of willing with the availability of the right sources of delight. To account for how volition can be caused through such coordination, Augustine appeals to the logic of consent. We consent only to things which in some way attract us or appeal to our interests, and we call consent to an object of attraction voluntary even if we must admit that the nature of what attracts us as well as its availability is often beyond our control. God knows the innermost machinations of the human will and has control over the sources of its delight. He is therefore in a position to arrange for our voluntary consent.[81] The central difference between ordinary instances of consent and divinely inspired ones is that in the latter the fit between disposition and environment is so good that no margin remains for hesitation or irresolution. We do not need to make a choice. Our choice is, as it were, built into God's offer.

The features of the suitable calling are undoubtedly present in Augustine's description of his own conversion, as a number of scholars have noticed.[82] In the "tolle, lege" episode, the verse and the voice are carefully situated vehicles of divine instrumentality. They define in operation the divine initiative that is working to open the impasse in Augustine's will. When that happens, we are led to see not two discrete moments – an offer and a choice – but a single moment of illumination, wherein divine cause issues in human effect. It would seem that the conversion of the *Confessiones* reflects itself in Paul when

the suitable calling as "his first recognition of a divine working which achieves its purpose without independent human consent, a grace which causes a person's assent and cooperation, an operative grace."   [81] *Ad Simpl.* 1.2.21.

[82] Brown, *Augustine of Hippo*, 170: "Surprisingly enough...the austere answer to the *Second Problem* of the *Various Problems for Simplicianus* is the intellectual charter for the *Confessions*. For both books faced squarely the central problem of the nature of human motivation. In both books, the will is now seen as dependent on a capacity of 'delight,' and conscious actions as the result of a mysterious alliance of intellect and feeling: they are merely the final outgrowth of hidden processes, the processes by which the 'heart' is 'stirred,' is 'massaged and set' by the hand of God." See also Burns, *The Development*, 46–47, Fredriksen, "Paul and Augustine," 23, and TeSelle, *Augustine the Theologian*, 197.

Augustine's exegesis of Romans 7 in the *Expositio* is wed to his exegesis of Romans 9 in *Ad Simplicianum*. Paul's representation of crisis under the law picks up Augustine on the brink of his conversion. The crisis yields to conversion as he responds to the intricate promptings of God's suitable calling. Finding Augustine mirrored in Paul may not exactly give us our desired inside look at his will's reintegration, but the reflection does cast considerable light on the surface.

To leave it at that, however, is to miss the conversion of *Ad Simplicianum*. With the *Expositio* there is some doubt whether Augustine meant his explication of a calling in the context of Romans 9 to mesh with his diagnosis of Paul's professed condition in Romans 7. Nevertheless, mesh they did, nearly perfectly, since free acceptance of a calling supplied the fitting dénouement to crisis under the law. When Augustine redesigned the calling in the context of the second question of *Ad Simplicianum*, his subsumption of consent under grace ruined the harmony between Romans 9 and his exegesis of Romans 7, which he had carried over from the *Expositio*. If grace anticipates our consent to our calling, then our acceptance of the spirit in faith cannot serve as the transition between law and grace. Grace by anticipation is on the side of the law. In order to mesh Romans 7 and Romans 9 in the context of *Ad Simplicianum*, Paul has to convert. He begins in the condition under the law in the first question. In the wake of the suitable calling developed in the second question, he must move in retrospect under grace.[83]

Notice what happens when we take the converted Paul of Romans 7 to the scene of Augustine's conversion. Paul still reflects in his tormented state of mind the prelude to the "tolle, lege" episode. But if Augustine's condition of internal conflict is mirrored in Paul's, Augustine is under grace *before* the supposed moment of his conversion. In beginning to look with book VIII, we have arrived too late to observe the entry of grace into Augustine's divided will. This is a surprising implication, but

---

[83] Augustine missed the conversion while he was writing *Ad Simplicianum*, but he noticed it later on. See *Retrac.* 2.1.1 and cf. *Retrac.* 1.22.1. The association of Paul's avowals in Romans 7 with the condition of someone under grace was to become crucially important for Augustine's case against Pelagian theology. See, for instance, *C. duas ep. Pel.* 8.14, 10.22, *Contra Iulianum* 2.3.5, and *De praed. sanct.* 1.4.8.

one which I think is well taken. If I were to speculate about the silence in Augustine's moment of inner illumination, when he reads the verse and finds peace, I would say that it contained his recognition that the divine presence had been with him all along. It did not have to enter from outside to resolve his crisis from within.

If there is merit to my speculation, then we have in the pages of the *Confessiones* our desired complement to the inside view of the divided will. We did not notice it before because we were too busy scrutinizing a moment. The inside story of Augustine's reintegration is the story of his disintegration told in retrospect. Conversion marks the moment when he has regained sufficient self-possession to tell his story.

Having set out to explore the work of grace at the scene of Augustine's conversion, we are left finally with the question of the beginning. When does grace begin to influence the pathways of human agency? It is a question of paramount importance for understanding how theology begins to reshape philosophy to fit the pursuit of beatitude. We will discover none the less that beginnings are the most elusive moments in Augustine's theology of grace.

CHAPTER 5

Virtue in retrospect

Towards the end of his life, Augustine sent forth a pair of treatises on grace in response to the written appeals of two lay admirers of his theology, Prosper and Hilary.[1] These men had voiced their concern to him that groups of monks in southern Gaul, Marseilles in particular, were attempting to secure places for human initiative inside the formidable edifice of predestinarian theology. Without wishing to be grouped with the discredited Pelagians, the monks nevertheless hoped to find some alternative to what they understood to be Augustinian fatalism, or theology which seemed to deny human beings any say over whether they would join and persevere in the company of the saints. Augustine's response to these fifth-column Pelagians, who would come to be known (misleadingly) as semi-Pelagians, took the form of the two aforementioned treatises, *De praedestinatione sanctorum* and *De dono perseverantiae*, finished and delivered sometime near the end of 429. These works, though enshrined in Augustine's corpus of writings against Pelagians, have not been favored by contemporary admirers of his theology, who tend to see in them the rigidity and exasperation of an old man worn out by continual challenges to his most deeply held views. John Burnaby catches the mood of the scholarship when he states, perhaps harshly, that "nearly all that Augustine wrote after his seventieth year is the work of a man whose energy has burnt itself out, whose love has grown cold."[2]

---

[1] *Epistulae* 225, 226.
[2] John Burnaby, *Amor Dei: A Study of the Religion of St. Augustine* (London: Hodder & Stoughton, 1938), 231.

For my part, I confess that the tedium of these works strikes me more than their rigidity. Scholars differ over the significance of the encounter between Augustine and the theologies he associated with the mind of Pelagius. But the logic of Augustine's position, as it emerged in clear (but not necessarily rigid) definition over the course of the controversy, is hard to miss. Paul's rhetorical question to the church at Corinth, "What do you have that you have not received?,"[3] assumes for Augustine the role of a logical operator for delineating divine agency in the process of human redemption. Take any moment in graced life, even if it should occur before a discernible conversion. Does this moment reflect movement towards redemption, such as petitioning for divine aid or accepting the gift of faith? If so, then on the basis of the presumed answer to Paul's rhetorical question, we have received what we have found the strength to accomplish. The initiative for conversion and the impetus for its lasting effect must always be understood to have had their source in the divine will. Augustine's correction of the erring monks of Marseilles amounts to a thorough and somewhat belabored application of this theological principle. In *De praedestinatione sanctorum* he strives to ensure that the beginnings of faith are understood to have been received rather than offered up by the believer, and in case anyone were in doubt concerning the continued receipt of faith's benefits over the course of time, in *De dono perseverantiae* he draws the obvious conclusion for the completion of the saintly life. Perseverance is God's gift too.

Even Augustine's contemporary readers may be excused, I think, for finding his line of argument frustrating. He mostly confines his attention to vindicating in Scripture and tradition the principle of God's anticipation of the human will in every aspect of its redemption. Concerning the logic of the principle's application, Augustine remains content with deducing that the termini of faith, start and finish, belong under grace. It is implausible to suppose that so unelaborated a clarification of the scope of grace would have addressed the profounder worries of the monks. Prosper requested of Augustine that he not only

[3] I Cor. 4:7.

vindicate his view of predestination and grace as the one in keeping with the tradition, but that he go on to explain to his skeptics why grace did not by anticipating and working through the human will impede free choice.[4]

It was assumed by Prosper, and rightly, that theological interpretations of Scripture would have to respect some role for human free choice in divine and human interaction, for Scripture spoke often of human responsibility and merit. Augustine did not disagree. Yet from the perspective of the dissenting monks in and around Marseilles, the elderly bishop erred when he insisted that no human contribution to redemption could be characterized independently of God's influence on human willing. That seemed to them to preclude respect for human choice and responsibility in all but name only. Augustine in turn defied his opponents to find in Scripture or tradition authentic descriptions of saints who were or had been in some meritorious sense emancipated from God.[5] But what he did not do with any seriousness, at least not in these two treatises, was to explain why it would not serve the cause of *libertas* to look for moments when human wills could be discerned oriented to God in anticipation of divine assistance.

The monks had agreed with Augustine against the Pelagians that human willing was too crippled by sin to rise on its own strength to the demands of virtue.[6] Nevertheless, they sought to confine the extent of God's intrusion into human willing to the time between the beginning of faith, when we choose to enter into God's grace, and the possible end of faith, should we decide ever to abandon the company of the spirit. Human choice thereby bounds the exercise of divine agency. The ironic effect of this "semi-Pelagian" modification of Augustinian theology of grace is that the coincidence of human and divine will marks the period of our consent to servitude under God. Once the life of virtue has been set off by human anticipation of God's grace,

---

[4] *Epistula* 225.

[5] The term *emancipatus a deo*, used by Julian of Eclanum to describe human freedom from either grace or temptation (see *C. Iul. op. imp.* 1.78), connotes the Roman son who has been released from social and financial dependence on the will of his father. The connotations have their source in Roman law. See Peter Brown, *Augustine of Hippo: A Biography* (Berkeley: University of California Press, 1967), 352.

[6] *De praed. sanct.* 1.2.

virtue under grace no longer expresses human self-determination. Its expression has been left to the choice that stands outside the influence of grace. Virtue under grace can by comparison represent only the diminution (if not the outright effacement) of our autonomy.

The young Augustine had endorsed a remarkably similar picture of free choice in the first part of his first book of responses to Simplician. There he had declared that "in this mortal life this remains to free choice, not that a person could be just whenever he so willed, but that a person could turn himself in suppliant piety to the one whose gift would enable him to be just."[7] As to the second response, however, this free choice moved under grace, and Augustine never again indulged the temptation to define freedom apart from the grace. He could invoke God in the *Confessiones* as the virtue of his soul ("virtus animae meae") and mean by virtue the source of his self-determination.[8] By 429 Augustine was acutely aware of the seductive but profoundly misguided tendency of the faithful to define human freedom against divine grace. The lure of the beginning of faith (*initium fidei*) posed the most formidable temptation, since the foothold afforded there to independent and meritorious choice seemed a relatively innocuous concession to the powers of an otherwise disabled will.

It is not surprising that Augustine would have chosen in *De praedestinatione sanctorum* to inform the monks of his change of heart in his responses to Simplician, for he situates them at the place where he was in the period of his *Expositio* on Romans.[9] They sought as he did to commend the grace of God, but in clinging to control over the beginning of faith, they failed to heed the testimony of the apostle, "What do you have that you have not received?" By his own reckoning, Augustine heeded the testimony for the first time in his discussion of election in *Ad Simplicianum*, where he had concluded that no antecedent merits distinguished the elect from the mass of sinners.

---

[7] *Ad Simpl.* 1.1.14 (CCSL 44, 18, 247–50): "Hoc enim restat in ista mortali uita libero arbitrio, non ut impleat homo iustitiam cum uoluerit, sed ut se supplici pietate conuertat ad eum cuius dono eam possit implere."   [8] *Conf.* 10.1.1.
[9] *De praed. sanct.* 4.8.

In attempting to solve this question [of election], I labored on behalf of the free choice of the human will, but the grace of God triumphed; and not until this point was reached could I understand the apostle's clearest meaning when he said: "Who is it that sets you apart? For what do you have that you have not received? And if you have received it, why boast of it as if you had not?"[10]

If the monks could follow Augustine's decisive meditation on election and append to their reading his revision of the first response in *Ad Simplicianum*, which has Paul in Romans 7 stand under grace rather than under the law (i.e., Paul converts), they would begin to view the beginning of faith in an utterly different way. The moment of faith simply could not then be supposed to remain outside the sphere of divine influence – not if election is gratuitous and the will divided between spirit and flesh has already come under grace. The beginning of the process of renewal would inevitably slip back to anticipate human response to grace.

Augustine returns the monks to the cardinal principle of his mature theology, which is God's necessary anticipation of human willing in matters redemptive. The treatise ends, nevertheless, on a peculiar note. Augustine excuses his prolix exposition in *De praedestinatione sanctorum* on the grounds that he has been exploring a new question (*nova quaestio*). Readers of his earlier works on the nature of grace will be surprised to learn that the new question is whether the beginning of faith (*initium fidei*) counts as God's gift.[11] That it does may come as news to certain monks, but it could hardly have come as a revelation to Augustine. In his companion meditation on predestination, *De dono perseverantiae*, he reaffirms his usual conviction that it was in *Ad Simplicianum* that he first "recognized and stated that the beginning of faith is also God's gift."[12]

---

[10] *Retrac.* 2.1 (CCSL 57, 89–90, 20–25): "In cuius quaestionis solutione laboratum est quidem pro libero arbitrio uoluntatis humanae, sed uicit dei gratia; nec nisi ad illud potuit perueniri, ut liquidissima ueritate dixisse intellegatur apostolus: Quis enim te discernit? Quid autem habes quod non accepisti? Si autem accepisti, quid gloriaris quasi non acceperis?" [11] *De praed. sanct.* 21.43.

[12] *De dono persev.* 20.52 (OSA 24, 728f.): "Quod plenius sapere coepi in ea disputatione, quam scripsi ad beatae memoriae Simplicianum episcopum Mediolanensis Ecclesiae, in mei episcopatus exordio, quando et initium fidei donum Dei esse cognovi, et asserui."

It would probably do little harm to our understanding of Augustine's theology to allow him the luxury of an occasional inconsistency. In this case, however, I find it telling that so late in his career he would have supposed (even for a moment) that the beginning of faith continued to bear a question mark for him. It is equally telling that he would have overlooked his own second response to Simplician as the obvious precursor to the supposed new question dealt with in *De praedestinatione sanctorum*. There is a certain insight in inconsistency here. The suitable calling of *Ad Simplicianum* builds human consent to God's calling into the structure of the call. That, in one way, settles the issue of the beginning of faith. The elect consent to the influence of grace because God has willed them to do so. Consent is a gift. In another way, it is precisely this sort of divinely informed consent which places the question mark next to the beginning of faith. If consent to grace is a graced act, so to speak, our entry into grace would seem to anticipate our consent to God's call. When, then, does faith begin?

The fate of this question in Augustine's theology of grace remains tied to his willingness to take Paul in Romans 7 as the representative voice of conversion. This connection lends the question an urgency it would not otherwise have. The graced Paul who fails to reconcile his habits of the flesh with his own consent to the spirit not only emerges at the heart of Augustine's polemic against the Pelagians, but he also lurks, as I indicated in the last chapter, at the threshold of Augustine's conversion. This persona of Paul's, which was largely Augustine's own creation,[13] obscured the divide between a sinful past and a redeemed present by bringing division into the very heart of the converted life. For Pelagius, the consequences of assimilating this kind of Paul into the tradition were intolerable, for at the very least Paul's representation of inner conflict under grace (as opposed to under the law) undermined the perfectionist energies of the Christian community of virtue. Individual efforts at virtue

---

[13] Augustine's interpretation of Romans 7 departed from tradition when he began to deny that Paul described there someone under the law. See J. Patout Burns, "The Interpretation of Romans in the Pelagian Controversy," *Augustinian Studies* 10 (1979), 48. A. C. De Veer summarizes the internal evolution of Augustine's exegesis in "L'Exégèse de Rom. VII et ses variations," Note complémentaire 27 (OSA 23, 770–78).

would continually suffer contamination from a discredited, sinful past.[14] Regardless of his use of Paul *sub gratia* against the Pelagians, Augustine did not find the assimilation of this figure into his theology much easier than his opponents did, though he was, unlike them, committed to the attempt. The challenge of moving Paul under grace was the challenge of finding some way to comprehend conversion as including rather than discarding the past, as throwing light back into a time of spiritual darkness. To meet such a challenge, Augustine will find himself constantly rethinking beginnings. If he presents us near the end of his life with the beginning of faith as a new question, in part we are given an indication that his efforts of assimilation remained unfinished.

If Augustine thought he had settled once and for all the question of the *initium fidei* in his work on predestination, then the work disappoints. He establishes there only that he has grounds in apostolic testimony for believing that God never waits upon human willingness to be redeemed before working redemption. Faith itself is worked. But the implications of having to give up the beginning of faith as a human initiative are left largely to the reader to work out. Their omission from *De praedestinatione sanctorum* gives the work its air of rigidity for those who are convinced that the implications cannot be for good for human moral striving and its tedium for those who wish that Augustine had spent less time asserting his principles and more time developing them. The most charitable reading of the work, however, allows him the right to leave to his audience the task of thinking for themselves under the rules he has fixed for the theology of grace. The rules themselves, variations on the principle that God always anticipates us in the quest for

[14] In coming to view Augustine's differences with Pelagius as in essence their disagreement over the nature of conversion, I have been much influenced by Peter Brown's characterization of their disagreement in "Pelagius and his Supporters: Aims and Environment," *Journal of Theological Studies* N.S. 19 (1968), 93–114, see 107: "Augustine, in a scrupulous examination of his abiding weaknesses, in his evocation of the life-long convalescence of the converted Christian, had tacitly denied that it was ever possible for a man to slough off his past: neither baptism nor the experience of conversion could break the monotonous continuity of life that was 'one long temptation.' In so doing, Augustine had abandoned a great tradition of Western Christianity. It is Pelagius who had seized the logical conclusions of this tradition: he is the last, the most radical, and the most paradoxical exponent of the ancient Christianity – the Christianity of discontinuity."

beatitude, must of course be accepted before they can guide investigation. To this end Augustine appeals to authority, not to end inquiry but to afford it a fruitful place to begin. The most charitable reading is probably the right one.

In taking the charitable reading, we are not left without guidance from Augustine as to how an inquiry into grace might proceed. But in following him, we must not be misled into closing questions prematurely. He advises us to turn to his responses to Simplician for his understanding of faith and works. Are we to suppose that the perplexing nature of the beginning of faith will be revealed there? In his second response to Simplician, he speaks of faith as the moment when someone is moved to believe in God.[15] He goes on to say, however, that in its beginnings faith is incomplete, and until faith matures into virtue, the beginnings are not enough.[16] Revelation will require some exegesis.

For Augustine, beginnings of faith are elusive mainly because they are discovered in retrospect from the graced perspective of virtue. Connections between virtue, faith, and time, which tend to become obscured in his polemical writings on grace, gain clarity once we have united Paul at the threshold of Augustine's conversion with the Paul whom he marshals against the Pelagians. Situating Paul under grace at the center of Augustine's theological perspective affords us our best vantage, I think, on the redemptive use of memory. Only then will it be appropriate to ask whether Augustine's appeal to divine power has preserved human self-determination in some recognizable form.

---

[15] *Ad Simpl.* 1.2.2 (CCSL 44, 25, 27–29): "Incipit autem homo percipere gratiam, ex quo incipit deo credere uel interna uel externa admonitione motus ad fidem. ("A person begins to take possession of grace from when he or she begins to believe in God, having been moved to faith by an interior or exterior admonition.")

[16] *Ad Simpl.* 1.2.2 (CCSL 44, 25, 43–47): "Fiunt ergo inchoationes fidei quaedam conceptionibus similes. Non tamen solum concipi sed etiam nasci opus est, ut ad uitam perueniatur aeternam. Nihil tamen horum sine gratia misericordiae dei, quia et opera si qua sunt bona consequuntur, ut dictum est, illam gratiam non praecedunt." ("Some beginnings of faith are incomplete and so resemble conceptions. It is necessary, however, not only to be conceived but to be born as well, if one is to attain eternal life. None of these things are without the grace of God's mercy, because good works, if there are some, follow and do not go before that grace, as has been said.")

CONVERSION'S PERSONA

The more Augustine insisted on the stubborn presence of misbegotten desires in the converted will, the more he opened himself to the charge that he remained the captive of his Manichaean past. Julian of Eclanum, Augustine's most gifted theological opponent, never tired of making the accusation.[17] Julian had a certain genius for making it seem that no one could refuse Pelagius without embracing Mani. On at least one issue, that of the transmission of original sin, he did catch Augustine attempting to occupy nonexistent middle ground.[18] For when Augustine allowed the guilt of Adam's sin to proceed through the generations by way of Adam's seed, he seemed unavoidably to confuse categories of nature and will. The confusion, as the younger Augustine would have readily admitted, was endemic to Manichaean views of sin as substance. Julian would connect Augustine's apparent relapse into Manichaean heresy with his lack of respect for the integrity of free choice. Much to Augustine's annoyance, Pelagians tended to view his theological development as an unfortunate departure from Pelagianism.[19]

Aside from the case of sin's transmission, however, Augustine could not have been convicted of mixing Pelagian spirit with Manichaean flesh. He had decisively turned from Manichaean metaphysics of sin once he had associated involuntary sin with captivity to habit. He was then able to reclaim Paul from the Manichees, who saw in Paul's struggles with the flesh the conflict between two opposed and irreconcilable natures.[20] Augustine recast Paul initially as the soul struggling under the law, torn between the tug of its habitual loves (flesh) and the pull of its desire for renewal (spirit).[21] Pelagians recognized habit, and so they could live with this Paul, but they also placed confidence in the power of rightly informed choice to discard

---

[17] See, for example, Augustine's citation of Julian's argument against original sin in *De nuptiis et concupiscentia* 2.29.49.

[18] For an illuminating investigation of the Manichaean resonances in Augustine's rendition of the myth of original sin, see Elizabeth Clark, "Vitiated Seeds and Holy Vessels: Augustine's Manichaean Past," in her *Ascetic Piety and Women's Faith: Essays on Late Ancient Christianity* (New York and Toronto: Edwin Mellen Press, 1986), 291–349. [19] *Retrac.* 1.8. [20] *C. Fortunatum* 21–22.

[21] *Propp.* 44–46.

habit as if it were some threadbare outer garment.[22] Paul under grace would emerge a wholly changed man. Because Augustine came to see in the converted life a halting struggle against sin, he worked to reclaim Pauline spirit from the Pelagians, just as he had taken Pauline flesh from the Manichees.

Julian forced Augustine to face the most provocative implications of his allowing past perversities to intrude upon the will's renewal. In one of two letters received by Pope Boniface on behalf of Pelagius, he accused Augustine and his allies of, among other things, believing that "all the apostles, even Paul, were always polluted by unrestrained desire."[23] The accusation stung because it was too close to the truth. Augustine did believe that habits of the flesh exercised influence on willing permanently, and in the absence of some specification of the limit of that influence, a clever polemicist could put the converted Paul in very bad company. Julian exploited this vulnerability in Augustine's presentation of grace, and Augustine found himself in the delicate position of having to defend the efficacy of grace in the conduct of the saints. It was a Pelagian's game to praise grace by praising the virtue of the life it enabled.

Augustine tries to beat Julian at his own game. He would praise Paul, but not overly much. The contest over conversion moved to the field of Romans 7. Where once he had assumed that Paul's avowals there were out of character and representative of the internal conflict of someone not yet under grace, he now identifies this kind of reading as Pelagian. The refusal to take Paul at his word, he offers, is the source of Julian's

---

[22] Brown, "Pelagius," 104, notes the contrast with Augustine: "Pelagius was undoubtedly influenced by the early anti-Manichaean works of Augustine; like Augustine, he used the force of habit, a force, that is, created by previous acts of the free will, as a way of rejecting determinism while facing the observed fact that men do find it difficult to control their actions. But, with Augustine, this force of habit became increasingly internal, deeply insidious. It established itself permanently in profound, unconscious layers of the personality."

[23] Cited in *C. duas ep. Pel.* 1.8.13 (CSEL 60, 433, 3–4): "Apostolum etiam Paulum," inquit, "uel omnes apostolos dicunt semper immoderata libidine fuisse pollutos." Of the two letters received by Boniface, one Julian wrote himself and sent to Rome, and the other represented the consensus of eighteen Italian bishops who dissented from Zosimus' papal condemnation of Pelagius. That letter went first to Thessalonica. Boniface forwarded both letters to Augustine through Alypius in the winter of 419–20. Augustine responded in four books, the first of which was specifically directed at Julian.

calumnious misrepresentation of conversion.[24] For the first time in his reading of Romans 7, Augustine argues that Paul speaks from personal experience when he confesses that the law has led him to recognize misdirected desire (*concupiscentia*) in his own person.[25] The presence of such desire, contrary to Pelagian hopes, plagues even the convert. On his fundamental revision of Paul's persona, Augustine holds his ground. Paul remains, regardless of seemingly intractable inner torment, the spokesman for grace.

Having established this much, Augustine attempts to distinguish conversion and captivity under the law so that Julian's stigma of "unrestrained desire" is removed from Paul's converted character. The attempt involves him in some exegetical acrobatics. He keys his reading of the quality of Paul's internal division to Romans 7:18, where Paul laments that he cannot perform (*perficere*) the good that he is willing to do. There are numerous avowals in Romans 7 of Paul's inability to follow through on his desire to will the good, but Romans 7:18 is the only verse which contains an intensified form of an action verb, *perficere* instead of the more common *facere*. Since *perficere* has the added nuance of an acting that is not simply performed but performed in its highest degree, it can sometimes mean "perform" in the sense of "perfect." It would be appropriate to give *perficere* this sense only if the effect intended in performance admitted of an ideal and the context of the intending suggested that the ideal effect was at issue. Neither condition seems to hold in the case of Romans 7:18, but Augustine works here against the obvious. He suggests the ideal of performance when he defines an incomplete action as an action performed under the disconcerting (but not constraining) influence of desires opposed to the action, "for the good is performed imperfectly when one covets, even if consent to the evil of coveting is withheld."[26] Complete action is by contrast action uniformly supported by the agent's desires. If Paul intends to effect good

---

[24] *C. duas ep. Pel.* 1.8.13.   [25] Romans 7:7–8; *C. duas ep. Pel.* 1.8.14.

[26] *C. duas ep. Pel.* 1.10.19 (CSEL 60, 441, 2–4): "inperfectum est autem bonum, quando concupiscit, etiam si concupiscentiae non consentit ad malum." Augustine offers this observation as a gloss on part of Romans 7:18, "velle enim adiacet mihi, perficere autem bonum non."

action in its completeness but fails, then *perficere* must refer to perfecting an action. Not only does Augustine contend that this is the correct reading of the verse in which *perficere* appears, but he assumes that the other, unadorned ways of expressing acting, as with the verbs *facere*, *agere*, and *operari*, carry implicitly the extended sense of acting in conformity to an ideal. So, for example, when Paul seems to admit straightforwardly in Romans 7:15 that he performs ("facio") what he hates, Augustine takes him to mean that he performs what he approves of (i.e., what the law demands), but not without the presence of some lingering sinful desires.[27]

On the face of it, Augustine's circuitous exegesis of the life of the spirit opens up a divide between conversion and captivity under the law. Paul cannot be said to suffer under grace with unrestrained desire, since to a very large extent his desires are restrained. They do not interfere with his actions, but only with the purity of his intentions. The captivity that he and others suffer under grace leaves them free to consent to what is good. The burden of their captivity is simply the burden of always having to restrain wayward desires from gaining control over willing.[28] By implication, the captivity to sin for those not yet

[27] Augustine arrives at this remarkably contrived interpretation by reading the verse in conjunction with the subsequent verse and drawing the following moral, *C. duas ep. Pel.* 1.10.18 (CSEL 60, 440, 8–12): "sed considerandum est quod adiungit: 'si autem quod nolo hoc facio, consentio legi quoniam bona.' magis enim se dicit legi consentire quam carnis concupiscentiae – hanc enim peccati nomine appellat –; facere ergo se dixit et operari non affectu consentiendi et inplendi, sed ipso motu concupiscendi." ("We must consider what he adds: 'If indeed I perform what I do not want, I consent to the law as good.' For Paul says that he consents more to the law than to carnal desire, the latter going for him under the name of sin. He has said in effect that he has labored and acted not under a disposition to consent to and gratify untoward desire but under the bare impulse of desire.")

I am assuming that the difference between having desire and consenting to desire turns here on whether Paul actually has acted on the desire. When Augustine claims, then, that Paul withholds his consent to carnal desire, Paul should be understood to have refrained from gratifying the desire. For confirmation of Augustine's odd use of Romans 7:18 to define a way for Paul to do what he hates yet act on what he approves of, one may turn to a slightly earlier work written against Julian, *De nuptiis et concupiscentia*, where Augustine performs precisely the same exegetical acrobatics. Note especially 1.28.31–32.

[28] *C. duas ep. pel.* 1.11.24. Augustine remarks in this section that the apostles refrained from consenting to their depraved desires by restraining them with humility and piety. Nevertheless, he adds, the apostles would have preferred not to have had the desires at all. Preference for purity over mastery comes out in Augustine's definition

under grace runs deeper, so that consent to evil desires becomes unavoidable. Paul under the law would worry about acting contrary to what he knows to be good. Augustine reads this Paul out of Romans 7 by mitigating his captivity to sin and shifting the interest of grace from actions to motives.

The victory over Julian is hollow, however. If we compare Augustine's redescription of Paul with his early understanding of the condition *sub gratia*, we will discover that Paul's conversion from law to grace carries little of substantive import for the nature of grace. In his *Expositio* of 394, Augustine looks at Paul's struggles against the flesh, surmises that his inability to act on knowledge of the law has its source in carnal custom, and concludes that Paul must be describing the condition of someone held captive to sin.[29] He introduces no subtlety of exegesis to suggest that acting means anything other than expressing will in external effect. Romans 7:18 is omitted from comment, but the omission is significant only in retrospect. At the time of the *Expositio*, Paul's avowals of distress still represented for Augustine the torment of someone in need of grace, and so he naturally did not feel the need to blunt the impact of verses where Paul confessed his perverse accomplishments of will and lamented his powerless approbation of the law.[30] It is not until the end of the chapter that Augustine begins to mark Paul's change of voice to one speaking under grace. By Romans 7:25 the transition has been made. Paul serves the law of God with his mind (*mens*), the law of sin with his flesh (*caro*). For Augustine this means that Paul no longer gratifies his misguided desires, but instead overrules their influence in his acting and serves the law of God. The desires nevertheless continue to inhabit his will. They are inoperative but dangerous, a constant

---

of our final state of freedom in paradise, *De nupt. et conc.* 1.30.33 (CSEL 42, 245, 12–13): "ibi sumus ueraciter liberi, ubi non delectamur inuiti." ("There we are genuinely free, where we delight without reluctance.")   [29] *Propp.* 41–46.

[30] In *Propp.* 44, Augustine exegetes verses 15–16 together, a conjunction he would insist upon later in *C. duas ep. Pel.* 1.10.18. But unlike the later exegesis, he does not suggest that Paul's avowal of consent to the law (*consentio legi*) alters the apparent meaning of his admission immediately preceding. Augustine understands Paul's consent to mean that he approves of the sort of life that the law promotes, and in the *Expositio* Augustine finds this approval consistent with Paul's acting contrary to the law ("quod nolo, hoc facio").

reminder to him of his mortal weakness.[31] At this point Augustine's exegesis meets his rejoinder to Julian. In responding to Julian, he extends the same description of what it means to be under grace back into the previous verses. The result is an understanding of grace that is remarkably consonant with the *Expositio*.[32] The only difference seems to be that Julian has incited Augustine to restrict Paul in Romans 7 to a single voice.

The voice that Augustine leaves to Paul carries none of the subtle transformations that have shaped Augustine's view of conversion. Largely this is due, I think, to Julian's success in tempting Augustine to compromise with Pelagian views rather than pursue his own insights. On the question of Paul's persona in Romans 7, Julian presented Augustine with two choices. Either he implicitly endorsed the Pelagian view of the converted life by having Paul assume the voice of the unconverted, or he left Paul in his own voice and risked slandering the church and her saints by failing to account for how his conversion had taken hold. For Augustine to accept the first part of the disjunction was, of course, for him to admit defeat, and this he steadfastly refused to do, but to take the second was to play right into Julian's hands. The challenge of having to secure Paul's graced condition from confusion with his life before conversion is set up so that if Augustine wins, he loses. This is so because widening the gulf between the time before and after conversion opens the royal road to Pelagian theology. Augustine will find it difficult to clean up Paul's conversion without creating the impression that grace severs all ties between the dark past of sin and the illuminated future of virtue. He does throw a bridge across conversion in the form of desires which carry over from the old life into the new. But so slender a bridge fails to support a viable

---

[31] *Propp.* 45–46.

[32] Against Julian, Augustine echoes his earlier exegesis in his use of the distinction between having a desire and consenting to a desire to set off the converted from the unconverted will. See *Propp.* 45–46 (CSEL 84, 20, 5–8): "In eo enim est damnatio, quod obtemperamus et servimus desideriis pravis carnalibus. Si autem existant et non desint talia desideria, non tamen his oboediamus, non captivamur et sub gratia iam sumus." ("For condemnation rests in this, that we obey and become subject to depraved carnal desires. If, however, such desires abide in us and yet do not receive our submission, we are not captured and now are under grace.") Cf. *C. duas ep. Pel.* 1.10.21 (CSEL 60, 442, 15–16): "non enim damnatur, nisi qui concupiscentiae carnis consentit ad malum." ("For condemnation falls only on the one who consents to the evil of carnal desire.")

alternative to Pelagius. If all that separated Augustine from Pelagius were the presence of some inoperative perversity in good works, Augustine could press his case against Pelagius only by obsessing morbidly on the purity of intentions (a not unknown temptation in the history of Augustinian ethics). At best he would come off as a Pelagian with an overweening conscience.

Augustine finds himself very nearly argued into a Pelagian corner. It would be a mistake, however, to view Paul's conversion from law to grace solely in its polemical context. Augustine tells us that he revised Romans 7 in an effort to understand these words of the apostle, "And now it is no longer I that do it..."[33] This particular avowal is framed on one side by Paul's recognition of the good of the law and on the other by his observation that sin works against him. In between, then, we have the confession of someone who recognizes but no longer identifies with his sin. For Augustine, the puzzle concerns the manner in which Paul manages to avoid identification with sin when sin is still clearly involved in how he wills. He looks for his answer in Paul's declaration of delight in the law, a delight having its source deep within his person ("secundum interiorem hominem").[34] Augustine will express the intimacy of Paul's delight in terms of the difference between fear of punishment (*timor poenae*) and love of justice (*amor iustitiae*). No one who delights in the law out of love, he concludes, can fail to be under grace.[35]

Because Augustine has Julian's complaint in mind when he rereads Romans 7 in light of this discovery, he focuses more attention on what delight facilitates – refusing consent to perverse desires – than on the delight itself. As a result, he obscures the direction in which his own theology of grace is evolving. We are left wondering whether being under grace is marked by having at least the beginnings of love for the life sanctioned by God, or by having enough love to avoid having to capitulate to discredited desire. Augustine's polemical insistence

---

[33] *C. duas ep. Pel.* 1.10.22. The verse is Romans 7:17, "Nunc autem iam non ego operor illud, sed quod habitat in me peccatum."   [34] Romans 7:22.

[35] *C. duas ep. Pel.* 1.10.22. Burnaby, *Amor Dei*, 219–52, is an extraordinarily good interpreter of Augustine on *delectatio iustitiae*.

on Paul's inability to *perfect* his actions lends support to the idea that conversion introduces the time when misguided loves of the past no longer rule us. On the other hand, too strenuous an insistence on the connection between conversion and continence would seem to rule out beginnings of faith which do not immediately break the volitional inertia of habit. Augustine will have brought back under the law persons who experience the first stirrings of delight in the recesses of a divided will. Any suggestion that delight, or love for justice, can appear in us prior to grace seems inconsistent with Augustine's professed motivation for revising Paul's condition under the law. When he finishes his lesson on the proper reading of Romans 7, he leaves the beginning of conversion, and hence the nature of conversion, oddly unsettled.

Some of the obscurity surrounding the beginning of conversion can be cleared up if we refocus attention on what Augustine has for polemical purposes hidden from view. Once Paul in Romans 7 converts in his exegesis from law to grace, we no longer have a description of what it means to be under the law. In his *Expositio*, it was clear that Augustine took this condition to be one in which sinful habits prevent us from acting on the good.[36] If our desires should conflict with our judgment, no reintegration could occur solely on the strength of our approbation of the law. Grace would have to cure our will's weakness before we could break the hold of oppositional desires. Paul's conversion from law to grace necessitated a fundamental revision in the *Expositio's* definition of internal division. Augustine could no longer identify internal division with weakness of will, or more precisely, he could no longer equate all forms of the will's infirmity with our inability to act on preference. Any lingering antagonism between affect and intent, regardless of its severity, constituted a measure of incontinence or internal division. The converted Paul manifested the sort of division that attends the triumph of intent over affect in action. He obeys the law, but traces of his old self remain in the form of suppressed desires. Augustine interprets Paul's laments as expressions of someone awaiting complete renewal, when no

[36] *Propp.* 13–18, 44–47.

part of himself would remain alienated from contemplation and enjoyment of God. But because he does not allow any of Paul's avowals in Romans 7 to express struggle under the law, Augustine seems to concede the *Expositio*'s description of the condition *sub lege* to the Pelagians. They are not asked to take account of the coercive power of habit in their view of conversion.

This concession is not one that Augustine can afford to make. The strength of his case against Manichaean psychology came down to his ability to describe the severest expression of internal division – our inability to withhold our consent to sin – without resort to metaphysical dualism. Success here enabled him to articulate sin in the language of volition and thereby to disallow independent creation of evil. Nothing fell outside the bounds of God's creation, not even the human creation of sin, which remained parasitic on the divinely established order of values. Still left to be settled, however, was the issue of sin's elimination. On this front Pelagian theology challenged Augustine for the right to delimit virtue. Both Augustine and Pelagius could agree that sinful habits needed to be uprooted before virtue could take hold, but for Pelagius the uprooting took effect through free choice. He assumed that we would turn from sin to God if when offered knowledge of the right path (the law) we approved of it. One good turn followed another, and as we appropriated knowledge in the choices we made, virtue would take root in place of sin. Augustine had to reject the Pelagian perspective if only because it turned a blind eye to involuntary sin. In placing the efficacy of grace in informed choice, Pelagius joined the company of pagan philosophers who saw in intellect sufficient check to unthinking affections.[37] Neither he nor the Stoics envisioned the overthrow of sin whose roots in will reached deeper than the immediacy of knowledge. Pelagius kept the route of grace open by delivering the law at baptism and by refusing to entertain the possibility of involuntary sin on the graced side of conversion.[38] Augustine was in an excellent

---

[37] See Brown, *Augustine of Hippo*, 366.

[38] In Pelagian theology the law supplied the convert with the knowledge of how to pursue Christian virtue. In the Rome of the 390s, a time when upper levels of Roman society were converting to Christianity in sizable numbers, adult baptism was still

position to challenge Pelagian assumptions, but when he accuses Julian and company of having to read Romans 7 as the description of someone prior to grace, he takes the bite out of the accusation by excluding consent to sin from Paul's graced condition. The one kind of internal division fatal to Pelagian theology – the kind that left Paul to lament, "I do not do what I want, but I do the very thing I hate" – Augustine graciously hides from view.

There are nevertheless hints in even the earliest of his works against Pelagius that Augustine worked steadily behind the scenes to reclaim for grace the time he once thought represented life under the law. His response of 412 to the imperial tribune Marcellinus ostensibly addressed the latter's request for clarity on the possibility of perfection in the Christian life.[39] The sinless life was one that Pelagius exhorted converts to achieve, and the issue of sin's elimination clearly divided Pelagius and Augustine. But since it was the source of perfection more than its moment that exercised Augustine, he chose to clarify the nature of grace. Specifically, Marcellinus is treated to a lesson on how to read II Corinthians 3:6, "For the letter kills, while the spirit gives life." Augustine uses Paul's contrast between law and spirit as the occasion to draw an invidious comparison between the killing power of the law (the letter) and the theology that placed grace (spirit) under the law's power to kill. Pelagius is never mentioned by name in *De spiritu et littera*, but his assimilation of grace to law stands condemned there as the attempted murder of the spirit.

In order to substantiate this sort of accusation against Pelagian theology, Augustine reserves for the law a time wholly outside the influence of grace. This is the killing time, when the law's revelation of sin has the ironic effect of increasing illicit

common. For the connection between adult baptism and reception of the law, see Brown, "Pelagius," 109–10.

[39] In an earlier treatise, his first written expressly against Pelagian theology, Augustine admitted that under the influence of grace, it was possible for someone to live without sin, but he also doubted whether anyone other than Christ himself could or would fit the description. When Marcellinus, who sided with Augustine against both Donatists and Pelagians, learned of this, he wondered whether Augustine had not in some way contradicted himself. He wrote Augustine for clarification, and *De spiritu et littera* came in reply. Cf. *De peccatorum meritis et remissione* 2.6.7, 2.7.8, and 2.20.34 for the view of perfection at issue.

desire. "For in some unknown way," he observes, "the desired object becomes more attractive for being forbidden."[40] To account for the quality of this effect, Augustine will suggest only an image, that of water rushing faster past an obstacle constricting its flow. The law proves a poor dam to desire. Yet as to the cause of the effect and the source of the law's ineffectiveness, Augustine is quite clear. Without the aid of the spirit, "drawing in good desire in place of bad" and "pouring love out into our hearts," prohibition alone fails to strike at the root of sin.[41] The springs of sinful motivation, illicit desires for mutable goods, continue to determine the character of the will. Prohibition may sometimes through fear of punishment suppress the expression of perverse desires in action, but Augustine discounts the value of coerced conformity to the law. Obedience based on fear has no root in the love of justice and hence indicates no advance of the soul towards virtue and the blessed life. "If what is enjoined is done out of fear of penalty, not love of justice, it is done servilely," Augustine argues, "not freely, and so is not done at all; for no fruit is good which does not emerge out of love's root."[42]

Although he wishes to reduce Pelagian emphasis on the efficacy of informed choice to this grim depiction of fear and carnal servitude, it is doubtful that Augustine has worked his *reductio* on Pelagian assumptions. For if the law brings knowledge of sin only in the superficial manner of identifying punishable behavior, there is no reason to believe that someone under the law in Augustine's sense has any appreciation for why the law circumscribes the life most worth living. Pelagius could escape the *reductio* simply by pointing out that Augustine

---

[40] *De spir. et litt.* 4.6 (CSEL 60, 159, 1–2): "nescio quo enim modo hoc ipsum, quod concupiscitur, fit iocundius, dum uetatur."

[41] *De spir. et litt.* 4.6 (CSEL 60, 158, 22–27): "sed ubi sanctus non adiuuat spiritus inspirans pro concupiscentia mala concupiscentiam bonam, hoc est caritatem diffundens in cordibus nostris, profecto illa lex quamuis bona auget prohibendo desiderium malum, sicut aquae impetus, si in eam partem non cesset influere, uehementior fit obice obposito." ("But when the holy spirit does not aid us, drawing in good desire in place of bad, or pouring love out into our hearts, the law, although good, actually increases longing for evil by prohibiting it; just as the force of water flowing in a single direction becomes more violent when opposed by some obstacle.")

[42] *De spir. et litt.* 14.26 (CSEL 60, 180, 22–25): "quod mandatum si fit timore poenae, non amore iustitiae, seruiliter fit, non liberaliter et ideo nec fit. non enim fructus est bonus, qui de caritate radice non surgit."

equivocates in his description of the knowledge of sin. Under the law such knowledge represents for him the sinner's fearful submission to a penal code; under grace it represents the saint's grief over failing to bring full will to bear on accepting the spirit and taking hold of God's wisdom. Only on the side of grace is there any genuine awareness of the links between virtue, the good life, and obedience to God. On the side of the law, obedience has been so stripped of wisdom that it counts as barely more than failure of nerve. The devaluation of obedience does not of itself, however, reduce Pelagian confidence in the power of disciplined knowledge to mere fascination with punitive sanctions. Until conformity to the law can be said to manifest at least a modicum of wisdom, it remains an open question whether knowledge and choice can carry the will to God. From the Pelagian point of view, Augustine's theology is obfuscating when it associates time under the law with servile fear of punishment and idle when it suggests that knowledge of the virtuous way to live needs to be motivated.

Compared with his description of the condition *sub lege* in the *Expositio*, Augustine's portrayal of time under the law has darkened considerably in response to the Pelagians. To be under the law in the *Expositio* was to possess virtues of justice and prudence in sufficient degree to know why the law deserved approbation. When Augustine robs the condition of these virtues in *De spiritu et littera*, he also robs it of its characteristic internal division. No longer does the person under the law stand divided between flesh and spirit, for nothing of either virtue or knowledge remains to indicate the presence of the spirit. Parodies of justice and prudence have taken the place of rudiments of the genuine virtues, so that when someone submits to the law, it is on the basis of a crude calculation of self-interest. External conformity to law results when the prospect of punishment takes priority over illicit gratification of some temptation in the person's private economy of pleasure. Because Augustine eliminates love of justice as a source of motivation for those under the law, it appears as if he simply collapses the condition under the law into the condition before the law. The assimilation is certainly peculiar as a polemical move, given that what drops out is the very internal division that drives Pelagian hopes to despair.

Augustine's unaccountable omission of involuntary sin from the perspectives of both law and grace is ultimately, however, the illusion created by his shifting focus on law and grace. Observe what emerges if we take his description of Paul under grace in *Contra duas epistulas Pelagianorum* (his response to Julian) and set it next to his description of the condition under the law in *De spiritu et littera*. Where we might have expected the conjunction of two sides of conversion, before and after, we are presented instead with a conundrum. The graced side of conversion has been purged of involuntary sin. Augustine's representative of grace, Paul in Romans 7, longs for perfection in grace, but is able, despite some residual desires to the contrary, to follow his approbation of the law. The alternative reading, that Paul's avowals of distress express his inability to *act* on his approbation, is by implication left to the description of someone under the law. But looking at what Augustine offers for this description in *De spiritu et littera*, we find that no room has been reserved for the alternative reading of Romans 7. The law's reign of fear excludes the sort of approbation that becomes involved in the conflict between two opposing sources of motivation, cupidity of habit (flesh) and love of God (spirit).[43] Augustine's exegetical habits have excluded involuntary sin from penal servitude (*sub lege*) and from genuine love of God (*sub gratia*). Caught between flesh and spirit, the involuntary sinner slips between the cracks of law and grace.

But as I said, involuntary sin's disappearance is the illusion of

---

[43] The juxtaposition between the law's reign of fear and grace's reign of justice could be set up using Augustine's dismissal of righteousness under the law in *C. duas ep. Pel.* 1.9.15 (CSEL 60, 436, 20–23): "aliud est enim uoluntate benefaciendi benefacere, aliud autem ad malefaciendum sic uoluntate inclinari, ut etiam faceret, si hoc posset impune permitti." ("For it is one thing to act well with a will for acting well, but quite another thing to act well with a will inclined to evil doing, where one would do the evil if it could be done with impunity.") Saul of Tarsus serves in this section as Augustine's illustration of empty righteousness under the law, and given that what he misses in Saul's behavior is genuine regard for justice, again the condition of the divided will seems to belong to neither law nor grace. I have chosen nevertheless to frame this puzzle with *De spiritu et littera*, because I believe that its solution requires attention to the genealogy of the condition *sub lege*.

a shifting focus. Augustine's equivocation on knowledge of sin in *De spiritu et littera* does not uniformly beg the question against Pelagius. The knowledge is question-begging only when the law operates "under the law" to send fear into the hearts of those who understand punishment, yet neither know nor love justice. Working under conditions of fear and vice, the law would without question be devoid of grace, but devoid as well of any resemblance to the Pelagian understanding of law. On the other side of conversion, the law reappears under grace and with an utterly transformed effect. In place of fear, the law sows love of God. More precisely, the law becomes the love of God, and this love is the gift of the spirit.[44] When discussing the work of grace, Augustine intends to identify law and grace, which were from the perspective of law alone radically different. In order to reunite the two under grace, he must speak of law no longer as a set of injunctions imposed upon us under threat of punishment, but as our inner disposition to seek happiness in God.[45] The shift of the law's operation from external obligation to internal disposition is paradoxical, of course, if we see in the move from law to grace an ethics of law being squeezed into teleology. But the better way to view the move is to notice how grace's subsumption of law begins the soul's recovery of virtue. Augustine has left no doubt about the soul's unabated time of

---

[44] In *De spir. et litt.* 17.29, Augustine contrasts old and new dispensations of the law, the first written on tablets of stone to terrify the unjust, the second written by the spirit on the hearts of believers. Concerning the change in dispensation, Augustine draws the following moral: "lex ergo dei est caritas. huic prudentia carnis non est subiecta; neque enim potest. sed ad hanc prudentiam carnis terrendam cum in tabulis scribuntur opera caritatis, lex est operum et littera occidens praeuaricatorem; cum autem ipsa caritas diffunditur in corde credentium, lex est fidei et spiritus uiuificans dilectorem" (CSEL 60, 183, 2–6). ("Thus the law of God is love, and to it the wisdom of the flesh is not subject, nor can it be. But when works of love are written on tablets to dismay the wisdom of the flesh, the law is of works and the letter kills the prevaricator. When instead love itself is poured into the hearts of believers, the law is of faith and the spirit enlivens the lover.")

Although my main purpose for citing the two operations of law is to indicate law's transformation into love, it is worth noting that Augustine's tendency to view the history of redemption through the lens of conversion sometimes gets him into trouble. If the condition under the law corresponds to the old dispensation and God's promises to Israel, then the conditions of fear and vice characteristic of an individual's time under the law suggest a corresponding darkness in Israel's time under the old covenant. The lens of conversion distorts here, as it presents more of a separation between old and new covenants than Augustine would intend. Cf. *De spir. et litt.* 25.42.   [45] *De spir. et litt.* 21.36 and 22.37.

ethical darkness under the law. Love of God, first received under grace, lays the foundation for the virtues. It renovates the springs of human motivation, replacing fear of punishment with love of justice. From the onset of grace to final perfection, knowledge of sin remains tied to our increasing appreciation for how the unjust life, lived in alienation from God, serves as its own punishment.

Once on the side of grace, Augustine's depiction of the law engages the concerns of Pelagian theology. Law and grace come together, we grow in virtue, and because love of God requires some measure of wisdom, our gain in virtue may be correlated with our appropriation of beatific knowledge.[46] Augustine and Pelagius will part company on the issue of appropriation, but they will not have crossed one another at all until knowledge of the law reflects wisdom rather than a debased form of prudence. Pelagius, in other words, must rejoin the company of philosophers in the late antique world who sought to put the good life, the life of virtue, wholly under human control. Holding him accountable for the life outside the influence of grace, when beatitude is sought in the enjoyment of temporal goods, is a waste of time, since there the convergence of virtue, beatitude, and self-determination has obviously been given up. Augustine's best challenge to Pelagian theology lies in his rebuttal of pagan philosophy. If knowledge of beatitude can find us lacking in will, then the convergence of virtue and autonomy seems impossible on either pagan or Pelagian terms.

Augustine does in fact quietly secure infirmity in willing from the oblivion of Pelagian exegesis. For as he darkens one side of conversion to extinguish virtue under the law, he rekindles virtue on the other side with our first glimmer of delight in God. Because he has in *De spiritu et littera* so thoroughly blackened the side of law alone, any such delight, regardless of its capacity to inform willing, represents the gift of the spirit.[47] Given that delight has its ultimate source in the redemptive power of God,

---

[46] As a general principle, Augustine believed that we could know without having to love what we knew, but we could not love without having to know (to some degree) what we loved. It therefore stands to reason that love of God, the source and end of the good life, involves knowledge of beatitude. See *De spir. et litt.* 36.64 for a brief description of the principle and *De Trinitate* x for more elaboration.

[47] *De spir. et litt.* 32.56.

the efficacy of grace will manifest itself over time. Gradually we are healed of internal division, as spirit gains ascendancy over flesh:

If there is faith, which works through love, one begins to delight in the law of God inwardly. Such delight is a gift not of the letter but of the spirit. It remains so even if another law in the members should war against the law of the mind until the old self, wholly changed, passes over into that newness which increases daily from within, as the grace of God liberates us from the body of this death through our lord, Jesus Christ.[48]

Augustine's choice of language to express the inward source of delight ("secundum interiorem hominem") and the struggle between two kinds of law, one in the members ("in membris") and the other of the mind ("mentis"), draws heavily from the final verses of Romans 7, or that part of the chapter which had always represented for him Paul's experience under grace. The effect is to move the conflict between willing and wisdom squarely under grace and to do so under Paul's authority. We have no reason to assume that inability to act on beatific knowledge or not to act against it cannot express a form of the conflict. Although the *Expositio* associates this sort of inability with being under the law, Augustine's subsequent revision of life under the law leaves even the dimmest comprehension of beatitude to grace. Paul must move under grace, if only by default of the law.

If there is any doubt after *De spiritu et littera* that someone under grace may yet find the spirit lacking when it comes to willing the good, it is answered in *De natura et gratia*, his rebuttal of 415 to Pelagius' *De natura*. As Augustine sees the main issue of contention, Pelagius errs in claiming that human nature can never lose its capacity to avoid sin: "He attributes the possibility of his not sinning to the grace of God for the reason that God is the creator of his nature, in which, he says, the possibility of his

---

[48] *Ibid.*, 15.26 (CSEL 60, 180–81, 25–27 and 1–4): "si adsit fides, quae per dilectionem operatur, incipit condelectari legi dei secundum interiorem hominem, quae delectatio non litterae, sed spiritus donum est, etiamsi alia lex in membris adhuc repugnat legi mentis, donec in nouitatem, quae de die in diem in interiore homine augetur, tota uetustas mutata pertranseat liberante nos de corpore mortis huius gratia dei per Iesum Christum dominum nostrum."

not sinning has been inseparably placed."[49] To disabuse him of his error, Augustine is only too happy to point out the possibility of involuntary sin on both sides of baptism. For involuntary sin, he has in mind those occasions when we cannot overcome the desires that we know to obstruct our beatitude. He invokes Galatians 5:17, "The flesh desires against the spirit and the spirit against the flesh, for these oppose one another and keep you from doing the things you would."[50] Strictly speaking this opposition in the will between flesh and spirit can only happen under grace, and Augustine freely admits that Paul speaks to the converted, but he does not feel the need to insist here on the restriction. Pelagius cannot accommodate involuntary sin on either side of conversion. For if we cannot act on our knowledge of the good before conversion, he has no way to account for conversion. And if internal division should appear after our conversion, he has no way to account for our perfection in virtue. He is forced to refuse the intelligibility of internal compulsion in order to preserve the efficacy of informed choice. That leaves Pelagians with a very shallow appreciation for the power of habit, as Augustine is well aware. He urges Paul in Romans 7 to the attention of Pelagius, knowing that the voice in the text subverts his claim for the inalienable power of human nature to avoid sin.[51]

The evolution of Augustine's polemic against Pelagius makes it all the more curious that he would have chosen to present Julian in *Contra duas epistulas Pelagianorum* with a Paul who was able to avoid sin. His most consistent reading of Romans 7 in 421 would have been to allow Paul's avowals to represent the full spectrum of internal conflict, ranging from involuntary sin to imperfect virtue. Instead Augustine unnecessarily complicates his exegesis to keep Paul, the text notwithstanding, from admitting that he in fact does what he hates and not what he approves of. His reading of the text does not exclude on

---

[49] *De nat. et gr.* 51.59 (CSEL 60, 276, 16–19): "ideo dei gratiae tribuit non peccandi possibilitatem, quia eius naturae deus auctor est, cui possibilitatem non peccandi inseparabiliter insitam dicit."

[50] "caro concupiscit aduersus spiritum et spiritus aduersus carnem; haec enim inuicem aduersantur, ut non ea quae uultis faciatis," as cited in *De nat. et gr.* 53.61 (CSEL 60, 278, 4–7).   [51] *De nat. et gr.* 50.58.

principle that someone under grace could sin involuntarily, but his representation of Paul does a pretty fair job of obscuring this possibility.[52] To all appearances, Augustine's polemic against the Pelagians takes an unexpected and defeatist turn when Julian launches his counterattack. Instead of admitting profound internal division into Paul's condition, he widens the divide between Paul and those who still consent to sin.

There is undoubtedly some measure of capitulation or at least compromise in Augustine's spirited apologia for Paul's life under grace. He simply protests too much. On the other hand, we need to consider why Augustine would have supposed his response to Julian to have held the line against Pelagian theology without compromise or capitulation. For although he continues in his writings to insist that delight in the law begins with the work of the spirit, he does not dwell on the convert's experience of incapacitation.[53] He could not, of course, have forced the Pelagians to face the issue of involuntary sin without having posed it for himself as well. If involuntary sin falls out of view in his redescription of Paul in Romans 7, its disappearance may indicate that he was in no better position than Pelagius to have grace answer profound internal division (as Julian suspected), or it may indicate on the contrary that he understood himself to have addressed the issue elsewhere.

One recurrent theme in his critique of Pelagius suggests where Augustine will have developed his view of grace to respond to the worst damages of sin. Beginning especially with *De spiritu et littera*, he emphasizes the spirit's gift of love over and against mere knowledge of the law. The contrast involves a certain equivocation on what knowledge of the law constitutes

---

[52] Paul does not cease to experience temptation, but Augustine accords him the power to resist it. The passive experience of temptation is sin only when the meaning of sin is extended to include what sin effects. Normally sin is taken in a more restricted sense: i.e., there must be consent to temptation for there to be sin. If Paul can always avoid having to give his consent to temptation, and Paul represents those under grace, we are not far, it seems, from an inalienable capacity to avoid sin. Cf. *Contra duas ep. Pel.* 1.11.24 and 1.13.27.

[53] He does not, however, leave it out of his account entirely. See, for example, *De gr. et lib. arb.* 17.33 (OSA 24, 164): "Qui ergo vult facere Dei mandatum et non potest, iam quidem habet voluntatem bonam, sed adhuc parvam et invalidam." ("The person who wants to do what God commands and is unable indeed already possesses a good will, but one still small and powerless.") This work, addressed to the monks of Hadrumetum, dates from 427.

before and after grace, as I have already discussed, but regardless of the equivocation, the necessity of the spirit's gift of love places an important restriction on any theory of conversion. The restriction is that no theory of conversion can assume that there is always a prior disposition on the part of the convert to accept grace. Pelagius violates the restriction in so far as he requires the human will to remain receptive to the knowledge that saves. Indeed, it is very hard to say on what basis he could account for someone's informed rejection of beatific knowledge. Augustine can account for it because his understanding of habit admits the possibility of involuntary sin. But whether he can also supply the corresponding theory of conversion depends on his conception of the spirit's gift. He must elaborate an operation of grace which brings to the scene of conversion someone having not only beatific knowledge but the will (or least the beginnings of one) to appropriate it.

MIXING MEMORY AND DESIRE

Commentators on Augustine have long noticed that towards the middle of his years of conflict with Pelagian theology, around 418 by most accounts, he begins to shift the operation of grace inward, so that its efficacy depends crucially on introducing new desires to the unconverted will.[54] There is no consensus in the scholarship on the import of the shift. Two modern commentators, Jean Lebourlier and J. Patout Burns, have offered the thesis that Augustine's new focus on grace's inward operation means that he must have abandoned his earlier view of conversion in *Ad Simplicianum*.[55] Lebourlier sees in

[54] For a review of the literature, see J. Patout Burns, *The Development of Augustine's Doctrine of Operative Grace* (Paris: Etudes augustiniennes, 1980), 7–15. In 418, Augustine finished *De gratia Christi* and there, apparently for the first time, detailed an inward operation of grace which actually infused human willing with new desires for beatitude. See, for instance, *De gr. Chr.* 24.25. Before 418, he seems to have restricted interior work to the spirit's strengthening of already existing desires for beatitude. Burns, *The Development*, 145–50, locates the decisive shift not in *De gratia Christi* but in Augustine's letter of the same year to Sixtus of Rome (*Epistula* 194). His view may be compared with that of Eugene TeSelle, *Augustine the Theologian* (New York: Herder and Herder, 1970), 333–35.

[55] Jean Lebourlier, "Essai sur la responsabilité du pécheur dans la réflexion de saint Augustin," *Augustinus Magister* 3 (Paris, 1954), 287–300, and Burns, *The Development*, 111–20.

Augustine's writings on grace a reversal in grace's *modus operandi*. Callings are no longer given to suit the disposition of those called; those called are instead given the disposition to accept their callings.[56] Burns agrees with Lebourlier, but sets the reversal in the context of a more elaborate hypothesis. He attributes to Augustine in *Ad Simplicianum* a theory of congruous vocation, which has God supply the appropriate motives to individuals having a prior disposition to convert. This theory is overturned with Augustine's letter of 418 to Sixtus of Rome, where he depicts conversion as the reversal of unabated perversity by God's internal renovation of human desire. Finally, in 427 a unified view of operative grace emerges in *De correptione et gratia*, where Augustine combines the environmental and interior work of the spirit in order to account for the perseverance of the saints. These changes in grace's operation never depart from Augustine's foundational assertion of God's sovereignty over the human will. But they do represent, as Burns sees them, significant development in how Augustine comes to understand that assertion.[57]

More than any other recent commentator, Burns has worked to reintroduce contours into the often flattened landscape of Augustine's theological development after *Ad Simplicianum*.[58] In this he has succeeded admirably, though not without succumbing on occasion to oversimplification. Because Burns understands Augustine to have completed his theory of operative grace in 427, his analysis, despite its careful attention to context, leaves too great an impression of a linear evolution towards closure. This is not to deny that the texts can sometimes suggest such an evolution. Augustine's increasing emphasis on the interior work of the spirit follows in the wake of his devaluation of the condition *sub lege*, the time before conversion. This condition, once denuded of all redeeming desires, places the burden of the missing desires on grace. It is not unexpected, then, that Augustine would turn his attention to the interior operation of grace in order to account for the efficacy of conversion, *contra Pelagianos*. He has to move to an ever more radical internal operation for the simple reason that grace must

---

[56] Lebourlier, "Essai," 299.   [57] Burns, *The Development*, 7–9.
[58] Only TeSelle's work in *Augustine the Theologian*, 185–338, is comparable.

answer an ever more radical condition of perversity. Before
conversion, Augustine allows us no vestige of merit to serve as
the basis for our election.[59] Not only does his stance respect the
gratuity of election, but it blocks the Pelagian route of grace.
The absence of regenerative desire in us prior to grace leaves
knowledge of the good begging futilely at the door. Having
reclaimed conversion from the Pelagians, Augustine can then in
his final works move human perfection securely under the
control of the spirit. He combines the interior and exterior work
of grace to bring the saints home. In sum, he steadily secures the
efficacy of grace against the ravages of sin and the delusions of
Pelagians.

Burns would never put the logic of Augustine's evolution so
baldly, for he is too sensitive to the way in which changing
polemical contexts elicit very particular developments. He
works hard to dispel the impression that it was all there
implicitly from the beginning. Nevertheless it is not unreasonable to hold him accountable for Augustine's logic. Though he
would deny that grace's means of operation changes in response
to a single explanatory principle, Burns does admit that the
scope of life under grace widens progressively in response to the
principle that God retains sovereignty over human willing.[60]
Frankly I do not see how Augustine's conception of the means
of grace can gain much independence from his comprehension
of the scope of grace. As his appreciation for the time-bound
character of human willing increases, he will have to find in
grace more than the conquest of a moment.

In fact, Burns does not keep means and scope wholly separate
when he examines Augustine's changing view of the means of
grace. He reunites the two in saintly perseverance. This belated
reunion, placed at the dénouement of the Pelagian controversy,
incorporates mechanisms of grace that have earlier been
associated exclusively with conversion. Since these mechanisms,
the inward and environmental operations of grace, have when
taken together secured the efficacy of conversion, the scope of
grace will emerge as the extension over time of the means of
conversion. Whatever his intention, Burns will have left

[59] See, for example, *C. duas ep. Pel.* 2.8.18.   [60] Burns, *The Development*, 8.

Augustine with the following response to Pelagius. Grace cannot effect conversion unless it supplies not only beatific knowledge but the knower's receptivity to moral transformation. To ensure receptivity, grace will have to work within as well as without, so that when the calling comes, the recipient will have been made ready to accept. The interior work of grace becomes less dramatic after conversion, having no longer to break up a monopoly of perverse desires, but grace's perfecting of conversion employs no new means of operation. Inwardly grace continues to control the recipient's sources of motivation, while outwardly it brings these sources into concrete expression. The converted life thus takes shape as the integration of graced moments, which, depending on their place in time, may involve creating, strengthening, or simply motivating desires for the good. Given the moment-by-moment intrusiveness of grace upon human willing, it is no wonder that Burns comes to view Augustine's reconciliation of grace and free choice as a zero-sum game.[61]

But this final picture of grace's operation depends on viewing the scope of grace as the temporal extension of its means, and in this Burns oversimplifies.[62] Augustine does not develop means effective for a moment and then add up the moments of grace over a lifetime. His reflections on means are bound from the first to considerations of scope. The means of conversion, for instance, never change operation in his thought without also displacing the moment of human entry into grace. Some of the intricacy of this effect can be detected in the fruitful confusion of *Ad Simplicianum*. In the second question on election, Augustine secures human consent to God's calling by having God anticipate the moment of calling. Having suited situation to person, God enables those called to acknowledge their own

[61] *Ibid.*, 169: "The logic of Augustine's interpretation of *Romans* 9, 16 which attributes salvific effects to the divine mercy rather than to human effort would eventually require that he eliminate all human autonomy."

[62] I am guilty of similar oversimplification in my article, "The Recovery of Free Agency in the Theology of St. Augustine," *Harvard Theological Review* 80 (1987), 101–25. After having explicated the function of the congruous vocation in eliciting consent, I attempted to extend the efficacy of this means of grace into the remainder of the converted life (see 120–21). It was through reading Burns's more nuanced views on Augustine that I came to see my own error. With the ingratitude of hindsight, I now charge him with similar error.

desires for beatitude. The scene of conversion does not, however, merely introduce them to grace, for no consent to grace would be genuine unless it also came with the recognition (necessarily in retrospect) of God's anticipation. Those who come to the scene of their conversion expecting to encounter God for the first time come too late. Augustine seems to have understood this well enough in his own case, for his address to God in the *Confessiones* offers belated acknowledgment to a previously unnoticed presence: "Late did I love you, beauty so ancient and so new...You were with me, and I was not with you."[63] It takes him longer to notice that the Paul of his first response to Simplician must come to make a similar confession. Paul may not sound in Romans 7 like someone who has settled accounts with his unconverted past, but the resolution of his internal struggle must (if it involves genuine love of justice) bring his struggle retrospectively under the care of God's spirit.

There is no consistent picture of conversion to be found in *Ad Simplicianum*. Augustine's remarks on the efficacy of God's calling in election offer tempting material for an early theory of conversion, but he never specifies in the second response whether the one called suitably has to have met certain dispositional preconditions. The omission leaves the fit between situation and person too vague to suggest more than a hint of grace's operation. Lebourlier and Burns find more than a hint because they tacitly assume that Paul's disposition under the law, discussed in the first response, represents the sort of disposition that callings were made to suit. But in absence of the dispositional precondition of having some delight (albeit suppressed) in the good, as Paul did under the law, the suitable calling is not unambiguously an external operation of grace, appealing to already existing desires for beatitude. The contrast of primary interest to Burns and Lebourlier, that between an early external and a later interior operation of grace, consequently becomes more difficult to sustain. But the fact that Augustine failed in 396 to notice any incongruity in his first two responses to Simplician does not mean that he would have intended at that time to have Paul set the stage for the suitable

---

[63] *Conf.* 10.27.38 (CCSL 27, 175, 1–4): "Sero te amaui, pulchritudo tam antiqua et tam noua...Mecum eras, et tecum non eram."

calling. He was then much too absorbed in his reevaluation of election to give a backward glance to his first response. The Paul who emerges on the brink of conversion at the end of the second response is not the man of Romans 7, but Saul of Tarsus, persecutor of Christians, whom Augustine describes as having a rabid will, one full of fury (*furiosa*) and blind (*caeca*).[64]

It is undeniable that over the course of his encounter with Pelagians, Augustine placed greater emphasis on grace's reversal of perverse dispositions, such as Saul's. In his reconsideration of *Ad Simplicianum* (2.1), coming in 427, he officially brought his earlier work in line with this emphasis by changing Paul's status in the first response. Having moved Paul under grace, Augustine leaves Saul in the second response free to represent the unconverted will.[65] This representation will be of someone in need of radical renewal, one whose perversity requires God's gift of a good will to include new desires. No doubt it would be rash to assume that Saul's persona in 396 harbored more than the vaguest presentiment of Augustine's interest in an interior operation of grace. It would, on the other hand, be equally rash to dismiss Saul altogether by supposing that Augustine imagined Paul in Romans 7 to have met dispositional preconditions for conversion by calling. There are two incompatible personae of the apostle offered in *Ad Simplicianum*, that of Saul and that of Paul under the law, and at least in the unrevised work their incompatibility cannot be resolved into a consistent theory of conversion.

During the Pelagian controversy, Augustine sorts out the two personae in an attempt to obstruct Pelagian exegesis of Paul's conversion. Saul comes to represent for him the time before conversion, and his condition of dire perversity divests this time of its last vestiges of beatific knowledge. Paul represents for him the time after conversion, and his condition of internal division drives a wedge between knowing and willing. Each persona in its own way undermines Pelagian theology. Stuck with Saul, the Pelagians cannot account for the beginning of conversion, and stuck with Paul, they cannot account for its completion. But regardless of Augustine's success in denying the Pelagians access

---

[64] *Ad Simpl.* 1.2.22.   [65] See, for example, *C. duas ep. Pel.* 1.19.37.

to a recognizable persona of the apostle, he cannot be said to have offered a viable alternative to their theology unless Saul and Paul fit together to form a single life. For his own theology of grace, the compatibility of the personae is as important as their separate polemical roles.

There is a deceptively simple answer to the question of compatibility. We could follow Augustine's advice to the monks of Marseilles and take *Ad Simplicianum* as the place to begin looking for grace's operation. We could also assume that his subsequent encounters with Pelagians will have resolved any inconsistency in his early work. What is it that we are left with? The unrevised early work brings consent to God's calling under grace, but only by obscuring the point of human entry into grace. Part of the time once held under the law moves retrospectively under grace, leaving conversion with no clear division of sides. The division reappears as Augustine progressively darkens the unconverted side. Upon revision, *Ad Simplicianum* offers Saul as the true representative of life without grace, and Paul emerges out of Saul with the first stirrings of delight in the good. We have a single life from Saul to Paul, though one divided on a moment of radical reorientation.

Before resting with this view of conversion, we would do well to examine more carefully just how the inconsistency in *Ad Simplicianum* gets resolved. If we allow Augustine's later emphasis on the interior work of grace to define the moment of human entry into grace, then we are assuming that the anachronism of conversion is only an accidental feature of the human perspective. In other words, when the means of grace changes in *Ad Simplicianum*, those called suitably to faith find themselves anticipated by God, but not anticipated in such a way that they could not trace grace back (at least in principle) to its beginning in their lives. Augustine was slow to recognize that his reformulation of the means of grace placed Paul after the beginning of grace, and by keeping Paul under the law, he left Saul and Paul at odds in his early work. One way to resolve their conflict would be for him to set the two apart at the moment of grace, and in many ways Augustine's writings against the Pelagians unfold as his attempt to meet the spirit at the beginning of its work. But I doubt whether success in his efforts at fixing the beginning of grace, if he can be said to succeed here, gives him his best answer to Pelagian theology.

The alternative response comes into view when we no longer assume that the anachronism of conversion is merely an accidental feature of human appropriation of grace. Taking it as a necessary feature would mean that no change in the operation of grace could be interpreted to give human beings the opportunity to anticipate their conversion.[66] If, for example, Paul's condition in Romans 7 no longer finds him anticipating grace, he will not be able to recover his view of the beginning simply on the knowledge that delight in justice puts him on the side of grace. Once he finds himself in the midst of redemption, the beginning of the process will elude the reach of his memory, much in the way that its completion extends beyond his expectation. Moreover, without discernible points of entry and exit in the converted life, desire for the good (the spirit's inward work) fails to join Saul and Paul at their moment of mutual divergence, when the divided will emerges out of pure perversity. It is apparent from the very experience of division that Saul cannot be left behind so easily, and any interior work of grace will have to reach back in time to claim him.

We will not be inclined to notice the anachronism that attends recognition of the spirit's gift of desire if we understand Augustine to have corrected for the anachronism of *Ad Simplicianum* by the simple expedient of moving Paul under grace. There are nevertheless many indications in his writings against the Pelagians that he supposed God to have prepared human willing to receive grace, before even the advent of new desires for the good.[67] By anticipation God moves into our

---

[66] When I speak of the necessarily anachronistic character of conversion, I mean something similar to but still different from what Paula Fredriksen, "Paul and Augustine: Conversion Narratives, Orthodox Traditions, and the Retrospective Self," *Journal of Theological Studies* N.S. 37 (1986) 33, identifies as anachronistic in conversion narratives: "The conversion account, never disinterested, is a condensed, or disguised, description of the convert's *present*, which he legitimates through his creation of a past and a self." Hers is a thesis about historical knowledge and, by extension, self-knowledge; mine is a thesis about knowledge of God and, by extension, self-knowledge.

[67] Augustine's frequent references during the Pelagian controversy to God's preparation of the will have been well documented in Athanase Sage, "Praeparatur voluntas a Domino," *Revue des études augustiniennes* 10 (1964), 1–20.

darkest times. The logic of this anticipation is most apparent, I think, in a reply that Augustine delivered around 428 to his friend Firmus. Little is known about this particular figure other than what can be gleaned directly from the letters recently uncovered by Johannes Divjak. In letter 2*, from Augustine to Firmus, Augustine addresses Firmus as a catechumen who is reluctant to be baptized.[68] He seeks to free Firmus from his excuses, and the excuse calling for the most interesting response concerns Firmus' contention that he must wait for God to give him the will to convert before he accepts baptism. Here is the substance of Augustine's reply:

Look no longer for the moment when God should will, as if you would offend him by willing before he did. At whatever time you will, you will with God's help and by his work. His mercy undoubtedly goes before you, that you may will. But when you do will, it is you in particular who wills.[69]

Firmus places himself in the time before grace in order to occupy a vantage for anticipating God. Augustine denies him any such perspective. If he has desires for conversion, then God has already entered the scene, and Firmus, having moved under grace, has no cause to postpone his baptism. If, on the other hand, he has no genuine desires for conversion, it would never have occurred to him to anticipate God. He would have remained held fast to the distractions of the moment, utterly oblivious of God's presence. The logic of divine anticipation consequently rules out human anticipation of the divine. The very capacities of will and recognition needed to anticipate grace are ones which God supplies. There will always be, given the means of grace, a temporal dislocation or anachronism between human recollection of God and God's recollection of humanity.

---

[68] For background on this particular letter, see René Braun, "Lettre 2*," Note complémentaire (OSA 46B, 427–29) and Herbert Frohnhofen, "Anmerkungen zum Brief 2* des heiligen Augustinus," *Vigiliae Christianae* 38 (1984), 385–92.

[69] *Epistula* 2*.7 (OSA 46B, 74, 167–71): "nec expectes quando uelit, quasi offensurus eum si ante tu uelis, cum ipso adiuuante atque operante uelis, quandocumque uolueris. Praeuenit quidem te misericordia eius, ut uelis, sed cum uoles, tu utique uoles."

We can discern some of the significance of this anachronism for Augustine's theology of grace if we return to the problem of Paul's continuity with Saul. At first glance, it seems to matter little whether the anachronism of conversion can be contained within a single lifetime. Suppose that the gift of new desire does set off Saul the persecutor from Paul the preacher. It certainly does not follow that Saul could have anticipated (even in principle) the onset of conversion. Prior to grace his desires left him no room to formulate any such expectation, however feeble. But in the logic of divine anticipation, it is not Saul's perspective that counts. From Paul's point of view there will be in looking back no time when God was wholly absent from his life. The bleak time of Saul becomes in retrospect not the time of abandonment by God, but the period of Paul's own perverse unwillingness to call to mind God's continual presence. The choice between these two perspectives carries enormous import for Augustine's conception of conversion. If Saul is allowed to define the time before grace, Paul's reception of grace consigns his old life to oblivion, and he never needs to turn back to face it in memory. The anachronism of conversion will have reached its terminus in the singular gift of new desire. If, however, Paul's perspective defines the scope of conversion, then his efforts at finding a beginning will bring even Saul under the recollection of grace. The anachronism of conversion will have swallowed up time in an asymptotic approximation of eternity.

Augustine attempted inconsistently to define conversion from both perspectives during the Pelagian controversy. His failure to notice the poor fit between the revised personae of Paul and Saul obscured his resolution of will's internal division – the one challenge neither Pelagius nor Plato had been able to meet. But it is abundantly clear which perspective served his purposes best. Saul's darkened visage plunged the sinful will into an irredeemable past and denied grace access to the very roots of sin. To the degree that Augustine allowed Saul to personify his case against the Pelagians, he was in no better position than they were to penetrate the mystery of iniquity. It is only when he took Paul as his point of departure that he gained his vantage on the redemption of the past. This Paul, the one who relived his sins under grace, Augustine had met with in himself, when he wrote of his own conversion and reclaimed for grace what once was lost to sin.

IRRESISTIBLE GRACE

Those who expect to find incoherence in Augustine's description of human freedom as the effect of grace, not its precondition, inherit the misgivings of Julian of Eclanum. To Julian's eyes, a will circumscribed on all sides by necessity could never be construed as free, however much the necessity shifted in favor of virtue. It was the very language of necessity that irked. Having no choice but to sin, the sinner sinned without responsibility (*sine reatu*), and having no choice but to pursue the good, the saint possessed glory without the bother of holiness (*sine cura sanctitatis*).[70] Augustine understood that the language of necessity could mislead the unwary into supposing that grace was something like an irresistible force meeting an immovable object. But once he had introduced the element of necessity into conversion in *Ad Simplicianum*, he never disowned it later on. If Julian insisted on calling its presence to everyone's attention, then Augustine was happy to admit that grace worked to efface the possibility of sin. As an end more than a present reality, this effacement would secure the blessed life from death and all manner of vulnerability to deleterious change, and for that reason the necessity of grace's effect was "an altogether most blessed necessity."[71] His main caveat to Julian was not to confuse necessity with force, for "what is more absurd than to say that someone unwillingly wills what is good?"[72]

---

[70] *C. Iul. op. imp.* 1.102.

[71] *Ibid.*, 1.103 (CSEL 85, 120, 7–12): "beatissima est ista omnino necessitas, qua necesse est feliciter vivere et in eadem vita necesse est non mori, necesse est in deterius non mutari. Hac necessitate, si necessitas etiam ipsa dicenda est, non premuntur sancti angeli, sed fruuntur; nobis autem est futura, non praesens." ("Altogether most blessed is the necessity which makes it necessary to live happily, and in this life of happiness never to perish or change for the worse. This necessity, if indeed it should be called such, does not press the holy angels but is enjoyed by them. For us, however, it is a future and not a present necessity.")

[72] *C. Iul. op. imp.* 1.101 (CSEL 85, 119, 24–25): "quid absurdius quam ut dicatur nolens velle quod bonum est?"

Augustine allowed for at least two ways for necessity to cancel choice, one of which clearly violated the will's freedom. The idea of being forced against our will runs counter to freedom of choice in that our power of choice is met and overwhelmed by an opposing power. Choice drops out because will drops out: "If one is forced, one does not will."[73] It is when necessity is allied with force that Augustine dissociates necessity and grace. But suppose, to take the other case, that our desires are all drawn towards a singular object of attraction. In that case choice disappears in our single-minded love for the beloved. There is no possibility of choice here, because alternative objects of attraction cannot be motivated. Nevertheless our power to will remains intact in the purity of our love.

Sympathetic interpreters of Augustine tend to latch on to the latter kind of necessity in order to charge Julian and other Pelagians with obtuse disregard of the dynamics of choice. Burnaby, for instance, has Julian worry about the loss of *libertas indifferentiae*, or freedom defined as "the absolute power of choice between alternatives," while Augustine offers the better understanding of free choice (*liberum arbitrium*) as "spontaneity, the self-determination inherent in the will as such." Spontaneity is threatened only in the face of force, the one face of necessity that Augustine refuses from his perspective on sin and grace. The moral of Julian's worry is that the Pelagians defend the power of choice in abstraction from the way in which we are actually motivated; hence they defend a baseless freedom.[74] TeSelle develops a critique very similar to Burnaby's. He views Augustine's interest in necessity as an interest in the motivational constraints on how we will. Because we are always oriented to act in particular ways and lack the power to change our fundamental orientations at will, we are incapable of acting without drawing upon a context of prior motivations. This sort of necessity does not abrogate freedom, but it does rule out "the complete arbitrariness ascribed to it by Pelagius."[75] Once again Pelagians are caught playing with the abstraction of naked possibility, leaving Augustine the psychologist to address the necessities of actual willing.

---

[73] *C. Iul. op. imp.* 1.101 (CSEL 85, 119, 23–24): "Si enim cogitur, non vult."
[74] Burnaby, *Amor Dei*, 227–28.   [75] TeSelle, *Augustine the Theologian*, 291.

A less sympathetic interpreter of Augustine, John Rist, does not find that the nuances of necessity compensate for the elimination of choice. He takes Augustine's claim that we cannot be forced to will (*cogi velle*) to mean that compulsion always pits us against an external opposing force: "What we should call psychological compulsions are not compulsions for Augustine. They are simply the individual working out his own nature."[76] Like Julian, Rist denies that any genuine description of freedom can consistently qualify choice as both necessary and free. The so-called liberty of spontaneity, which would have us single-mindedly pursue some object of attraction, is akin, to use his image, to iron filings being drawn to a magnet.[77] Unless the saints have the option to reject the advances of the spirit, their freedom under grace is a cruel sham. Rist's emphasis on the integrity of choice does not commit him, however, to what Burnaby calls the liberty of indifference. The possibility of rejecting God's call does not require those called to feel absolute indifference to the calling; it merely requires that whatever attraction it holds for them, they retain the option of refusing their assent. Rist's Pelagius enjoys a "state of love for God made the greater for the possibility of rejection."[78]

On his interpretation of Pelagius, Rist is surely closer to the truth than either Burnaby or TeSelle, who lend greater credibility to Augustine by attributing a crude libertarian view of freedom to his opponents.[79] Their attribution is implausible because it has Pelagians unaccountably adopt a position far more extreme than their theoretical needs would warrant. In order to highlight freedom of choice, Pelagians need to maintain a margin of distinction between how we will and how we are

---

[76] John Rist, "Augustine on Free Will and Predestination," *Journal of Theological Studies* N.S. 20 (1969), 420–47, here 422.   [77] *Ibid.*, 430.   [78] *Ibid.*, 442.
[79] Guy De Broglie has suggested that it is anachronistic for modern commentators to pose liberty from necessity, with its emphasis on choice, against Augustine's freedom from constraint, with its emphasis on desire. See his "Pour une meilleure intelligence du *De correptione et gratia*," *Augustinus Magister* 3 (Paris, 1954), 319–21. If liberty from necessity is taken to mean freedom from the claim of any kind of reason or motive for acting, De Broglie is right. No one in late antiquity would have envisioned so radical (and empty) a freedom. Short of radical independence from motivating desires and reasons, however, the ability to choose expresses a form of freedom Augustine should in some way have been able to address. The Pelagians gave him plenty of opportunity.

motivated to will. But an absolute distinction, expressed as indifference to motives or as arbitrariness, undercuts the role that choice is supposed to play in appropriating action.

When Julian criticizes Augustine for freeing sinners from responsibility and saints from sanctity, the source of his objection is his belief that we cannot be identified with what we do if in our acting we must always follow the lead of our strongest desires. The intuitions governing his view of the appropriation of grace are something like this. Whenever we recognize the good in action through our knowledge of God's law, the good moves us to desire it. If it did not, we could hardly be said to have recognized the good. Desire for the good nevertheless does not overwhelm our capacity for choice. We choose to act upon our desires and without having our choice determined wholly by their influence. The limited independence that our act of choice has from what we may happen to know or desire emerges out of two necessary preconditions for appropriating grace. First, knowledge of good must motivate as well as inform us, and second, we must not be determined by this motivation. Without the first condition, grace cannot initiate action, and without the second, we have no stance outside the initiative from which to act on our own. It is important to Pelagians such as Julian that after knowledge of the good has elicited the appropriate desires in us there remain something left over in us – free choice – to be able to identify with those desires. The same should hold true with the appropriation of sin, the only difference being that the knowledge involved is of a good inferior to one delimited by God's law. In neither case would it make sense, however, to drive Pelagian intuitions toward libertarian independence from motivating desires. For unless the good engages us, there is nothing for us to appropriate.

Once free choice has been returned from the ethereal abstraction of motiveless choosing, there turns out to be remarkably little to distinguish Rist's Pelagius from the Augustine advocated by Burnaby and TeSelle. Both TeSelle and Burnaby would gladly emend Augustine's view of the reception of grace with the possibility of refusal. They recognize, as did

Rist, that the texts do not support such a possibility. Augustine's development of the suitable calling is explicitly directed against the notion that the elect can reject their callings. Nevertheless, Burnaby thinks that only the old Augustine, the one "whose love has grown cold," would have insisted on the point, and TeSelle believes that the spirit of Augustine's theology is respected if a revised operation of grace infallibly gives the inclination to act, but leaves the final decision to the recipient.[80] Their principal difference from Rist seems to be that Rist takes Augustine's insistence on the irresistibility of grace to poison his entire theology, right down to its foundations, while Burnaby and TeSelle introduce the right of refusal as an attractive emendation of an otherwise healthy point of view.[81]

Both sides are mistaken, though Rist's mistake is less profound than the one made by Augustine's admirers. The issue of resistibility is a nonstarter for explicating the appropriation of grace. A little reflection on the nature of our reserve towards grace bears this out. Suppose that grace gives us delight in justice, as Augustine says it does when the spirit introduces us to a new order of desires. This order, the order of justice, sets knowledge of the good before our reckoning. Given that Augustine emphasizes God's gift of delight in justice, leaving the cognitive aspect of delight implied, approbation must always be a part of our recognition of the good. No Pelagian need object to this, however, since, as I have tried to indicate, it is important to the Pelagian view of grace that knowledge of the good be able to motivate us. Pelagians then, of course, go on to say that we may resist this motivation from our position outside God's gracious initiative. Augustine does not say against this that we

---

[80] Burnaby, *Amor Dei*, 230–31, and TeSelle, *Augustine the Theologian*, 330–31.

[81] Rist's engaging article bristles with indignation. In an appendix to his analysis of predestination and freedom of the will ("Augustine on Free will," 442–47), he explores the possibility of a connection between Augustine's understanding of the reception of grace and his (notorious) justification of the use of force to compel schismatics to rejoin the fold. It is clear that Rist finds complicity between theology that fails to respect free choice and ecclesiology that accepts coercive force as a prod to instruction. The connection between Augustine's theology and power politics has been more recently explored by Elaine Pagels in "The Politics of Paradise: Augustine's Exegesis of Genesis 1–3 versus that of John Chrysostom," *Harvard Theological Review* 78 (1985), 67–99.

have no capacity to resist, but for him the source of that capacity is not some special reserve we maintain to protect our autonomy, but our will held back in mortgage to its past. What Pelagians see as a source of freedom, a way to make knowledge of the good our own, Augustine sees as bondage, the resistance that habit offers to renewal. From Augustine's point of view, our reserve towards grace must be eliminated altogether before we can be said to be genuinely liberated. Pelagian fascination with resistibility rests on unanalyzed intuitions about the appropriation of knowledge, and if TeSelle and Burnaby wish to emend Augustine's view of grace to make grace resistible, they are endeavoring to do surgery with a meat ax. Little of Augustine's thought after 396 will survive the operation. If resistibility is as indispensable a feature of grace as they seem to think it is, it would be better to have an honest Pelagius than a mutilated Augustine.

But Rist is no more correct than TeSelle and Burnaby to assume that resistibility must always be a feature of the appropriation of grace. His sharp criticism of Augustine for omitting it merely begs the issue of appropriation in favor of Julian. Commentators with very different sensibilities, who profess to reject Julian's refined Pelagianism, end up begging the very same issue against Augustine, largely because Augustine has given them so many red herrings to chase. It was, for instance, obfuscating and unresponsive of Augustine to inform Julian and other Pelagians bothered by the necessity of grace's effect that human consent can be voluntary and necessary at the same time. But when in 1946 Xavier Léon-Dufour published his opinion that Augustine's psychology of willing ruled out God's usurpation of human consent to grace, he epitomized the hope some scholars had for resting the appropriation of grace on the necessarily voluntary character of consent.[82] This hope lay behind Portalié's attempt to reconcile Augustine's emphasis on

---

[82] Xavier Léon-Dufour, "Grâce et libre arbitre chez saint Augustin: A propos de *Consentire vocatione dei...propriae voluntatis est*," *Recherches de science religieuse* 33 (1946), 129–63. His line of thought has been expounded more recently and with great insight by Isabelle Bochet, in her *Saint Augustin et le désir de Dieu* (Paris: Etudes augustiniennes, 1982), 302–34.

the efficacy of grace to freedom of choice,[83] and Gilson's claim, criticized by Rist, that "grace can be irresistible without being constraining."[84] And although Burnaby felt that the old bishop had lost sight of the voluntary character of responsive love, he continued to think that Augustine's rejection of *cogi velle* as a contradiction in terms carried implicitly his recognition that grace could be refused. The necessity of having an unforced will for willing led him to surmise on Augustine's behalf that "all choice is free choice, all will is free will."[85]

However much Augustine may have encouraged his readers to take these leaps of interpretation, his actual analysis of the power behind all expressions of will cannot be read to establish free choice as an inherent attribute of willing. His analysis appears in *De spiritu et littera* as *obiter dicta* to resolving the question of whether faith falls under human power.[86] Because Augustine takes faith to mean consent to the knowledge that love of God brings, he is working to put faith under human power in the sense that any act of will (in this case, consent) qualifies as an expression of power. But before he can come to this conclusion, he must make sure that his readers understand why expressions of will are always expressions of power – hence his aside on the nature of the connection. To understand Augustine's argument it is helpful to note that he has in mind the connection between successful acts of will and expressions of power. He is aware that we can will what we have no ability to accomplish. But whenever we will successfully, our willing expresses our power to act. Doubtless for many cases of acting, this is not a terribly profound revelation – our power to will is trivially our power. Yet when action is performed unwillingly or

[83] Eugène Portalié, *A Guide to the Thought of Saint Augustine*, trans. Ralph J. Bastian (Chicago: Henry Regnery, 1960), 196–204. His original work appeared as the encyclopedia article "Augustin," in *Dictionnaire de Théologie Catholique*, vol. 1 (Paris: 1902), cols. 2268–2472.

[84] Etienne Gilson, *The Christian Philosophy of Saint Augustine*, trans. L. E. M. Lynch (New York: Random House, 1960), 155. See also Rist, "Augustine on Free Will," 434–35: "Though Gilson does not say it, his Augustine is a moral determinist: fallen men are puppets." Gilson's original study, *Introduction à l'étude de saint Augustin*, predated Léon-Dufour's 1946 study on grace and free choice.

[85] Burnaby, *Amor Dei*, 227.   [86] *De spir. et litt.* 31.53.

under coercion, acting might be supposed to negate rather than express the power of the person coerced to act.

Augustine clarifies the connection between willing and having power to act under compulsion in his analysis of compulsory action:

We are not accustomed to saying that someone who acted unwillingly acted under his own power. Although, if we should attend to the matter more precisely, even what someone is forced to do he does by means of his will if he does it at all. But since he would prefer to do otherwise, he is said for that reason to act against his will; in other words, he acts unwillingly. Obviously some evil compels him to act in that he does unwillingly what willingly he would avoid or remove from himself. For if his will were such that he should prefer not acting to not suffering the evil, no doubt he would resist the source of compulsion and not act. And so if he does act, even without a full or free will, he acts nevertheless in no other way than by means of his will. And because his will issues in effect, we cannot say that the power for acting was lacking to him.[87]

As is clear from his redescription, Augustine does not claim that it is impossible for someone to act unwillingly (*nolens* or *inuitus*). Forced willing (*cogi velle*), as opposed to unwilling action, is incoherent. External opposition sets limits to what we can will, but does not influence how we will within those limits.[88] When physical forces or impediments have reduced agents to mere objects of nature, the external limits on willing have closed to exclude the domain of willing altogether. To force willing is to eliminate it altogether, which is why "forced willing" is an oxymoron. Compulsory acting is an entirely different phenomenon from the specter of forced willing, and its relation to

---

[87] *Ibid.*, 31.53 (CSEL 60, 210, 4–14): "neque enim dici solet quispiam potestate fecisse, si quid fecit inuitus. quamquam, si subtilius aduertamus, etiam quod quisque inuitus facere cogitur, si facit, uoluntate facit; sed quia mallet aliud, ideo inuitus, hoc est nolens facere dicitur. malo quippe aliquo facere conpellitur, quod uolens euitare uel a se remouere facit quod cogitur. nam si tanta uoluntas sit, ut malit hoc non facere quam illud non pati, cogenti procul dubio resistit nec facit. ac per hoc, si facit, non quidem plena et libera uoluntate, sed tamen non facit nisi uoluntate; quam uoluntatem quia effectus consequitur, non possumus dicere potestatem defuisse facienti."

[88] The distinction between compulsion and force is, as far as I can tell, consistently reflected in Augustine's use of terms. Although he will speak of "being forced or compelled to act" (*cogi facere*), he does not conflate this locution with "being forced to will" (*cogi velle*).

external force is incidental at most. Take as illustration a case that troubled Aristotle.[89] The captain of a ship encounters a storm at sea, and in order to protect the lives of his crew, he decides to lighten his ship's load by throwing cargo overboard. Aristotle had some difficulty deciding whether the captain acted voluntarily. For Augustine, however, the answer is evident. The captain is the man who is compelled by some evil to do unwillingly what willingly he would avoid. His action is compelled, but in so far as any action must be done by will, his action is also voluntary.

In order to appreciate the import of Augustine's answer, we need to recognize that it is not the storm that compels the captain to dump his cargo. The storm merely sets the stage for possible action. It is what the storm occasions *within* the captain, his fear of shipwreck and death, that compels him to act against his desire to protect his cargo. If the value of the goods to be lost were to weigh greater for him than his own life or the lives of his crew, then he would not act, even in the face of the storm. But if he does act, he manifests both power and will in achieving his effect. Compelled action, such as the captain's, counts as "voluntary" (*voluntate*) because all forms of compulsion, *contra* Rist, originate from within. They may be occasioned externally by the threat of an outside power, but compulsions always have their immediate source in the conflicting desires of the agent. Augustine would not then be contradicting himself to claim that a saint sometimes sinned both unwillingly (*nolens*) and voluntarily (*voluntate*). That would be an oblique way of describing the unhappy resolution of an internally divided will.

In their rush to reclaim free choice for Augustine, his interpreters have tended to insist on the connection between acting and willing out of the context of compulsory action. That allows them to claim that, necessity notwithstanding, we choose to accept grace; it is not forced upon us. And having chosen successfully, our act of choice, per Augustine's analysis, expresses what we had the power to do. But taken out of the context of compulsory action, the bare insistence on the voluntary quality

---

[89] *Nicomachean Ethics* 3.1 (1110a1–19).

of acts of will amounts to no more than the uninformative tautology that acts of will engage the will. Augustine himself is not always above this kind of tautology mongering. When he resolves to answer whether faith rests in our power, he ignores the complexity of his own analysis of power and rests human appropriation of faith on the necessarily voluntary character of consent:

Now see whether anyone will believe if he wills not to believe, or not believe if he wills to believe. But this is absurd, for what is it to believe if not to consent to the truth of what has been said? And consent is always an expression of will. Faith is certainly in our power.[90]

But lest anyone read too much human autonomy into the tautology, he claims that the will to believe is always given by God in anticipation of human consent,[91] a qualification which led Léon-Dufour to read *De spiritu et littera* as Augustine's definitive statement on the reconciliation of grace and free choice. He takes Augustine to have sorted out divine and human roles in redemption as pure giving and pure receiving, roles whose irreducible natures would emerge in the analysis of the act of faith.[92] In this, Léon-Dufour tries to turn obfuscation into a virtue. Augustine offers his readers the tantalizing suggestion that consent holds the answer to how recipients of grace manage to appropriate grace into their own willing, but he also misleads his readers into thinking that the tautologous connection between consenting and willing can somehow be made to serve as the answer. That it can never do so is obvious if we remember that compulsory action is just as necessarily an expression of will as consent is.

ALIENATION AND AUTONOMY

Grace issues in freedom, but not the freedom to resist grace. "Freedom" to resist grace is not, however, genuine freedom but bondage to sin. Somehow grace, freedom, and virtue all come

---

[90] *De spir. et litt.* 31.54 (CSEL 60, 211, 12–16): "uide nunc utrum quisque credat, si noluerit, aut non credat, si uoluerit. quod si absurdum est – quid est enim credere nisi consentire uerum esse quod dicitur? consensio autem utique uolentis est –, perfecto fides in potestate est."   [91] *De spir. et litt.* 34.60.
[92] Léon-Dufour, "Grâce et libre arbitre," 143.

together for Augustine. But how? The answer to this must be as much constructed as inferred from what he says about the nature of grace and its appropriation. Right up to his death, he continued to ponder the work of grace and its influence on human agency. Many unresolved tensions in his reflections remained with him as he broke ranks from antique philosophy and Pelagian theology to square virtue with his conception of grace. We expect too much if we want a tidy resolution to so radical a break. Nevertheless, with a little digging the essential features of Augustine's originality emerge in relief. We might profitably begin with the remark in *De spiritu et littera* that so captivated the attention of Léon-Dufour: "Assuredly God works in us even the very will to believe and in all things does his mercy anticipate us, but consenting to God's calling or dissenting from it belongs, as I have said, to our own will."[93]

Léon-Dufour was selective in his attention, keeping his focus squarely on consent and its anticipation by God's mercy, leaving dissent out of his account entirely. He did of course notice that Augustine paired consent with dissent, but he assumed, not unreasonably, that dissent had to do with reprobation, a topic that was best left to an investigation of predestination.[94] If Augustine did intend to have dissent from God's calling denominate the reprobate, then Léon-Dufour could hardly be blamed for wanting to avoid the topic. The issue of reprobation has always been the bane of scholarship on Augustine, conjuring up as it does images of condemned infants and helpless sinners cut off from the mercy of God. Back in 1892 the Benedictine monk Odilo Rottmanner set out the logic behind Augustine's understanding of predestination. There are two classes of human beings, one saved and one damned, which respectively exemplify God's mercy and God's justice. God

---

[93] *De spir. et litt.* 34.60 (CSEL 60, 220, 17–20): "profecto et ipsum uelle credere deus operatur in homine et in omnibus misericordia eius praeuenit nos, consentire autem uocationi dei uel ab ea dissentire, sicut dixi, propriae uoluntatis est."

[94] Léon-Dufour, "Grâce et libre arbitre," 158–59: "Le lecteur aura sans doute remarqué que les rapports de la grâce et du libre arbitre ont été exposés sans faire appel à la théorie de la prédestination. Aussi bien notre enquête n'a-t-elle eu pour but que de préciser avec saint Augustin quelle était la *structure* de l'acte de foi (informée par la charité, selon le langage de l'École)."

alone determines who will fall under mercy; those not selected remain in the mass of sinners on account of divine judgment.[95] The problem for Augustine's apologists has been that there is no accounting for divine judgment other than by the unhappy device of original sin.[96] This is to explain the obscure by the more obscure. I have no intention of entering the morass of confusion that awaits the investigator of reprobation. Léon-Dufour was right to assume that the predestination of reprobates plays to different interests in Augustine's theology than his better-developed views of the work of grace. But I do not suppose that reprobation necessarily goes along with dissent, and in the passage in question, the placement of dissent next to consent associates both acts of will with the anticipatory mercy of God.

If it can be allowed that God's calling of the elect represents not the hypothetical moment of an offer to be accepted or refused, but divine care for the shape of an entire human life, then dissent remains a possibility for the graced will. The saints do sin, even when grace abounds. They act on desires displeasing to God, and so dissent from the way God calls them to live. Whether or not Augustine meant to bring dissent under grace at that precise moment in *De spiritu et littera* (and I doubt that he did), he will not be able to avoid the difficulties for his theology raised by the conjunction of grace and sin. He cleans up Paul's life under grace for Julian's benefit, but his darkening of the time before conversion, when not even the beginnings of virtue are apparent, commits him to placing the divided will and the possibility of involuntary sin in the time of grace. Since it is in *De spiritu et littera* that Augustine moves virtue root and

---

[95] Odilo Rottmanner, *Der Augustinismus* (Munich, 1892), 9–12. His study has been rendered into French by J. Liébaert as "L'Augustinisme: Etude d'histoire doctrinale," *Mélange de science religieuse* 6 (1949), 31–48. For a critique of Rottmanner's interpretation, to my mind unsuccessful, see François-Joseph Thonnard, "La Prédestination augustinienne et l'interprétation de O. Rottmanner," *Revue des études augustiniennes* 9 (1963), 259–87.

[96] Lebourlier, "Essai," 298, notes that Augustine commits himself in *Ad Simplicianum* to a theory of mass condemnation in Adam, and he believes that this turn in Augustine's thought hopelessly obscures human responsibility for sin. For sanguine accounts of the connection between original sin and human responsibility, see De Broglie, "Pour une meilleure intelligence," 317–37, and Malcolm Alflatt, "The Responsibility for Involuntary Sin in Saint Augustine," *Recherches augustiniennes* 10 (1975), 171–86.

branch under grace, he faces even there the issue of virtue's vulnerability to unredeemed desires. These desires have in the move from law to grace become alien to the agent's perceived interests, but as Augustine's own analysis of compulsory action requires, "alien" does not mean that they do not express the agent's will. To clarify Augustine's logic, if not his intentions, it is useful to take him at his word and keep the association between dissent and mercy, moving sin under grace.

Once under grace, sin is a source of some theological discomfort for Augustine. If God has sovereignty over the human will and grace is efficacious, then why does sin continue to be part of the lives of the saints? Two equally unacceptable conclusions suggest themselves. Either saints have the power to refuse grace, in which case its efficacy is thrown into doubt, or God becomes the author of sin, in which case his sovereignty is maligned. Wishing to protect both sovereignty and efficacy, which together seem to crowd out the reality of sin, Augustine is inclined to thread the needle. He introduces to his conception of God's sovereignty over the human will a distinction that allows sin narrow passage into the saintly life. The distinction is well presented to Firmus the catechumen, who, as you will recall, planned to postpone his baptism until God delivered up the will to faith:

It is, of course, true that nothing happens unless either God does it or permits it to be done, and since God wills both in doing and in permitting, nothing at all happens should he not will it. Nevertheless it is correct to say that whatever displeases God happens against his will. God yet permits evil things to happen, for he has the power to make from the evil that is not his the good that is his.[97]

The idea that God wills sin without really willing it, that is, by permitting it and then turning it to good effect, is of some vintage in Augustine's outlook. In the second response to Simplician, he cautions his readers to understand that God's hardening of Pharaoh's heart means that God withholds mercy from Pharaoh, not that God induces Pharaoh to sin.[98] Back then

[97] *Ep.* 2*.8 (OSA 46B, 78, 217–23): "Nihil enim prorsus fit, nisi quod aut ipse facit aut fieri ipse permittit, et quoniam uolens facit, uolens et permittit, nihil fit omnino, si nolit. Vere tamen dicitur quidquid ei displicet contra eius fieri uoluntatem. Permittit tamen, ut fiant mala, quia potens est etiam de malis non suis sua facere bona."
[98] *Ad. Simpl.* 1.2.15.

Augustine was using the distinction between production and permission to give God a controlling but innocent interest in the sin of reprobates. Out of the evil permitted to hardened sinners God has harvested the dubious good of instructing the godly with someone else's punishment, a benefit which looks rather too much like spiritual cannibalism.[99] But by the time he addresses his friend Firmus, his use of the distinction has broadened. No longer does God's will to permit sin single out those abandoned to judgment. To the saints, God permits sin in order to produce virtue. This reversal of sin's effect turns on the spirit's gift of love for God. "To such as love God, God works to turn all things to their good; utterly all things," Augustine reassures us, "to the point that if some should lose their way and stray, God makes even this very thing serve their good, for they return further humbled and instructed."[100]

Firmus receives the sum of Augustine's wisdom on God's two forms of willing in a rule for differentiating human and divine roles in sin and virtue respectively. We act on our own when we sin; jointly with God when we recover from sin. Thus whenever his love fails, either because he is taken in unwittingly by his vice ("uitio tuo nesciens deciperis"), or because he is a knowing slave to it ("sciens uinceris"), Firmus is to attribute this failure to himself and not to God. Otherwise God's love goes along with him to win virtue, and the credit is God's.[101]

Augustine's theological fix to the problem of sinning saints is not without ambiguity. In distinguishing two different operations of divine willing, he does nothing to discourage the idea that God acts in successive moments, at one time drawing the human will irresistibly towards spirit, at another allowing it to slip back into habits of the flesh. The victory of grace begins to look suspiciously like fate, a resemblance remarked upon often by the Pelagians, and sin under grace, because it affords saints a vehicle for independent self-expression on the way to a predetermined end, emerges as the arena of human freedom.

---

[99] *Ibid.*, 1.2.18.

[100] *De corr. et gr.* 9.24 (OSA 24, 320): "Talibus Deus diligentibus eum omnia cooperatur in bonum; usque adeo prorsus omnia, ut etiam si qui eorum deviant et exorbitant, etiam hoc ipsum eis faciat proficere in bonum, quia humiliores redeunt atque doctiores."   [101] *Ep.* 2*.11.

Augustine disavows the analogy between fate and grace on the grounds that fate determines good and evil wills alike, whereas grace leaves sin its own agency.[102] But his disavowal retains the very asymmetry that threatens to turn redemption into self-effacement. John Freccero captures the irony superbly when he observes that Augustine's most influential readers – Dante, Petrarch, and Rousseau – invert his intended message in the *Confessiones* by "making sin the principle of individuation."[103]

The test for Augustine's theology is not whether sinners can refuse their introductions to grace but whether saints already under grace can recall their sins without invoking a lost freedom. Obviously Augustine did not intend conversion to begin the romance of sin. He meant grace to individuate the soul and restore to it the identity it was losing to sin. We can still wonder, however, whether human entrance into the cosmic plot of redemption, whose ending has all the saints bear the image of God, does not in retrospect lend the life of sin an identity and interest all its own.

Augustine's most memorable recollection of sin is doubtless of his theft of pears in the company of other young adolescents, an episode he recounts at unusual length in the second book of the *Confessiones*. Freccero believes that the pear tree stands in allegorically for the biblical Tree of the Knowledge of Good and Evil.[104] Augustine's theft of *poma*, also the Vulgate's expression for forbidden fruit, is thus taken to reenact the elemental human desire to claim God's freedom from all restriction or limitation as its own. The relative worthlessness of Augustine's object of desire, pears of unexceptional taste and form, underscores his

---

[102] *C. duas ep. Pel.* 2.6.12.

[103] Here is Freccero's observation in greater detail: "All that happens in a confession happens to the sinner; as every reader of Dante knows, the truly interesting people are in hell. Similarly, Petrarch's portrait of himself as sinner is essential for his characterizing himself as unique. By the time the genre reaches Rousseau and uniqueness seems more and more elusive, the claim to sinfulness requires virtuoso efforts. This turning-around of Augustine's avowed purpose marks the origin of what might be called the hagiography of the sinner. Because saints are meant to represent the image of God, they all look pretty much alike." Cited from p. 21 of his "Autobiography and Narrative," in *Reconstructing Individualism: Autonomy, Individuality, and the Self in Western Thought*, ed. Thomas Heller, Morton Sosna, and David E. Wellbery (Stanford: Stanford University Press, 1986).

[104] Freccero, "Autobiography," 27.

delight in sinning itself, the savor of freedom from God: "I loved my falling away, not what I was falling away to, but the very falling away itself I loved."[105] His delight in the illicit autonomy of sin was a moment of conversion to self, to be revealed later in book VIII, under the shade of a fig tree, as an aversion from self. Freccero contends that the logic of the conversion narrative will require the identification of the two trees in the *Confessiones*, pear (the fall) and fig (the return), so that in a single turning from aversion from self to conversion to God, conversion is completed and its story may be told.[106] Viewed from the perspective of his conversion to God in book VIII, Augustine's autobiography moves under the eternal eye of biblical allegory. His converted self narrates all that remains to autobiography proper – the story of his time-bound self, undone by sin and mortality. In recounting conversion, "the story-teller," Freccero wryly notes, "pretends somehow to have survived his own death."[107]

Unlike Freccero, however, I do not believe that conversion closes the book on sin. For if I am correct in my suggestion that Paul's inner conflict under grace shows up in Augustine just prior to his conversion, rumors that Augustine survived his own death are greatly exaggerated. There is, to be sure, a radical change in point of view associated with his conversion, and it is expressed in how he recollects sin. We can follow Freccero and take the episode of the pear tree as his paradigmatic recollection. Stealing from the Tree of the Knowledge of Good and Evil, usurping freedom enjoyed by God alone, what does Augustine learn looking back at his original sin about the nature of sin?

At first glance, very little. He does recognize that because sin begins in forgetfulness of God, sin gets expressed in the sinner's perverse and unwitting imitation of God. We tend in being moved to sin, in other words, to put ourselves in place of the standard of value we have abandoned. In his own iniquitous

---

[105] *Conf.* 2.4.9 (CCSL 27, 22, 18–19): "amaui defectum meum, non illud, ad quod deficiebam, sed defectum meum ipsum amaui."

[106] Freccero, "Autobiography," 22, 28. Neil Forsyth's analysis of the *Confessiones*, under the subheading "The Two Trees" (*The Old Enemy: Satan and the Combat Myth*, 409–18), also emphasizes the way in which autobiography becomes allegory for a cosmic plot.

[107] Freccero, "Autobiography," 20. Cf. Forsyth, *The Old Enemy*, 413.

assertion of freedom, Augustine claims to have mimicked God's freedom in form but not in substance.[108] God acts without motives, for having motives implies being moved to act in response to some perceived good. If God were moved to act, that would be as if the good originated from outside its source. God creates *ex nihilo*, and so must be free from motives. Augustine attributes a similar freedom to himself when he insists that he sinned without motivation. Looking back at his theft, he denies that he was moved either by the promise of material gain or by the threat of material loss. His was wholly an act of self-will, done in the company of others, but no more motivated by their approbation than by any other external standard of value.[109] Thus he mimics God's freedom in form. But Augustine is not God, and his willing does not furnish its own motives. He must have been moved to steal, if he is to have acted intelligibly. Yet having acted under a shadowy similitude of omnipotence ("tenebrosa omnipotentiae similitudine"), he cannot recall having had sufficient motive to sin. He is left with the mystery of unmotivated evil.

Augustine never solves this mystery in book II, anywhere else in the *Confessiones*, or indeed anywhere in his writings prior or subsequent to the *Confessiones*. "Voluntary sin" remained a highly problematic conception for him; for unless compulsion were involved, sinning seemed to violate the principle that acts of will must be motivated by reasons the agent would find compelling. If acts of sin were in fact unmotivated or at least insufficiently motivated by how their agents perceived the end of acting to be good, then by virtue of his own critique of Pelagianism, Augustine would seem forced to conclude that voluntary acts of sin are not intelligible as actions and therefore cannot be attributed to agents. Matters seem even worse for him when we consider that involuntary sin must originate in voluntary sin (the mystery of original sin). The specter of unmotivated evil threatens to unhinge his entire philosophy by rendering sin *as a reality* unintelligible.

But it is easy to draw the wrong moral from Augustine's allegory of (his) original sin in *Confessiones* II if we fail to keep in

---

[108] *Conf.* 2.6.14. [109] *Ibid.*, 2.5.10.

mind the perspective from which he tells it. It is only *in retrospect* that he is able to discover that the motives he had in sinning were insufficient to rationalize his sin as good. This is certainly not the sort of insight he could have attributed to himself at the time of his theft. Then he acted for what he supposed were good reasons, and in recollection he suggests indirectly what they were – his need for friends, his desire not be ridiculed, his sense of adventure. When he adds to those reasons the caveat, "but these were not enough to make sense of my sin," we ought to take his sense of bemusement at his past self as indicative of a more profound gain in intelligibility. Augustine comes to understand that his actions, when represented under the good of his own creation, lose their intelligibility; they no longer add up to a life worthy of choice, one able to be represented as good. I noted in my opening remarks to chapter 1 that he would need to account for our cognitive access to God's paradigmatic representation of our individual lives as fully intelligible.[110] We have no direct access to this representation, to be sure, but in the knowledge of sin Augustine gives us a way to disavow the false unity of a sinful life, to recognize its disorder. When he recollects his own sin as sin, he discredits its ability to serve as the principle of his life's ordering. This may leave him bemused at having sinned, but his bemusement does not obfuscate his recognition that what he once represented as good was, in retrospect, a misrepresentation. Better knowledge of sin, by a *via negativa*, enables him over time to bring his imperfect representation of himself into conformity with its perfected paradigm in God. Having been made aware of this gradual convergence (the recovery of his self-knowledge), Augustine can recall his delight in sinning and conclude with hindsight, "I was made a wasteland to myself."[111]

Augustine does not romanticize sin, because he never gives his converted self the opportunity to eulogize his past. Sin carries into his conversion as self-alienation, the internal division that grace heals over the course of a lifetime's labor in love. In this life conversion is always unfinished business. Freccero insists on giving temporal closure to conversion because an endless

110 See p. 25 above.
111 *Conf.* 2.10.18 (CCSL 27, 26, 8): "factus sum mihi regio egestatis."

turning to God would run the continual risk of being blocked at any moment – a magnificently Pelagian evocation. "No story of the self," he submits, "can be built on such a threat."[112] What Freccero fails to appreciate is that the timeless perspective of creation, in which individuation over time comes to perfection, is not the narrator's but God's. Augustine's self-knowledge in the *Confessiones* amounts to his (limited) grasp of himself as God knows him. In God's eternal present the internal conflicts of his time-bound will have already been recollected to reflect the triumph of love of justice over iniquity, a condition of freedom that he will later describe, without paradox, as the inability to sin (*non posse peccare*). God's time, however, is not Augustine's time, and he is left to trace the effect of divine action imperfectly in his memory.[113] No temporal being will be able to appropriate the gift of eternity without feeling that it has arrived at the scene of the offer too late. Love's labor begins in the field of memory. The inescapable failure of the saint to complete this labor marks not the limit of God's power to redeem, but the incongruity of time-bound and timeless points of view. Grace's efficacy is never in doubt because God has anticipated (necessarily) all the saint's failures of will. From God's point of view, conversion does have closure. Human beings, having limited access through grace to God's way of viewing things, nevertheless have no way of anticipating their own lives. Because we remain bound to time while in time, we cannot convert or consent to grace simply by entering into an eternal present. Instead consent must be renewed continually, as our minds reach into the past to recollect how our sins have been reclaimed by grace.[114] Freccero can be excused for wanting to end the process prematurely.

---

112 Freccero, "Autobiography," 22.

113 Dominique Doucet takes up the theme of memory as the mirror of divine action when she reads the *Confessiones* as Augustine's Christian adaptation of the classical art of memory. See her "L'*Ars Memoriae* dans les *Confessions*," *Revue des études angustiniennes* 33 (1987), 49–69.

114 Forsyth, *The Old Enemy*, 141, has a keen understanding of the redemptive use of memory: "Memory is the great transforming power once it is graced. The graced mind can begin, as Augustine begins in the second part of his *Confessions*, to extend itself, to comprehend the universal pattern perceived first in the particular life. Personal memory transcends personal time and becomes an image of the timeless, what was for Augustine the eternal present in the mind of God. The fallen past is redeemed and transformed by memory, as sin is redeemed by grace." Needless to say, my understanding of Augustine owes much to his insights.

Augustine himself was never entirely content with only the thread of eternity.

My part reconstruction, part interpretation of Augustine on the appropriation of grace brings us finally to the vexed issue of autonomy. To put it baldly, I am claiming that in terms of how grace operates, the saints live out their lives as the effect in time of an eternal cause. The effect is necessary in the way that events, once they have occurred, are fixed. On this analogy, our lives are set out in advance, predestined in God's eternity, and many philosophers would argue that predestined lives cannot also be free. Augustine, however, is not one of them, and since I happen to think that he is right, nor am I. But the issue of contention is not whether grace and freedom are compatible, but whether freedom is even intelligible apart from grace.[115] Augustine denies that it can be, and his reasoning is as follows. Our acts are genuinely ours if our motives fully account for our having committed them. Our motives have their source in what we perceive to be good. If any account of freedom makes it impossible for us to attribute acts to agents based on their motives, it must be rejected as incoherent, for it would have us designate as "free" actions which are not genuinely attributable to their agents. This is precisely the form of incoherence generated by Pelagian attempts to characterize freedom apart from grace. Agents must choose to be moved by their perceptions of the good, and this involves them in a motiveless choosing of motives. Augustine never dissociates choices from motives in his understanding of freedom, and so does not fall prey to Pelagian incoherence. He characterizes free will as our being moved to act wholly in accordance with the good. This adds to the basic condition of attribution the stipulation that our perceptions of the good suffer from no sinful distortion (i.e., distortion caused by our having measured the good on some standard other than God's). When we represent the good intelligibly, we are moved by God. Hence freedom coextends with grace.

From Augustine's point of view, there are two basic forms of

---

[115] If it were a matter only of their compatibility, freedom could be characterized apart from grace, and Augustine's analysis of grace would have no direct relevance for his understanding of human autonomy.

unfreedom, both of which have their source in rejection of God. One is involuntary sin, and this ranges broadly over internal conflict, finding expression in compulsion, temptation, and weakness of will. The other is voluntary sin, and this refers to our acting without conflict on some misrepresentation of the good. We do not recognize our misrepresentation as such (sin as sin), for otherwise we could not fail to have some experience of internal conflict. Involuntary sin is a form of unfreedom because in it our desires are at odds with one another, and the conflict prevents our motives from fully rationalizing our actions. There always remains a part of us that moves against what has moved us to act. Our actions fail, under such circumstances, to be fully attributable to us, and in that we lack free will. Voluntary sin is a form of unfreedom because in it our motives once again fail to rationalize our actions, not because our motives conflict, but because they fail to correspond to an intelligible representation of the good. We can recognize having experienced this sort of unfreedom only in retrospect, from the perspective of involuntary sin.[116] Grace moves us from voluntary sin to involuntary sin to voluntary adherence to good. To say that it does so of necessity (the doctrine of predestination) is simply to say that knowledge of the good is fully and finally motivating.[117] In being reconciled to God our autonomy is consummated.

The measure of Augustine's originality must be taken against the continuity he shares with the philosopher's quest for

---

[116] Augustine is at a loss to account for the origination of voluntary sin, but I am unconvinced that this weakens his position. He cannot account for why we would have abandoned God and misrepresented the good because there can be no *good* reason for having abandoned God, not if God is the source and measure of the good. Having set out the logic of sin's origination in *De civ. Dei* 12.6, Augustine declares in 12.7 that it would be misguided for anyone to seek an efficient cause (*efficiens causa*) for the evil will. It has its origin in deficiency. See William Babcock, "Augustine on Sin and Moral Agency," *Journal of Religious Ethics* 16 (1988), 45–48 for an adroit discussion of Augustine on deficient causality. The problems raised by sin's origination are, to say the least, far from resolved, but I will say no more about them in this book.

[117] It is axiomatic for Augustine that being determined for the good is part of what it means to be self-determining. Autonomy from God, the source of goodness, rests on the illusion that we define ourselves by creating our own values *ex nihilo*. Because Pagels, "The Politics of Paradise," 93, assumes that Augustine rejected autonomy from God for the dubious reason that he understood God to prefer slaves, much of her interpretation of Augustine is vitiated. For a contemporary defense of the compatibility between freedom and determination for the good, see Susan Wolf, "Asymmetrical Freedom," *Journal of Philosophy* 77 (1980), 151–66.

beatitude. Grace gives the saints greater liberty than either
Pelagius or Plato could have supplied them with, for grace
reaches over time to fortify them with perseverance, "so that
this world, with all its loves, terrors, and delusions, may be
surpassed."[118] There is preserved in the necessity of grace's
effect the ability of virtue to define and maintain the boundaries
of the self against the intrusive chaos of the world. Because
Augustine underwrites human virtue with divine power, he
appears to have excluded human power from virtue. But a
closer look reveals that he has invoked God (creator of value) to
reconnect human power to the perception of order. Love of
justice, the gift of God's spirit, is nothing other than representing
and willing the order of creation. Saints are empowered in will
in so far as they can recollect the ordered self that God has
created them to be. What Augustine has that Pelagius lacks is
appreciation for the blindness in human self-knowledge and the
trial of having to overcome it. Having seen through a glass
darkly his eternal image in God, Augustine abandons all hope
of perfecting his life in a moment of vision. Grace must lay claim
to his entire life, sacrificing none of its intelligibility to the
entropy of sin. But even the graced life, in having to reclaim the
past from sin, remains vulnerable to time. Augustine leaves
virtue to its temporary vulnerability, but not without revealing
the image of eternity in time – the unity of a redeemed memory.

[118] *De corr. et gr.* 12.35 (OSA 24, 348): "ut cum omnibus amoribus, terroribus,
erroribus suis vincatur hic mundus."

Conclusion: Free will

I think it fair to say that my reading of Augustine on human freedom is controversial both as an interpretation of his texts and as a theory of free will. I have already offered a detailed analysis of his texts, and I stand by it as an interpretation of Augustine. In conclusion, I would like to consider more directly the question of theory, or whether Augustine offers us an adequate and illuminating perspective on free will. Here I raise the question of theory explicitly, but I have touched upon it many times over the course of my attempt to articulate the different lines of argument that come together in his conception of will. The task of interpreting him properly on free will could not have been accomplished with much success without having had to engage him over the proper view of free will. I assume as an interpreter of Augustine that he intended to speak the truth, and so when I attribute meanings to his utterances, I draw upon my own sense of what is true and what is not and seek, on a reasonable principle of charity, to attribute to him the least amount of false utterances. This is not to imply that Augustine ought to be forced into the mold of contemporary wisdom. We cannot learn from him if we refuse to respect the integrity of his thought. On the other hand, the fluidity of contemporary wisdom on free will and the strangeness of fourth-century theological discourse make it inevitable that viable interpretations of Augustine on freedom merge our wisdom with his. We cannot interpret him without in some way engaging with him philosophically.

It has been difficult, however, for Augustine's more philosophically minded interpreters to establish the basis for genuine engagement, and consequently what begins as critique ends as eulogy. To take a recent example, Gerard O'Daly has put Augustine's notion of freedom of the will to the test of cogency, found it wanting, even indefensible, and accorded it a suitable epitaph: "it remains a glorious and influential failure."[1] In supposing Augustine to have identified free will with liberty of spontaneity, or freedom from constraint, O'Daly follows a well-established tradition of interpretation in the scholarship. His obvious precursor is Rist, who in 1969 deplored in print the psychological determinism of Augustine's doctrine of grace. If we really have no alternative but to will as God would have us will, then, Rist thinks, freedom from constraint is at best the freedom to be programmed by God, and "this would make us little more than living puppets."[2] O'Daly is more tentative in his conclusions. He grants that Augustine's deterministic account of grace does, in a manner of speaking, admit the possibility of having alternatives for acting. Say that God implants sufficient motivation not to sin in those predestined to salvation; still it would be true that they could have chosen to sin had they motive and opportunity. But O'Daly doubts whether Augustine could commit himself to a deterministic account of grace without also having to commit himself to a deterministic account of sin, and so he can preserve human freedom only at the intolerable cost of having to attribute sin to God. He implies the moral that Rist states outright. Augustine should have stuck with an indeterministic account of grace and based free will on our freedom not to be determined by our desires (the liberty of indifference).[3]

But Augustine never identified free will with freedom from

---

[1] Gerard O'Daly, "Predestination and Freedom in Augustine's Ethics," in *The Philosophy in Christianity*, ed. Godfrey Vesey (Cambridge: Cambridge University Press, 1989), 85–97, see 97.

[2] John Rist, "Augustine on Free Will and Predestination," *Journal of Theological Studies* N.S. 20 (1969), 420–447, see 424–25.

[3] O'Daly has alluded to a serious incoherence in Augustine's theology, but has drawn the wrong moral from it. If, as Augustine insists, some of us are predestinated not to be redeemed, then from God's eternal point of view, there are some of us whose lives are by nature unintelligible. This is inconsistent with his doctrine of creation, but it has no obvious bearing, as far as I can tell, on his account of free will. To remedy the inconsistency, Augustine needs to abandon his doctrine of reprobation, or eternal damnation.

constraint. The latter he generally referred to as *liberum arbitrium*,[4] and we have *liberum arbitrium* by virtue of being able to act on desire. Compulsory action (as in involuntary sin), blindly sinful action (as in voluntary sin), and virtuous action (as under grace) all express *liberum arbitrium*. Only the last, however, expresses free will. Rist and O'Daly were aware of Augustine's distinction between freedom from constraint and free will, and yet when they moved from interpretation to critical evaluation, they could do nothing with it. They could not imagine that being determined to respond to the good was a form of freedom, irreducible to either liberty of indifference or freedom from constraint. Having no other option but to attribute one of these recognizable forms of freedom to Augustine, they went on to test it for compatibility with his deterministic account of grace. Augustine fails their test, not because they judge his particular conception of free will to be inadequate, but because they believe his account of grace to have distorted freedom beyond recognition. Two of his most philosophically minded commentators find his conception of free will simply unintelligible.

Augustine's reception in Rist and O'Daly brings up the two obstacles that stand in the way of our philosophical rapprochement with him on the matter of free will. He seems to dissociate having free will from having more than one possible course of action. Many contemporary philosophers, on the other hand, have advanced the power of alternative action as at least a necessary condition for free will. If we cannot act other than as we act, it is assumed that we cannot be free. Much inconclusive analysis has been heaped upon the meaning of "can" and "cannot" in statements about actions, but the intuition has nevertheless remained strong that our free actions cannot be actions fixed in advance of our decision to act. Augustine lacks this basic intuition. Moreover, he seems to associate not having

---

[4] But not always. In *De spir. et. litt.* 30.52, for example, *liberum arbitrium* refers to free will. For more on Augustine's use of terms in the area of freedom, see John Burnaby, *Amor Dei: A Study of the Religion of St. Augustine* (London: Hodder & Stoughton, 1938), 227, and Etienne Gilson, *The Christian Philosophy of St. Augustine*, trans. L. E. M. Lynch (New York: Random House, 1960), 323–24 n. 85.

free will with having acted contrary to the good. He would insist, for instance, that sinning voluntarily is acting unfreely, even given an agent's unconflicted pleasure in having fallen away from God. Many contemporary philosophers, on the other hand, have kept the question of whether some action is free separate from the question of whether it is good or bad. The answer to the first is not presumed by them to imply the answer to the second. They lack Augustine's basic intuition that normative and metaphysical concerns meet in free will. Differences in basic intuition, or orientation, threaten to rule out the possibility of an intelligible conversation between Augustine and contemporary philosophers. Recent literature on free will nevertheless holds out some hope for thinking that the obstacles are not as insurmountable as they may at first seem.

Philosophers who insist on the connection between free will and the availability of alternatives for acting tend to situate action within a sequence of events causally connected over time (for instance, by natural laws). Then they ponder whether actions thus situated could have been otherwise. If they decide to grant the possibility, they defend free will under compatibilism; if not, under incompatibilism.[5] Free will is either accommodated to external determination or spared from it, but in neither case has it been made terribly clear what is being defended or why it is so valuable. Harry Frankfurt, in his much-admired and frequently cited article, "Freedom of the Will and the Concept of a Person," has helped to clarify the nature of free will by adopting a psychological focus on the will and characterizing its freedom as a function of the internal coherence of a person's motivations.[6] We have as persons, Frankfurt argues, the unique capacity to reflect on the desirability of our desires, and therefore in addition to the first-order desires that move us to act, we have second-order desires to be moved by certain desires. First-order volitions carry our first-order desires

---

[5] For detailed compatibilist and incompatibilist defenses of free will, see respectively Bernard Berofsky, *Freedom from Necessity: The Metaphysical Basis of Responsibility* (New York: Routledge & Kegan Paul, 1987) and Peter Van Inwagen, *An Essay on Free Will* (Oxford: Clarendon Press, 1983).

[6] *Journal of Philosophy* 68 (1971), 5–20; reprinted in Harry G. Frankfurt, *The Importance of What We Care About: Philosophical Essays* (Cambridge: Cambridge University Press, 1988).

into action. We act on desire. In second-order volitions, we decide to be moved to action by the desirability of our desires. We orient ourselves to act. Volitions of higher order are also possible, for we can reflect on the desirability of our higher-order desires, especially when they are in conflict. But only second-order volitions, Frankfurt submits, are necessary for having a will and being a person. Protopersons, or what he refers to as "wantons," never orient themselves to act, but remain passive to their desires. They always act in response to the strongest desire that they happen to have. Persons structure their motivations, and they can experience, as wantons cannot, a conflict between how they decide to be moved and how they are in fact moved. Compulsory action is for Frankfurt as well as for Augustine a paradigmatic form of unfreedom, and it has nothing to do with the external determination of action.

Frankfurt's conception of the will and its freedom dovetails with Augustine's in its differentiation of free action and free will. For Frankfurt, the distinction is roughly between acting on desire and acting on the desire we desire to act upon. We act freely when nothing constrains us from doing what we want to do. Animals and small children share this sort of freedom with fully rational persons. We act with free will when our actions are consistent with the person we would like to be. Our motivational structure, in other words, has internal coherence. Higher-order volitions line up to confirm the desirability of our manner of acting. For Augustine, the distinction between free action and free will is very similar. Once external constraints have established the domain of what we can will effectively, we act freely in so far as we act at all. But all that amounts to for him is the truism that our actions are intentional movements, whose individuation requires reference to what we desire. Augustine would agree with Frankfurt that free will refers to the integration of volition and desire in action. We can act on desire without acting of our own free will, if the strength of our desires leads us to will what we would have preferred not to have willed. The similarities between their respective views on free will suggest that neither Frankfurt nor Augustine would be inclined, strictly speaking, to describe external constraints on our action as limiting our freedom of will. From outside of us, we can have limitations put on what we can do (to the extreme of ruling out action altogether), but it is within those limitations that we are more or less free, depending on the coherence of our motivations. Neither Augustine nor Frankfurt feel the need, then, to tie free will to alternative possibilities for acting. Philosophers who insist on the connection have confused limitations on action with limitations on freedom.

In one regard, however, Augustine and Frankfurt think very differently about free will. For Frankfurt we can lack free will by default if we happen to be thoroughly wanton, and we can lack it unwillingly if we happen to suffer from internal conflict. But as long as we have a motivational structure to speak of, its coherence suffices for free will. For this reason, Frankfurt professes neutrality on the problem of determinism. It makes no difference to our having free will whether we are caused to have it, whether we have it by chance, or whether we cause ourselves to have it.[7] To Augustine's way of thinking, it makes on the contrary a profound difference. Motivational coherence, or having an unconflicted will, counts for him as a necessary condition for free will, but not a sufficient one. Had Augustine known of Frankfurt's wantons, I think he would have acknowledged a degree of wantonness in those who sin with an unconflicted will, but by no means would he have identified them with wantons.[8] We can as far as Augustine is concerned reflect on the desirability of our sinful desires, approve of them, will them into effect, and still lack free will. If we were wantons, the reflection and approval would be impossible; if we were able to acknowledge our sinful desires to be sinful, the approval would be impossible. Knowledge of sin brings in its wake disapprobation of sinful desires and thereby wrecks the motivational coherence of the sinful will. For Frankfurt disruptions of motivational coherence necessarily diminish free will; but for

---

[7] When Frankfurt says that "my conception of the freedom of the will appears to be neutral with regard to the problem of determinism," he is being somewhat misleading. He does not see determinism as a *problem*, not at least for free will. His neutrality refers only to the issue of *whether* we are determined to have free will. See Frankfurt, *The Importance*, 25.

[8] For further elaboration of the connection between sin and wantonness, see James Wetzel, "The Recovery of Free Agency in the Theology of St. Augustine" *Harvard Theological Review* 80 (1987), 113–15.

Augustine the move from voluntary to involuntary sin is a step towards free will. One form of unfreedom, unacknowledged by Frankfurt but considered by Augustine to be the essence of bondage, is to have an evil will. We are free, Augustine insists, only when we are determined by God to have a good will.

Most contemporary philosophers would concede that virtue and free will are necessarily connected, if what we mean by this is that free will is a condition of virtue. But the connection becomes obscure and controversial if, on the contrary, we mean to imply that virtue is a condition of free will. Augustine seems to think that we express ourselves in action most fully and most freely when we act virtuously in response to grace. Internal analyses of willing, such as Frankfurt's, seek to explicate free will without having to take into account the broader metaphysical context of human agency. This is misguided, if Augustine is right to connect questions of freedom to questions of value. Frankfurt is not unamenable to a normative focus on freedom. He deems it important for philosophers to elucidate the value of our having free will. Yet this for him is not the issue of whether there are values in nature or creation that orient human agency to the good. The second-order volitions that are basic to persons and relevant to free will involve us in evaluating our desires as good or bad only in the minimal sense that in volition we come to prefer some of our desires over others. It adds nothing to free will, he contends, to qualify the evaluations as moral.[9]

Frankfurt's internal analysis of free will, though ingenious, is not unproblematic, and its most dogged problem has, I will argue, much to do with his disinclination to move in Augustine's direction and link freedom to being determined for the good. Frankfurt and his critics have noticed that his assignment of desires to different levels in a hierarchy fails to differentiate higher-order volitions from desires.[10] Consider the case of

---

[9] Frankfurt, *The Importance*, 19 n. 6.

[10] Frankfurt, "Identification and Wholeheartedness," in *Responsibility, Character, and the Emotions: New Essays in Moral Psychology*, ed. Ferdinand David Schoeman (Cambridge: Cambridge University Press, 1987); reprinted in Frankfurt, *The Importance*, 159–76, see 165–67. The most trenchant criticism of Frankfurt on this issue is in Gary Watson, "Free Agency," *Journal of Philosophy* 72 (1975), 205–20; reprinted in *Free Will*, ed. Gary Watson (New York: Oxford University Press, 1982), 96–110, see 107–109. Note as well Eleonore Stump's criticism and revision of Frankfurt in

internal conflict between second-order volitions and first-order desires. In order to experience this sort of conflict, we need to have identified ourselves with some desires (of the second order), disavowed others (of the first order). But what defines our commitment to a desire or set of desires? It cannot be the highest order of our volition, for volitions are still desires, and it is futile to base commitment to a desire on a further desire.[11] To do so is to invite regress to ever higher orders of volition.

In his initial response to this problem, Frankfurt appealed to mental acts of identification with desire, or decisive commitments, that end the regress of volition.[12] But because he left unspecified the nature of this decisive commitment, or volition to end all volitions, his solution seemed patently *ad hoc*, and Gary Watson, for one, supposed him to have set up decisive commitment as the arbitrary refusal to regress to a higher order of volition.[13] Frankfurt's response to Watson has been to define the nature of person-constituting decisions (volitions) against two types of volitional incoherence.[14] In the first type, we have yet to identify ourselves wholeheartedly with any one of our competing desires, and until we establish a preferential order for their satisfaction, we lack coherence in our higher-order volitions. This sort of conflict, Frankfurt contends, divides the person, for all desires contend for some place *within* the person's volitional structure. In the second type, we have identified ourselves wholeheartedly with some preference, but we discover that our first-order desires move us contrary to how we would prefer to be moved. This sort of conflict takes place *between* the person and external desires. The external desires, having been disavowed, no longer have a legitimate claim to a place in the

"Sanctification, Hardening of the Heart, and Frankfurt's Concept of Free Will," *Journal of Philosophy* 85 (1988), 395–420, see 396–411.

[11] Watson (ed.), *Free Will*, 108 discredits the explanatory value of higher-order volitions as follows: "But why does one necessarily care about one's higher-order volitions? Since second-order volitions are themselves simply desires, to add them to the context of conflict is just to increase the number of contenders; it is not to give a special place to any of those in contention. The agent may not care which of the second-order desires win out. The same possibility arises at each higher order."

[12] Frankfurt, *The Importance*, 21–22.　　　　[13] Watson (ed.), *Free Will*, 108.

[14] Frankfurt, *The Importance*, 167–72; cf. his earlier article "Identification and Externality," in *The Identities of Persons*, ed. Amélie Rorty (Berkeley: University of California Press, 1976); reprinted in Frankfurt, *The Importance*, 58–68.

person's volitional structure; they must be eliminated or at least suppressed if volitional coherence is to be restored. Having contrasted these two forms of volitional incoherence (indecision and weakness of will), Frankfurt believes himself to have given substantive definition to a person-constituting decision. To my mind, however, he has not advanced far from his original position. In saying this, I do not deny that there are person-constituting decisions; nor do I doubt the usefulness of his two forms of volitional incoherence for setting them in relief. If we were, say, to move from indecision to weakness of will, we would have to decide to treat some of the desires we happened to have as truly our own and some as alien to us. This would certainly count as a person-constituting decision. But remember that Frankfurt needs to explain what it means for us to *identify* with our desires. Higher-order volitions fail to do this because either they are themselves motivated by desire, and so we never get to the bottom of our commitment to desire, or they are unmotivated, and we get to the bottom by arbitrary fiat. Decisions fare no better. What makes us decide to commit ourselves to some desire if not some other desire that moves us? Frankfurt cannot account for acts of volition or decision by dissociating them from the desires that motivate them; nor, however, can he attribute desires to us solely on the basis of the other desires we happen to have. He has reached an impasse.

Two of Frankfurt's admiring critics, Gary Watson and Eleonore Stump, have felt the need to interject an element of intellectualism into their respective accounts of free will. Our evaluative judgments must be invoked, they claim, to make sense of our identification with desires or ends we have for acting. Watson eschews the hierarchical characterization of motivation into lower and higher orders of desire and adopts in its place what he refers to as a Platonic conception of the psyche. "The doctrine I shall defend," he notes, "is Platonic in the sense that it involves a distinction between valuing and desiring which depends upon there being independent sources of motivation."[15] Watson's idea is roughly that some of our

---

[15] Watson (ed.), *Free Will*, 100.

desires, call them passions or appetites, move us independently of what we judge to be good. Irrational appetites can come into conflict with desires we judge to be worthy of satisfaction, and when we are torn between what we desire and what we value, we lack freedom of the will. Where Frankfurt speaks of a conflict between second-order volitions and first-order desires, Watson speaks of a conflict between two independent sources of motivation, one rooted in reason, the other in appetite. The problem that dogs Watson concerns his distinction between valuing and desiring. He has difficulty making it. Granted that valuing must involve judging something good; still, what is it to judge something good? Watson suggests tentatively that when we value or judge something to be good, we make use of principles and ends which we would recognize, in moments of rational lucidity, as definitive of the good.[16] Stump has criticized Watson for being overly intellectualistic in his characterization of values. They should not be identified, she argues, solely with the agent's rational principles and ends.[17] Watson himself has recently abandoned his earlier intellectualism. He admits that we may value in particular cases what we would refuse to endorse from a general evaluational standpoint, and in that way we would fail to identify ourselves with our evaluational judgments. These perverse cases, he submits, leave us "with a rather elusive notion of identification and thereby an elusive notion of self-determination."[18]

Watson, I think, too hastily dismisses his earlier identification of valuing and judging good as a conflation. His problematic case for identification – our wholehearted identification with what we would not value – is at best ambiguous. He claims that we can identify ourselves with what we would not sanction from a general evaluational standpoint that we *would* be prepared to accept. If he means by this that we do not actually operate under this standpoint, but would be prepared to do so if presented with it, then in acting "perversely" we still identify ourselves with some evaluational judgment, only it is defeasible in light of new knowledge. (This is the case with voluntary sin.) If he means, on the contrary, that we actually make use of this

[16] *Ibid.*, 105.   [17] Stump, "Sanctification," 402 n. 11.
[18] Watson, "Free Action and Free Will," *Mind* 96 (1987), 145–72, see 150–51.

general evaluational standpoint, then we cannot act contrary to our evaluative judgments without being internally conflicted. For while it is true that we sometimes identify wholeheartedly with what we *would* not value, it makes no sense to say that we sometimes identify wholeheartedly with what we *do* not value. I concede to Watson that the complexities of volitional incoherence, as in perversity, compulsion, and weakness of will, complicate the attribution of actions to agents enormously. It is a mistake, however, to surrender the basic connection between identifying with a desire or end in acting and judging the desire or end to be good. The question is not whether we should be intellectualist about actions, but to what extent.

Stump believes that we can get by with being minimally intellectualist. In her revised account of Frankfurt's hierarchical structure of motivation, we have second-order desires by virtue of our capacity to represent actions or first-order volitions as the good to be pursued. Having rounded out Frankfurt's account of willing with the role of intellect, Stump takes care of his problem of identification. Desires associated with what an agent represents as good are quite plausibly thought of as the agent's own. She further modifies his definition of second-order volitions. For Frankfurt they are essentially decisions to act (or not to act) on certain first-order desires, and because not all decisions are effective, it is possible for us to have second-order volitions without having them move us to act. For Stump, volitions are always effective desires. If we have second-order volitions, we have been able by definition to translate our desires for the good into action. In comparison to Frankfurt, she has a simpler conception of higher-order volitions and a more complex conception of higher-order desires. In both cases this is because she has allowed intellect to do the work of identifying us with our desires. Her revision of Frankfurt yields her the following definition of free will: "An individual has freedom of the will just in case he has second-order desires, his first-order volitions are not discordant with his second-order desires, and he has the first-order volitions he has because of his second-order volitions."[19] To take her example, if Patricius (Augustine's father)

---

[19] Stump, "Sanctification," 401.

beats his wife but deems this wrong and wishes not to have such
desires, God can free his will if God gives him the strength to
bring his actions (first-order volitions) into agreement with his
judgments (second-order desires).

Stump's definition of free will, although couched in Frankfurt's language, is nearly identical in content to Watson's
definition of free will as the integration of valuing and desiring.
If my second-order volitions determine my first order volitions,
this means that I am moved by what seems valuable to me. My
values give me my reasons for acting, and for both Watson and
Stump, my reasons more than my desires are constitutive of my
actions. Watson at one time held that values differed from
simple desires in being subject to rational defense. We can give
reasons for our values. In the spirit of a leaner intellectualism,
Stump observes that "an agent's intellect may formulate a
reason for an action in a manner that is hasty, thoughtless, ill-
informed, invalid, or in any other way irrational."[20] She allows
intellect to structure the will and give content to its freedom
wholly independently of the agent's recognition of some
objective order of values. I think that this is a mistake. Internal
analyses of free will at best are able to identify necessary
conditions for free will, but by failing to take into account the
objective order in which agents are situated, they miss something important. Part of what makes us free is our ability to
recognize good reasons for acting. Someone who significantly
lacked this ability – a paranoid schizophrenic, for instance –
would lack free will, even though he or she might well be able to
meet the conditions of Stump's definition.

Among contemporary philosophers, Susan Wolf has been the
vox clamantis for a maximally intellectualist conception of free
will.[21] We are free and responsible, she contends, when we are
able to sort out good values from bad ones and respond
appropriately. Being determined for the good is as necessary for

[20] *Ibid.*, 400.
[21] Her major statement of her position is *Freedom Within Reason* (New York: Oxford
University Press, 1990). But see also "Asymmetrical Freedom," *Journal of Philosophy*
77 (1980), 151–66; "The Importance of Free Will," *Mind* 90 (1981), 386–405; and
"Sanity and the Metaphysics of Responsibility," in *Responsibility, Character, and the
Emotions: New Essays in Moral Psychology*, ed. Ferdinand Schoeman (Cambridge:
Cambridge University Press, 1987).

freedom as light is necessary for seeing. Wolf's has been a minority voice partly because philosophers have tended to look to natural science for their ontology and have found it difficult to square the objectivity of values (The Good) with a scientific picture of the world, and partly because philosophers have tended to view threats to freedom in the form of constraints, either internal ones as in compulsion or external ones as in being caused to act by natural forces. Of the first tendency I have little to say other than to point out that theism is a viable metaphysics for explicating the objectivity of value, and theism is not, as I see it, incompatible with the virtues and method of science. If we should have independent reason for thinking that free will is unintelligible apart from an objective order of values, we should have reason for being theists. Of the second tendency, I would say that philosophers have become so accustomed to setting free will against determinism that they have missed its essential connection to rationality. The cogency of maximally intellectualist views of freedom, such as Wolf's and Augustine's, can be made salient if we cast the problem of free will not as the problem of whether we are determined to act, but as the problem of whether we can be said to act intelligibly. Thomas Nagel has set up the problem of free will this way, and I intend, after reviewing his reasoning, to reformulate his analysis from Augustine's maximally intellectualist point of view.

In recent work, Nagel has emphasized the importance to philosophy of two irreducibly discrete, incompatible, and yet necessary points of view – external and internal.[22] In the internal view I encounter the world as the subject of my experience, and what I see of the world therefore depends on the place I occupy within it. To lose this perspective is to lose my identity as a particular person. In the external view, or the view from nowhere, I encounter myself as an object in the world. To move to this impersonal view of myself, I need to detach myself as much as possible from my first-person perspective and attempt to see the world from no particular place within it. To give up this attempt is to give up objectivity, or my sense of

[22] Thomas Nagel, *The View from Nowhere* (New York: Oxford University Press, 1986). See also "Subjective and Objective," in *Mortal Questions* (Cambridge: Cambridge University Press, 1979).

being only one item among many in the world I inhabit. These
two perspectives are for Nagel indispensable and irreconcilable,
and their antagonism is at the source of much philosophical
perplexity.

To take the case of interest, I am struck with the problem of
free will when I take an external or objective view of my
actions.[23] My autonomy is impossible unless I can claim some of
my beliefs, desires, and actions as my own, but as I detach
myself from my internal view, allowing my beliefs, desires, and
actions to have conditions in the world at large, my life merges
seamlessly into an impersonal succession of events. In the view
from nowhere, or as it has more commonly been called, the view
from eternity, I will have objectified my life to the point where
nothing remains to my subjectivity. Nothing remains, in other
words, to the self that sees itself as object. Our drive to view
ourselves objectively is motivated in part by our desire to move
beyond aspects of our lives that are conditioned by the world
outside of us and arrive at the source of our own autonomy. But,
as Nagel observes, our ambition ends in irony, "for to be really
free we would have to act from a standpoint outside of ourselves,
including all our principles of choice – creating ourselves from
nothing, so to speak."[24]

Nagel does not abandon free will; he anguishes over its lack
of intelligibility. His problem of free will comes down to our
seeming inability, either from an internal or external point of
view, to solve the problem of identification. To explain an
action is to rationalize it in terms of reasons and purposes that
the agent had for acting. But what makes the motivation of
some action the agent's *own*? Not every action we undertake is
freely undertaken, and it must be possible, then, to distinguish
between desires we happen to have and desires we claim as our
own. It should be fairly obvious why Nagel's external perspective on action fails to illuminate this distinction. The
objective order, viewed externally, is a world of matter in
motion and things in space and time, a sound and fury,
signifying nothing. The world signifies nothing because it no
longer expresses anyone's intentions and purposes. When

---

[23] Nagel, *The View from Nowhere*, 110–20.   [24] *Ibid.*, 118.

explanations of action are divested of the language that agents use to describe their intentions, actions become indistinguishable from other events in the objective order. The internal perspective, on the other hand, retains the agent's point of view and allows us to individuate actions intelligibly, but still Nagel denies that this is enough to render free will intelligible. Suppose, to use his illustration, I have decided to accept a job offer.[25] My action is explicable in terms of the reasons I had for making my decision. The same would be true if I had decided not to take the offer. Since both options were open to me and either would have been intelligible in terms of my reasons, the intelligibility of my actual decision fails to explain why I opted for one option over the other. The point Nagel is trying to make is that the internal view of action does not tell us why the reasons that move us to act, rather than other reasons we might have acted upon, are genuinely *our* reasons and desires. Again this is the problem of identification.

From an Augustinian point of view, Nagel's approach to free will is unworkable because he segregates internal and external determinants of action into two irreconcilable forms of analysis. Neither form of analysis can in isolation from the other be adequate to its object, for autonomy takes in not only the internal coherence of our motivations but also the quality of our response to the objective features of our situation. Whatever autonomy turns out to be, it must be situated in the world. Augustine's and Wolf's way of handling the problem of identification is to take the minimally intellectualist insight that we identify ourselves with what we value and set it in the context of an objective order of values. My reasons and desires are most my own when they are the product of my perception of the good, and I value what is in fact of value. It matters to my free will, then, whether my reasons for acting are good ones. Lunacy, inattention, self-deception, and vice impair my judgment, and this impairment impacts upon my freedom to act, however unconflicted I may be in my motivations.

To be fair to Nagel, it must be admitted that if values disappear in the external view of things, such that no objective

[25] *Ibid.*, 115–16.

order of values remains to inform our actions, then he is quite right to insist on the antagonism between internal and external analyses of actions and the mystery of free will. Augustine and Nagel differ in their conceptions of free will because they differ in their conceptions of the objective order. Augustine philosophizes within a theocentric universe, and Nagel pays his respects to the disenchanted world of science. This sort of difference is too profound to be immediately resolvable, but if we bear in mind that conceptions of objectivity can be relevant to conceptions of free will, we can at least illuminate Augustine's much misunderstood conjunction of voluntary sin and bondage of will.

Bondage in the case of involuntary sin is unproblematic. It is compulsion, and the nature of compulsion can be readily described in internal analyses of action. Bondage in the case of voluntary sin is problematic, however, for it suggests that we can compromise our freedom simply by valuing what we ought not to value. This is a hard intuition for most contemporary philosophers to assimilate, and even the intellectualists among them minimize their intellectualism to avoid it. Nevertheless the intuition makes perfect sense in the context of an objective order of values. In order to sin voluntarily, we would have to abandon the objective order of values and set in its place some imposed order of our own making. If we find ourselves having to impose values upon the world, one of two conclusions is possible. Either the world has no discernible value of its own, and we have to create value for ourselves, or it does have one, but we have been unable or unwilling to see it. The first conclusion assumes the perspective of sin, under which the world's sensibility has been sundered from its intelligibility. The logic of sin divests the objective order of its significance and gives to human beings the ultimate power of creation – to create the good. But because human beings remain a part of the objective order even while they create, sin's logic sets up an irreconcilable antagonism between internal and external analyses of action. Free will ceases to make sense for exactly the reasons that Nagel identifies. When we sin voluntarily, we operate under assumptions that make our freedom unintelligible. The blindness continues until we are able to embrace the second conclusion, and that is to assume the perspective of grace.

Nagel claims that what we really want when we want autonomy is to be able to create ourselves from nothing, that we will never be satisfied with less than this, and that consequently we will never be able to understand ourselves as having autonomy. Augustine would have agreed with him up to a point. If we seek to create *ex nihilo* as God creates *ex nihilo*, then we confuse ourselves with what we seek and make a mockery of our freedom. But when we regain a sense of the difference, we can begin to recreate ourselves from the nothingness of sin. There is under grace a creation *ex nihilo* within our reach.

Editions

Confessionum libri XIII. Ed. Lucas Verheijen. Corpus Christianorum Series Latina. Vol. 27. Turnholt: Brepols, 1981.

Contra duas epistulas Pelagianorum. Ed. Karl F. Urba and Joseph Zycha. Corpus Scriptorum Ecclesiasticorum Latinorum. Vol. 60. Vienna: F. Tempsky, 1913.

Contra Fortunatum. Ed. Joseph Zycha. Corpus Scriptorum Ecclesiasticorum Latinorum. Vol. 25. Vienna: F. Tempsky, 1891.

Contra Iulianum opus imperfectum. Ed. Michaela Zelzer. Corpus Scriptorum Ecclesiasticorum Latinorum. Vol. 85/1 (Libri I–III). Vienna: Hoelder-Pichler-Tempsky, 1974.

De beata vita. Ed. W. M. Green and K. D. Daur. Corpus Christianorum Series Latina. Vol. 29. Turnholt: Brepols, 1970.

De civitate Dei. Ed. Bernard Dombard and Alphons Kalb. Corpus Christianorum Series Latina. Vols. 47 and 48. Turnholt: Brepols, 1955.

De correptione et gratia. Ed. Jean Chéné and Jacques Pintard. Bibliothèque augustinienne: Œuvres de Saint Augustin. Vol. 24. Paris: Desclée de Brouwer, 1962.

De diversis quaestionibus ad Simplicianum. Ed. Almut Mutzenbecher. Corpus Christianorum Series Latina. Vol. 44. Turnholt: Brepols, 1970.

De doctrina christiana. Ed. Joseph Martin. Corpus Christianorum Series Latina. Vol. 32. Turnholt: Brepols, 1962.

De dono perseverantiae. Ed. Jean Chéné and Jacques Pintard. Bibliothèque augustinienne: Œuvres de Saint Augustin. Vol. 24. Paris: Desclée de Brouwer, 1962.

De duabus animabus. Ed. Joseph Zycha. Corpus Scriptorum Ecclesiasticorum Latinorum. Vol. 25. Vienna: F. Tempsky, 1891.

De gratia Christi et de peccato originali. Ed. Karl F. Urba and Joseph Zycha. Corpus Scriptorum Ecclesiasticorum Latinorum. Vol. 42. Vienna: F. Tempsky, 1902.

De gratia et libero arbitrio. Ed. Jean Chéné and Jacques Pintard.

Bibliothèque augustinienne: Œuvres de Saint Augustin. Vol. 24. Paris: Desclée de Brouwer, 1962.

De libero arbitrio. Corpus Christianorum Series Latina. Vol. 29. Turnholt: Brepols, 1970.

De moribus ecclesiae catholicae. Ed. B. Roland-Gosselin. 2nd ed. Bibliothèque augustinienne: Œuvres de Saint Augustin. Vol. 1. Paris: Desclée de Brouwer, 1949.

De natura et gratia. Ed. Karl F. Urba and Joseph Zycha. Corpus Scriptorum Ecclesiasticorum Latinorum. Vol. 60. Vienna: F. Tempsky, 1913.

De nuptiis et concupiscentia ad Valerium. Ed. Karl F. Urba and Joseph Zycha. Corpus Scriptorum Ecclesiasticorum Latinorum. Vol. 42. Vienna: F. Tempsky, 1902.

De peccatorum meritis et remissione. Ed. Karl F. Urba and Joseph Zycha. Corpus Scriptorum Ecclesiasticorum Latinorum. Vol. 60. Vienna: F. Tempsky, 1913.

De praedestinatione sanctorum. Ed. Jean Chéné and Jacques Pintard. Bibliothèque augustinienne: Œuvres de Saint Augustin. Vol. 24. Paris: Desclée de Brouwer, 1962.

De spiritu et littera. Ed. Karl F. Urba and Joseph Zycha. Corpus Scriptorum Ecclesiasticorum Latinorum. Vol. 60. Vienna: F. Tempsky, 1913.

De Trinitate. Ed. W. J. Mountain. Corpus Christianorum Series Latina. Vols. 50 and 50A. Turnholt: Brepols, 1968.

De vera religione. Ed. Joseph Martin. Corpus Christianorum Series Latina. Vol. 32. Turnholt: Brepols, 1962.

Epistula ad Firmum 2*. Ed. Johannes Divjak. Bibliothèque augustinienne: Œuvres de Saint Augustin. Vol. 46B. Paris: Etudes augustiniennes, 1987.

Expositio quarundam propositionum ex epistula ad Romanos. Ed. Johannes Divjak. Corpus Scriptorum Ecclesiasticorum Latinorum. Vol. 84. Vienna: Hoelder-Pichler-Tempsky, 1971.

Retractationum libri II. Ed. Almut Mutzenbecher. Corpus Christianorum Series Latina. Vol. 57. Turnholt: Brepols, 1984.

Soliloquia. Ed. Wolfgang Hörmann. Corpus Scriptorum Ecclesiasticorum Latinorum. Vol. 89. Vienna: Hoelder-Pichler-Tempsky, 1986.

Translations

The translations appearing in the text are my own. Although Augustine does not lack for translators, I have judged it important for readers to have direct access to my interpretation of his Latin. In trying to explicate his conception of will, for example, I discovered that too many philosophical questions were tied to questions of syntax and word use for me to rely comfortably on the translations of others. This is not to say that I have not benefited enormously from the work of other translators, and I acknowledge those whom I have consulted below.

Bettenson, Henry, trans. *City of God*. Penguin, 1972.

Braun, René, trans. *Lettre 2* à Firmus*. Bibliothèque augustinienne: Œuvres de Saint Augustin. Vol. 46B. Paris: Etudes augustiniennes, 1987.

Burleigh, John H. S., trans. *Augustine: Earlier Writings*. Philadelphia: Westminster Press, 1953.

Burnaby, John, trans. *Augustine: Later Works*. Philadelphia: Westminster Press, 1955.

Holmes, Peter and Robert Ernest Wallis, trans. *Saint Augustine: Anti-Pelagian Writings*. Rev. and ed. Benjamin B. Warfield. A Select Library of the Nicene and Post-Nicene Fathers. Vol. 5. Grand Rapids: Wm. B. Eerdmans, 1971.

Landes, Paula (née Fredriksen), trans. *Augustine on Romans*. Chico: Scholars Press, 1982.

McKenna, Stephen, trans. *The Trinity*. The Fathers of the Church. Vol. 45. Washington, DC: Catholic University Press, 1963.

Stothert, Richard and Albert H. Newman, trans. *Writings in Connection with the Manichaean Controversy*. A Select Library of the Nicene and Post-Nicene Fathers. Vol. 4. Grand Rapids: Wm. B. Eerdmans, 1983.

Warner, Rex, trans. *The Confessions of St. Augustine*. New York: New American Library, 1963.

References

Alflatt, Malcolm E. "The Development of the Idea of Involuntary Sin in St. Augustine." *Revue des études augustiniennes* 20 (1974), 113–34.
"The Responsibility for Involuntary Sin in Saint Augustine." *Recherches augustiniennes* 10 (1975), 171–86.
Arendt, Hannah. *The Life of the Mind.* Vol. II (Willing). New York: Harcourt, Brace, Jovanovich, 1978.
Armstrong, Hilary. "Neoplatonic Valuations of Nature, Body and Intellect." *Augustinian Studies* 3 (1972), 35–59.
Babcock, William. "Augustine on Sin and Moral Agency." *Journal of Religious Ethics* 16 (1988), 28–55.
"Augustine's Interpretation of Romans (A.D. 394–396)." *Augustinian Studies* 10 (1979), 55–74.
Berofsky, Bernard. *Freedom from Necessity: The Metaphysical Basis of Responsibility.* New York: Routledge & Kegan Paul, 1987.
Bochet, Isabelle. *Saint Augustin et le désir de Dieu.* Paris: Etudes augustiniennes, 1982.
Braun, René. "Lettre 2*." Note complémentaire. In Œuvres de Saint Augustin. Vol. 46B. Paris: Etudes augustiniennes, 1987.
Broglie, Guy De. "Pour une meilleure intelligence du *De correptione et gratia*." *Augustinus Magister* 3 (Paris, 1954), 317–37.
Brown, Peter. *Augustine of Hippo: A Biography.* Berkeley: University of California Press, 1967.
"Pelagius and his Supporters: Aims and Environment." *Journal of Theological Studies* N.S. 19 (1968), 93–114.
Burnaby, John. *Amor Dei: A Study of the Religion of St. Augustine.* London: Hodder & Stoughton, 1938.
Burns, J. Patout. *The Development of Augustine's Doctrine of Operative Grace.* Paris: Etudes augustiniennes, 1980.
"The Interpretation of Romans in the Pelagian Controversy." *Augustinian Studies* 10 (1979), 43–54.
Clark, Elizabeth. *Ascetic Piety and Women's Faith: Essays on Late Ancient Christianity.* New York and Toronto: Edwin Mellen Press, 1986.

"Vitiated Seeds and Holy Vessels: Augustine's Manichaean Past." In Clark (1986).

Cochrane, Charles Norris. *Christianity and Classical Culture: A Study of Thought and Action from Augustus to Augustine*. Rev. ed. New York: Oxford University Press, 1944.

Colish, Marcia. *The Stoic Tradition from Antiquity to the Early Middle Ages*. Vol. II. Leiden: E. J. Brill, 1985.

Cooper, John M. "Aristotle on the Goods of Fortune." *The Philosophical Review* 94 (1985), 173–96.

Courcelle, Pierre. *Recherches sur les Confessions de saint Augustin*. Nouvelle édition augmentée et illustrée. Paris: E. De Boccard, 1968.

Davis, G. Scott. "The Structure and Function of the Virtues in the Moral Theology of St. Augustine." In *Congresso internazionale su S. Agostino nel XVI centenario della conversione*. Volume III. Rome: Institutum Patristicum Augustinianum (1987), 9–18.

Dihle, Albrecht. *The Theory of Will in Classical Antiquity*. Berkeley: University of California Press, 1982.

Dillon, John M. and A. A. Long (eds.). *The Question of "Eclecticism": Studies in Later Greek Philosophy*. Berkeley: University of California Press, 1988.

Doucet, Dominique. "L'*Ars Memoriae* dans les *Confessions*." *Revue des études augustiniennes* 33 (1987), 49–69.

Evans, G. R. *Augustine on Evil*. Cambridge: Cambridge University Press, 1982.

Ferrari, Leo C. *The Conversions of Saint Augustine*. Villanova: Villanova University Press, 1984.

Forsyth, Neil. *The Old Enemy: Satan and the Combat Myth*. Princeton: Princeton University Press, 1987.

Frankfurt, Harry. "Freedom of the Will and the Concept of a Person." *Journal of Philosophy* 68 (1971), 5–20; reprinted in Frankfurt (1988).
  "Identification and Externality." In Rorty (1976); reprinted in Frankfurt (1988).
  "Identification and Wholeheartedness." In Schoeman (1987); reprinted in Frankfurt (1988).
  The Importance of What We Care About: Philosophical Essays. Cambridge: Cambridge University Press, 1988.

Freccero, John. "Autobiography and Narrative." In Heller, Sosna, and Wellbery (1986).

Fredriksen, Paula. "Augustine's Early Interpretation of Paul." Ph.D. dissertation. Princeton University: 1979.
  "Paul and Augustine: Conversion Narratives, Orthodox Traditions, and the Retrospective Self." *Journal of Theological Studies* N.S. 37 (1986), 3–34.

Frohnhofen, Herbert. "Anmerkungen zum Brief 2* des heiligen Augustinus." *Vigiliae Christianae* 38 (1984), 385–92.

Gilbert, Neal W. "The Concept of Will in Early Latin Philosophy." *Journal of the History of Philosophy* 1 (1963), 17–35.

Gilson, Etienne. *The Christian Philosophy of Saint Augustine.* Trans. L. E. M. Lynch. New York: Random House, 1960.

Heller, Thomas C., Morton Sosna, and David E. Wellbery (eds.). *Reconstructing Individualism: Autonomy, Individuality, and the Self in Western Thought.* Stanford: Stanford University Press, 1986.

Holte, Ragnar. *Béatitude et sagesse: Saint Augustin et le problème de la fin de l'homme dans la philosophie ancienne.* Paris: Etudes augustiniennes, 1962.

Irwin, T. H. "Stoic and Aristotelian Conceptions of Happiness." In Schofield and Striker (1986).

Jordan, Robert. "Time and Contingency in St. Augustine." *Review of Metaphysics* 8 (1955), 394–417.

Kahn, Charles H. "Discovering the Will: From Aristotle to Augustine." In Dillon and Long (1988).

Kristeller, Paul Oskar. Review of *Christianity and Classical Culture.* *Journal of Philosophy* 41 (1944), 576–81.

Lacey, Hugh M. "Empiricism and Augustine's Problems about Time." *Review of Metaphysics* 22 (1968), 219–45.

Lebourlier, Jean. "Essai sur la responsabilité du pécheur dans la réflexion de saint Augustin." *Augustinus Magister* 3 (Paris, 1954), 287–300.

Léon-Dufour, Xavier. "Grâce et libre arbitre chez saint Augustin: A propos de *Consentire vocatione dei…propriae voluntatis est.*" *Recherches de science religieuse* 33 (1946), 129–63.

Long, A. A. and D. N. Sedley. *The Hellenistic Philosophers.* Vol. 1: *Translations of the Principal Sources with Philosophical Commentary.* Cambridge: Cambridge University Press, 1987.

McEvoy, James. "St. Augustine's Account of Time and Wittgenstein's Criticisms." *Review of Metaphysics* 38 (1984), 547–77.

McTaggart, John. *The Nature of Existence.* Vol. II. Cambridge: Cambridge University Press, 1927.

Marrou, Henri Irénée. *Saint Augustin et la fin de la culture antique.* Paris: E. De Boccard, 1938.

Retractatio. Paris: E. De Boccard, 1949.

Meijering, E. P. *Augustin über Schöpfung, Ewigkeit und Zeit: Das Elfte Buch der Bekenntnisse.* Leiden: E. J. Brill, 1979.

Mitsis, Phillip. *Epicurus' Ethical Theory: The Pleasures of Invulnerability.* Ithaca: Cornell University Press, 1988.

Mundle, C. W. K. "Augustine's Pervasive Error Concerning Time." *Philosophy* 41 (1966), 165–68.

Nagel, Thomas. *Mortal Questions*. Cambridge: Cambridge University Press, 1979.
"Subjective and Objective." In Nagel (1979).
The View from Nowhere. New York: Oxford University Press, 1986.
O'Connell, Robert J. "*De libero arbitrio I*: Stoicism Revisited." *Augustinian Studies* 1 (1970), 49–68.
St. Augustine's Early Theory of Man, A.D. 386–391. Cambridge: Harvard University Press, 1968.
O'Daly, Gerard. *Augustine's Philosophy of Mind*. Berkeley: University of California Press, 1987.
"Predestination and Freedom in Augustine's Ethics." In Vesey (1989).
"Time as *distentio* and St. Augustine's Exegesis of *Philippians* 3:12–14." *Revue des études augustiniennes* 23 (1977), 266–68.
Pagels, Elaine. "The Politics of Paradise: Augustine's Exegesis of Genesis 1–3 versus that of John Chrysostom." *Harvard Theological Review* 78 (1985), 67–99.
Portalié, Eugène. *A Guide to the Thought of Saint Augustine*. Trans. Ralph J. Bastian. Chicago: Henry Regnery, 1960.
Ricœur, Paul. *Time and Narrative*. Vol. 1. Trans. Kathleen McLaughlin and David Pellauer. Chicago: University of Chicago Press, 1984.
Time and Narrative. Vol. III. Trans. Kathleen McLaughlin and David Pellauer. Chicago: University of Chicago Press, 1988.
Rist, John. "Augustine on Free Will and Predestination." *Journal of Theological Studies* N.S. 20 (1969), 420–47.
Rorty, Amélie (ed.). *The Identities of Persons*. Berkeley: University of California Press, 1976.
Rottmanner, Odilo. *Der Augustinismus*. Munich, 1892; translated by J. Liébaert as "L'Augustinisme: Etude d'histoire doctrinale," *Mélange de science religieuse* 6 (1949), 31–48.
Russell, Bertrand. *Human Knowledge: Its Scope and Limits*. New York: Simon and Schuster, 1948.
Sage, Athanase. "Praeparatur voluntas a Domino." *Revue des études augustiniennes* 10 (1964), 1–20.
Schoeman, Ferdinand (ed.). *Responsibility, Character, and the Emotions: New Essays in Moral Psychology*. Cambridge: Cambridge University Press, 1987.
Schofield, Malcolm and Gisela Striker (eds). *The Norms of Nature: Studies in Hellenistic Ethics*. Cambridge: Cambridge University Press, 1986.
Sorabji, Richard. *Time, Creation, and the Continuum: Theories in Antiquity and the Early Middle Ages*. Ithaca: Cornell University Press, 1983.
Stump, Eleonore. "Sanctification, Hardening of the Heart, and

Frankfurt's Concept of Free Will." *Journal of Philosophy* 85 (1988), 395–420.

Suter, Ronald. "Augustine on Time with some Criticisms from Wittgenstein." *Revue internationale de philosophie* 16 (1962), 378–94.

Taylor, Charles. *Sources of the Self: The Making of the Modern Identity.* Cambridge: Harvard University Press, 1989.

TeSelle, Eugene. *Augustine the Theologian.* New York: Herder and Herder, 1970.

Testard, Maurice. *Saint Augustin et Cicéron.* Vol. II: *Repertoire des textes.* Paris: Etudes augustiniennes, 1958.

Thonnard, François-Joseph. "La Prédestination augustinienne et l'interprétation de O. Rottmanner." *Revue des études augustiniennes* 9 (1963), 259–87.

Van Inwagen, Peter. *An Essay on Free Will.* Oxford: Clarendon Press, 1983.

Veer, A. C. De. "L'Exégèse de Rom. VII et ses variations." Note complémentaire 27. Œuvres de Saint Augustin. Vol. 23. Paris: Desclée de Brouwer, 1974.

Verbeke, Gérard. "Augustin et le stoïcisme." *Recherches augustiniennes* I (1958), 67–89.

Vesey, Godfrey (ed.). *The Philosophy in Christianity.* Cambridge: Cambridge University Press, 1989.

Watson, Gary. "Free Agency." *Journal of Philosophy* 72 (1975), 205–20; reprinted in Watson (1982).

"Free Action and Free Will." *Mind* 96 (1987), 145–72.

(ed.). *Free Will.* New York: Oxford University Press, 1982.

Wetzel, James. "The Recovery of Free Agency in the Theology of St. Augustine." *Harvard Theological Review* 80 (1987), 101–25.

Wolf, Susan. "Asymmetrical Freedom." *Journal of Philosophy* 77 (1980), 151–66.

Freedom Within Reason. New York: Oxford University Press, 1990.

"Sanity and the Metaphysics of Responsibility." In Schoeman (1987).

"The Importance of Free Will." *Mind* 90 (1981), 386–405.

Index